The Book of

WINSCOMBE

A Changing Mendip Community

MARGARET TUCKER

HALSGROVE

First published in Great Britain in 2004

British Library Cataloguing-in-Publication Data
A CIP record for this title is available from the British Library

ISBN 1 84114 344 8

HALSGROVE

Halsgrove House
Lower Moor Way
Tiverton, Devon EX16 6SS
Tel: 01884 243242
Fax: 01884 243325
email: sales@halsgrove.com
website: www.halsgrove.com

Frontispiece photograph: *Empire Day march through the village, c.1930. Mr Searle is behind the band as John Bull.*

Printed and bound by CPI Bath

Contents

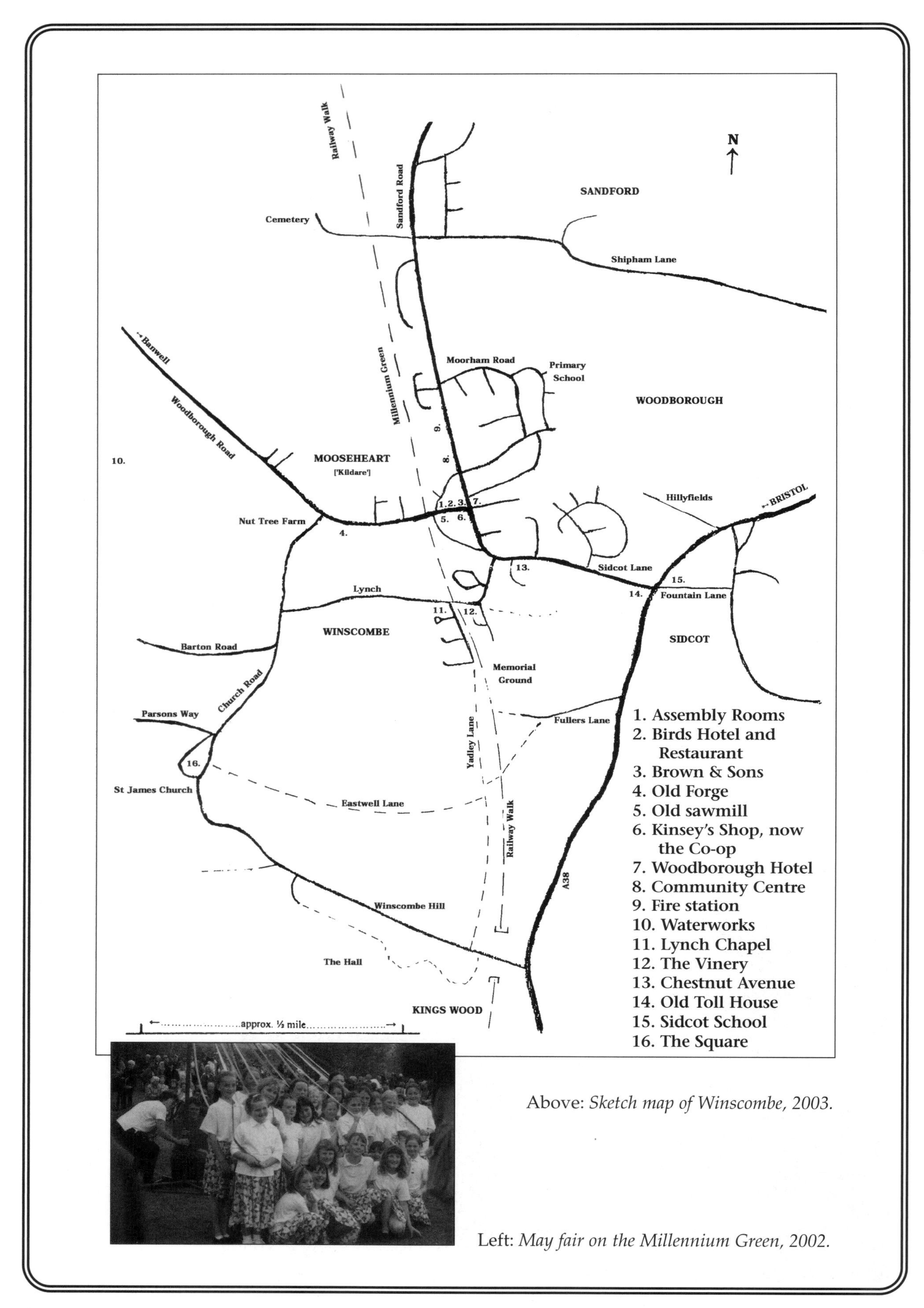

Above: *Sketch map of Winscombe, 2003.*

Left: *May fair on the Millennium Green, 2002.*

Acknowledgements

I have to thank the various local people who have told me of their younger days, and hunted out numerous photographs for me. They are: Mr P. Alletson, Mrs E. Averis, Mrs A. Bailey, Mrs A. Baldwin, Mrs M. Best, Mr P. Binding, Mr B. Bowen, Messrs Bird and Son, Mrs A. Bishop, Mr J. Blewitt, Mrs L. Brenchley, Mr and Mrs W. Brown, Miss G. Burman, Mrs J. Conibere, Mrs N. Cooper, Mrs P. Cram, Mrs L. Crook, Mr R. Dew, Mr P. Duckett, Mr I. Duthie, Sqn-Ldr J.V. Evans, Mrs J. Evans, Mrs M. Forbes, Mr H. Fountain, Mrs C. Gibbons, Miss C. Gladwin, Mr P. Griffin, Mr P. Griffiths, Mrs S. Gunn, Mr D. Hares, Mr and Mrs E. Hares, Mr D. Hembery, Miss P. Hopkins, Mr D. King, Gr. Cpt. J.E. Kirk, Miss M. Kinsey, Mr P. Knight, Mr and Mrs A. Langford, Mr D. Langford, Ms M. Lecomber-Paish, Mrs J. Lindley, Mrs J. Lister, Mr and Mrs G. Lloyd, Mr J. Mabbett, Mr J. Matthews, Mr J. Newsham, Mr A. Nipper, Mrs B. Pain, Mr M. Peters, Miss R. Richards, Mr P. Sayzeland, Mrs J. Searle, Mr A. Shephard, Mrs G. Smith, Revd C. Speed, Mr I. Tabrett, Mrs J. Thresher, Miss 'Bunty' Tracy, Mr E.J. Tucker, Mr M. Turner, Mrs R. Uffindell, Miss M. Weeks, Mrs W. Weeks, Mr J. Westlake, Mr and Mrs C. Wheller, Mr P. Whicher, Mr P. White, Mrs D. Whitear, Mrs M. Winchester, Mr D. Wyatt.

Thanks also to Weston-super-Mare Museum, Winscombe Library, Winscombe Women's Institute, Winscombe and Sandford Local History Society and the *Cheddar Valley Gazette*.

There are a couple of sources that perhaps I should mention more fully: a gentleman named Orion Charles Caple lived at Sidcot and he has left a record of his family and himself in his 'Reminiscences'. Another valuable source were the reports written by the Women's Institute in 1933 and 1985, together with the old scrapbooks and diaries from the Yatman family kindly lent to me by Mrs S. Gunn. The Local History Society (LHS) have also provided me with access to their many records.

Apologies for any names which have been omitted.

MARGARET TUCKER
WINSCOMBE 2003

A picture of Edwardian childhood. Left to right: *Arthur Mabbett, 'Effie' Mabbett, Norman Bird, Ronald Mabbett and Kenneth Bird.*

Above: *Winscombe Church, seen from Church Lane, showing the old Sunday School, c.2000.*

Inset above: *'Ready for Work' – Arthur Bird, c.1907.*

Winscombe Church from The Square, c.1881.

Woodborough Road showing Birds shop and Brown Bros, c.1920.

Introduction

... it would be hard to find [a village] *more thoroughly rural. Though it boasts of a 'street'; and even a 'square' there is not a row of houses in the village. The street is without a shop, a foot-path or a lamp-post, and the square is simply the meeting of four lanes, with a small farm-house at the corner. The nearest approach to a shop is a little cottage with a few pipes and lollipops in the window, and an intimation over the door that the occupier is licensed to sell tobacco... our village is without assembly room of any kind, except the parish church, and the whole parish is without either lawyer, doctor or dissenting minister.*

Theodore Compton, *Winscombe Sketches Among the Mendip Hills*, 1882.

This is the story of a small village in the heart of Somerset's Mendip Hills, a village much changed since it stood at just a few hundred, mainly farming, souls at the end of the eighteenth century. At that time the outstanding property was the thirteenth-century church on the hill; nearby was the Parsonage and here the village 'squire', the Revd J. Yatman, built a large house called Winscombe Hall. Apart from a handful of other substantial buildings, the original village of Winscombe was farmland and little else. The main centre of population was the surrounding hamlet of Woodborough which Compton described thus:

The central hamlet of Woodborough has a Railway Hotel and a Congregational Chapel, as well as a Board school, a Literary and Scientific Institute and Temperance Hall, besides a steam saw-yard and two smithies. The principal shop and two others are also here, and more than one deserving widow has opened what some call a coffee tavern, others a toffee cavern.

Little by little more families arrived, set up in business and had their own children; Winscombe as we know it today began to grow into a cohesive village.

The Book of Winscombe is the story of that community, of the villagers themselves; how they have lived, worked and played through a period of great upheaval and change in their history. They not only lived through the two worlds wars, but also adapted to the rapid growth of new technologies and the hard times of the Depression of the 1920s and '30s. The story that emerges is one of compassion and tolerance. It demonstrates the way in which people learned to accept and make the best of what they had, and to find means of enjoying themselves whatever the circumstances. There are many light-hearted moments, some of which illustrate the manner in which village life differs from that of a large town, particularly in earlier days, and the stories are a compilation of many different memories drawn from villagers past and present, hopefully to be treasured by those of the future.

In retrospect, one could say that Winscombe has lost little of its original character. Although the population has increased considerably, the area has still retained its 'village' atmosphere, whilst at the same time taking an active interest in world affairs and life in general. This being said, the village of today, in 2004, is different in so many ways from that of the nineteenth century.

Winscombe Church
Anon. c.1850

And there Winscombe's tower-hills rising high
Beyond it – fast behind a steep knoll meets the eye,
Oft times with sheep its ferny sides among,
And when the days of autumn haste along
Brown hues it gathers, and are scattered, too
The yellow furze-flowers, cheering to the view.
The old church bells – these send a merry bell
One marriage fête – or toll at funeral.
In years by-gone, upon a summer day,
The villagers bedecked in best array,
I saw thick scattered round upon the green,
A pretty sight! The old with crutch were seen;
Mothers with laughing babe, and maiden fair,
All met expectant round the old walls there;
The old grey walls, and here it may be said
'Tis told six centuries have o'er them sped,
And well nigh o'er the yew, whose bough so widely spread.

Somerset Record Office DD/SAS PR 54/7

Top left: *William Yatman, aged about 70.*

Above: *Alexandra Victoria Yatman.*

Left: *The stables at Winscombe Hall.*

Right: *The dining-room, Winscombe Hall, c.1920.*

One

Gentry

Winscombe Hall, c.1910.

The Yatman Family

Divisions between different 'classes' of society were a tangible characteristic of everyday life in England until well into the twentieth century, and this was as true for the community of the small village of Winscombe as any other. The 'gentry' who lived in the original parish around the church on the hill had, generally speaking, large properties, and owned a considerable amount of land. One family in particular has left us with a picture of their way of life. In 1847 Revd J.A. Yatman decided to settle in Winscombe, being drawn by the 'mild climate and hilly country', and he began work on a large property on top of Winscombe Hill that became known as 'The Hall'. In 1858 he married the daughter of the vicar of an adjoining parish, Alexandra Victoria Turner.

The Yatman residence was every inch a Victorian property, and boasted 11 bedrooms, each with its own dressing-room. The ground floor comprised living-room, morning-room and drawing-room, as well as a library. The rooms were, to many modern tastes, overfilled with furniture, and every wall or shelf was covered with pictures, photographs and mementoes.

The property, encompassing some 134 acres, also had a large garden, with statues, and walks on different levels. There was even a heated swimming-pool! Indoors, an unrecorded number of servants were hard at work; one family photograph shows a number of females, and there was certainly a nurse. Apparently, there were six men whose only job was to keep the drive clear – this was long and semi-circular

Above: *Statues in the grounds.*

Right: *Nurse, c.1910.*

Below: *Servants at The Hall; these people were probably all indoor staff.*

Below: *Staff at work in the woods.* Left to right: *Messrs Brooks* (with horse), *Brown, ?, Carter, Heal and Phillips.*

This picture: *Samuel Heath with cart and vegetables.*

Right: *James Heal sweeping the grounds.*

in shape, and went from one lodge to another.

Revd Yatman also built a farm on the hill where he produced vegetables and one photograph shows Samuel Heath harvesting a fine crop from the plot, whilst others show several 'Weeks' men working on timber in the plantation that was also created. Being on top of a hill, the question of a water-supply proved difficult. Most of the villagers used one of the several springs around the area, but at The Hall two wells were dug. This must have been hard work; the Revd Yatman's diary includes the following entry from 1849: '… sunk second well. Both men asphized [became unconscious] one after the other, but eventually quite well again.' Having had the well dug, he then built a large water tank on the property and also a very large sewage tank. This system worked very well for a number of years and the water from the tank could apparently be pumped all the way to the bedrooms.

Naturally the family moved and married within its own circle of acquaintances and the diaries tell of visits to and from other well-known (and usually extensive) families in the area, among them the Folletts, Edmundses, Leacrofts, Tiarkses, Graves-Knyftons, Barstows and Turners. Sometimes such visits were just for tea, and at other times to arrange some game such as hockey or tennis.

Revd Yatman and his wife had three sons, William, Arthur and Charles, and four daughters, Alice, Mabel, Emily and Fanny. When the sons and daughters of such families intermarried, as occurred with the Yatman children, the whole village participated in the event. The *Weston Mercury* newspaper printed the following article when Frances Mary Yatman was married to William Henry Slatter:

Fashionable Wedding at Winscombe 17 April 1881

In the picturesque and prettily situated village of Winscombe it seems that everyone decided that they would help to make this day memorable.

A handsome arch was erected at the New Lodge entrance by Mr & Mrs Arthur Phillips. The inscription on this was 'God Bless Them Both' and 'Long Life and Happiness'. Large and handsome clusters of primroses, bluebells and cowslips, and a double wreath of the same flowers... hung from the bordering. Opposite the main entrance to the house was a large scroll bearing in light straw letters on a blue ground the words 'Please accept our united wishes for long life, health and happiness.'

The fine old Parish Church and churchyard also received marked attention at the hands of the skilful decorators. An arch of evergreen spanned the roadway leading to the main entrance and in the centre in straw-coloured letters on a scarlet background was 'God Bless the Happy Pair'... The inside of the Church was most elaborately decorated, and the odours from the profusely sweet smelling flowers were as strong and varied as they were pleasant...

This was followed by highly detailed descriptions of the clothes worn by the bride and her seven bridesmaids, and also the manner in which the 'important' guests were dressed. The article continues:

In the afternoon the happy pair were driven to Winscombe Station, where the scholars of Sidcot School... gave the bridegroom an ovation (which they did right heartily!!)... The villagers crowded around the station and the platform to witness the happy couple's departure... the Bride's travelling dress was of dove coloured cashmere, trimmed with ruby corduroy, with jacket, hat and muff to match.

... the presents were displayed at Winscombe Hall for several days prior to the wedding, and at the invitation of Mrs Yatman they were inspected by the parishioners, generally at their convenience. The gifts were numerous, elegant and costly... The bells of the Parish Church rang out many 'merry peals' immediately after the ceremony, and the 'golden music' was repeated at intervals throughout the day... At night there was a very successful ball... and on Thursday the workmen

Left: *Mrs Yatman with sons Arthur, William and Charles.*

Below: *The swimming-pool on the roof of Winscombe Hall.*

Left: *Yatman sons and daughters.*

The gardener's lodge at Winscombe Hall.

Home Farm.

and their wives and families, together with the school children, were entertained to tea...

When Revd Yatman's daughter Emily was married to Hugh S. Tyssen on 26 April 1888, similarly well-orchestrated celebrations were put in place as they were for the wedding of Effie Edmunds and Mr Arthur Gregory, and Jessie Follett, the daughter of Winscombe's vicar, and Mr Herman Alexander Tiarks of Webbington.

It is no surprise that, after her death in 1922 (as the result of a fall), Mrs Yatman was greatly missed, for her contribution to village life did not stop at 'high days and holidays'. She set up a school for the children in the grounds of the The Hall; the only record of this comes from a 'comment' penned by H.S. Chapman and printed in a 1954 edition of the *Somerset Herald*:

I attended for three years... a small school attached to the laundry in the park below 'the big house' in which the Revd J.A. Yatman lived. The teacher was an elderly French lady named Mrs Curthoise. Near our small playground there was a high tower and from the top to the level of the courtyard of the big house was a walk like a pier. The tower was fitted with a lift to enable Mrs Yatman to visit the school and laundry without going down and up a great number of floors. Below the school and laundry were the stables approached by a long drive, with lodge gates about half a mile apart.

The 'walk' no longer exists, but the remains of the tower can still be seen. Apparently, Mrs Yatman, particularly during the period of her pregnancies, sat in a specially woven basket, which was raised or lowered in the tower as required and saved her from having to climb up and down the hill to visit the school.

Revd Yatman also took an active interest in the lives of the local children. As well as making a contribution to the building of the school at Sandford, he organised a 'shoe club' whereby children would be given a stamp for every penny that they managed to save; on saving sixpence their sum would be added to by the Revd to the tune of a similar amount, to go towards the cost of a pair of shoes.

When Revd Yatman died, his son William took over the farm management and running of the property. The younger son, Arthur, was a colonel in the Army and served in the Boer War. When he returned in 1902 the family donated a stained-glass window to

Alice Leacroft (née Yatman) with her bicycle.

the church to mark the event. Both sons played a large part in village life, serving on the Parochial Church Council as well as on various other committees. The third son, Charles, suffered from poor health, and died of consumption at the young age of 22.

It was not only the men of the family who were interested in the life of their neighbours. Alice Leacroft (née Yatman), who lived at the nearby hamlet of Rowberrow, decided to set up several groups for the benefit of local women, including the Women's Institute, the Red Cross and the Women's British Legion. This not only gave the women a common interest but also established an ideal platform from which they could achieve a great deal to help with the war effort.

The Parsonage

Also central to any community of course was the vicar, and when the Revd R.F. Follett was married to Mary Ann Rawlison the entire village joined in to see the bridal party. Revd Follett and his wife lived at the Parsonage where they raised a large family, although sadly one son died at the age of 14 months. When the vicar retired in 1895 he and his family joined his sister Mrs Lethbridge at Winscombe Court. He died in 1907 and was apparently well liked throughout the district. 'On the day of the funeral,' wrote Maria Forbes in her publication *The Church in Winscombe*, 'the minute bell at Winscombe Church tolled and the Ensign was lowered to half-mast. The bearers were the sexton and three workmen from Winscombe Court.'

Winscombe Court

At the end of the nineteenth century, this property, which may have originally been part of a monastery, was the residence of Fanny Lethbridge (née Yatman), a widow who was also without children. The property remained a single residence for several years, but was later divided into a number of flats and, at the time of writing, is home to a number of families.

Originally the property contained the buildings in Eastwell Lane, and Court Cottage – opposite the Vicarage – was the coachman's cottage. The Court land opposite, where there are now houses, was also part of the estate.

One elderly resident remembers, as a tiny child, helping with a fête in the garden when she was just four or five. She was given a small basket with posies in it, and people were supposed to give her the exact amount of money for their purchases, as she wasn't old enough to give the right change! Her mother, and other ladies of the parish, ran stalls to raise money for the church. Inside the house meanwhile there was a concert, featuring local singers and musicians.

Revd Follett's daughters, Debbie, Jennie and Mary.

The Parsonage.

Above: *Garden party at The Court, c.1920.*

Top right and right: *The entrance to The Court, 2003.*

Below: *Staff at Kildare; Wilfred Pain is on the far left of the back row.*

Below: *Kildare (now Mooseheart) in 2003.*

Kildare

Another central family at this time was that of Mr and Mrs William Henry Edmunds. In 1891 they bought a farmhouse called Kildare on the edge of the village, the building and gardens of which were well preserved and maintained. During 'spring-cleaning' the family would move out and live in a property on the opposite side of the road (the A371), at that time known as 'Beta' (its garden was used as a kitchen garden for the main house). The site is now called 'Corner Close'.

Wilfred Pain, whose grandfather had started 'The Vinery', went to work at Kildare as head gardener, and took his wife Charlotte with him. They lived at The Lodge with their sons Leonard and Jack and when their third son Edward was born in 1901 Mrs Edmunds took him for her godson. The Pains stayed at Kildare until the outbreak of the war when Wilfred joined the Army and Charlotte joined the Red Cross so that, working at Winchester Military Hospital, she could be near her husband. By the end of the conflict Wilfred was Acting Sergeant Major and Charlotte was head cook.

Later, John and Mary Hopkins joined the staff at Kildare as coachman/chauffeur and cook/housekeeper, and by the time of Mrs Edmunds' death they had been there for 30 years, living in a flat over the stables. In 1927 their only son, Harry, moved into Kildare temporarily with his wife Gladys, and daughter Betty, just before the birth of the couple's twin daughters – Phyllis and Margaret.

Betty Hopkins later married Norman Pain and lived at The Vinery. After the Second World War, her sister Phyllis was asked to work at 'Mooseheart' as secretary to the Loyal Order of Moose – a job which she did for over 30 years.

One photograph shows the coachman for Kildare, Mr George Seabright, who used to fetch the young daughters of the Follett family and bring them to the village; apparently they used to tease him unrelentingly.

Mr Edmunds died in 1900, and his wife presented the church with a tenor bell, which strikes the hour, in his memory. She continued to live at Kildare until her death in 1932 and became an important figure in the village, not only because she provided employment for many local people, but also because of her support for numerous voluntary organisations. Her sudden death was the subject of considerable publicity due to the unusual circumstances. Apparently she died from shock after hearing that her sister, Mrs Sarah Phillips, who was staying with her at the time, had had a sudden heart attack. They both died on the same evening and were given a joint funeral. A tribute to Mrs Edmunds in the *Weston Mercury* confirms her work with those less well off than herself:

Although outwardly she possessed an austere manner, this was merely a cloak of a warm heart, for nothing was too much trouble for her if she felt that by her actions she would be helping to brighten the lives of those around her, and the love she engendered in this way will be a lasting memorial of her.

How 'Kildare' became 'Mooseheart'

After the death of Mrs Edmunds the property was put on the market and was spotted by Cardiff architect, Mr E.C. Morgan Willmott, as he passed through the valley in 1933. He decided that this would be an ideal place to bring up orphaned children, and that it should become a site for the Loyal Order of Moose, hence the new name for the house – 'Mooseheart'. However, it never in fact became an orphanage. It was resolved instead that the prime purpose of this lovely house and grounds should be to serve as a holiday home and a place of convalescence for members of the Order and their widows and children.

The following is taken from '1935 Mooseheart Holiday Regulations':

Weekly charges for holidays are: – Adults £1.5s.0d.
Child £1.0s.0d.

All guests should bring house shoes; changes of underwear, toothbrush, dentifrice, face flannel and night wear. Guests will be subject to the authority of the Matron, or her assistant in her absence. All Guests will be present at Breakfast, which will be at 8.30a.m. Evening prayers will be said at 9.00p.m. All guests are expected to retire at the latest by 10.30p.m. Lights out at 11.00p.m.

Despite a certain level of strictness, it was a popular destination where visitors found themselves in beautiful peaceful surroundings, with a village which was most welcoming on their doorstep.

However, the building was destined to play yet another role in the life of Winscombe. In September 1939 47 boys and two masters from the Polytechnic Craft School were evacuated from London. Some of the children lived at 'Mooseheart', while the larger rooms were used for lessons. One of the teachers was the father of the well-known film star Jean Simmons. Jean went to the village school for a short period and, later in the war, both she and her sister took part in concerts staged for the soldiers in the local Drill Hall. The school returned to London in July 1945.

In 1952 a vocational and guardianship scheme was instituted at the property which proved very useful for young people starting out on a new career.

Through the years many alterations have taken place to improve the property. Members of the Ladies Circle provided a new vocational training building, and some old stables have been converted into offices.

Mr W.H. Edmunds, pictured in 1900.

Mrs Edmunds with her godson Edward Pain, c.1903.

Left: *The garden of 'Beta'. Mr Weeks is standing in the garden with gardener Mr Veale.*

Right: *The coachman at Kildare, George Seabright.*

Above: *Sandford Quarry.*

Above right: *Sheep in 'The Meadow'.*

Right: *Sandford Quarry, c.1880.*

Hillcrest Farm, the home of Mr Herbert Weeks. The building had previously been thatched.

Two

Farming

Highbridge & District Herds Competition, in which F. Mabbett emerged as the winner, 1921.

Whilst arable and dairy farming were the main occupations in the area, this does not seem to have always been the case; the Women's Institute scrapbook of 1933 includes the following:

> *... in years gone by, not only corn, but flax and teasels were extensively grown. One elderly resident recalled that her uncle used to take his harvest of teasels by road in his dilley, and went from this parish to one of the cloth districts in Yorkshire. Another villager made dolls and wax flowers from candles obtained from an Italian warehouse in Bristol at 2s.6d. per pound. A special journey was made to town to buy them.*

In the 1851 census several other trades were given a mention, including dressmaking, saddlery, guilding, carpentry, masonry and cooperage (barrel making). A bailiff, a laundress and a cordwainer were also listed, to name but a few. A great deal of quarrying was carried out at Sandford, where the limestone was extracted for the building of the Avonmouth Docks, and, very much later, the stone was used for the building of the motorway. Another mining area was Shipham, where calamine was extracted.

Agriculture was, however, the major industry in this predominantly rural area and the greatest source of employment. Luckily for local historians, a gentleman by the name of Mr Herbert Weeks was thoughtful enough to write some 'notes' on village life as he knew it as a boy, which provide us with a fascinating glimpse of village and farm life in the early-twentieth century. These were published in the *Weston Mercury* by Mr John Bailey and comprise an interesting mix of recorded history and personal recollections. The following are extracts:

> *There was a placid contentment about the place among folk and a solidarity and steadiness that might well be envied today. Queen Victoria was on the throne: Gladstone was a great star in the political world and Mr W.G. Grace was making history on the cricket field. There was no sound of war alarms.*
>
> *Our home was a long thatched farmhouse, and I was the eldest of four children. We lived mostly in the*

kitchen where a long settle and table filled one side of the room. Overhead hung hams and sides of bacon, and in the corner stood a sack of flour. When this got low, father and I loaded a sack of our own wheat into the cart and drove to the old water mill at Cheddar. It was then dragged to the top storey by a chain, and then we watched the flour pouring into a bag, which was then sent down a chute into the cart.

On baking day the large brick oven was heated with faggot wood, and then the ashes were raked out. Seven monster loaves of dough – one for each day of the week – were popped in, and the door closed until the baking was complete.

My brothers and I often helped in the farm work, especially in the hay fields. Good humour and fun always seemed to prevail and hay-making was looked upon as a sport in spite of the hard work. An old farm-hand had strong views on the use of machinery in the hay fields. He would say the grass didn't shoot as quickly as it did after the scythe, and he did not approve the use of the tedder because it knocked the seeds out of the hay. At the end of the day, we had supper in the kitchen where the men passed round a two-handed cider cup on which was inscribed the following rhyme:

Let the wealthy and great live in splendour and state
I envy them not, and I declare it.
I eat my own lamb, my own chicken and ham,
I sheer my own fleece and I wear it.
I have lawns, I have bowers, I have fruit, I have flowers,
The lark is my morning alarmer.
So jolly boys now, Here's God speed to the plough
Long life and success to the farmer.

To conclude, Mr Weeks sums up his youthful years as follows: 'Those were happy and carefree days for us all – the days of our childhood.'

Cider has been made locally for a great many years either in small quantities by a farmer for his workers or, later, by several well-known producers. Cider was the main drink of the farm workers but one would not want to look too closely at the ingredients of this potent form of refreshment! One long-term villager remembers that it was usual for the farmers to come to 'The Railway' on their horse at the end of the day, tie the horse up outside and, after a 'few' drinks, they would climb on and go home. One day, someone changed the order in which the horses were tied up, and several farmers arrived back at the wrong farms!

An old farm rake.

Not everyone was a cider advocate. In his book *Heart of Mendip* Knight writes:

> *... while the manufacture of cider, for which the country as a whole is celebrated, has of late materially declined to the moral and physical advantage of the community at large. If farmers could only be brought to see it, it would be to their interest in every way to grow apples for household use, instead of making them into cider.*

His idea does not appear to have been generally accepted.

It was not only in the upper classes that marriages took place between local families. The same thing happened among the farming and business folk locally, like those from the hamlet of Woodborough (originally separate from Winscombe and consisting mainly of farms, with fields and lanes between them, interspersed with a few private houses). Of course, such marriages also led not only to a further enlargement of the families involved, but also, in many cases, to the beginning of new businesses (a number of which are discussed below).

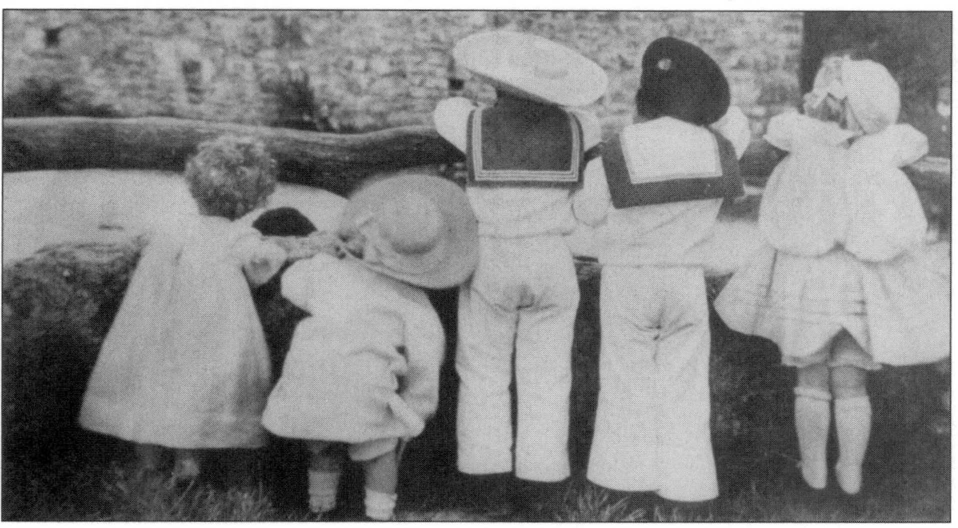
Left: *A picture of Edwardian childhood, seen from behind. The children in the photograph are the same as those on page 5.*

Sandford Road before the houses were built, c.1920.

Below: *Sidcot School seen from the hay fields, c.1880.*

A view of Crook's Peak.

Above: *Building new shops in Woodborough Road.*

Left: *Miss Hilda Amesbury.*

Below: *Old farmhouses which today are shops in Woodborough Road.*

Three

The Main Street

Woodborough Road, modern-day site of Winscombe's shops, banks and offices, was the original road through the hamlet of Woodborough. Geographically it has changed little since the early-twentieth century, but in almost every other way the area has been transformed, for through the years it has been subject to constant change due to the developing needs of the villagers. In the early 1900s the road was narrow, there were no pavements, and many of the properties faced directly on to the road. As can be seen in the photograph of the street viewed from the railway bridge, there is an open drain on the right-hand side which, as rumour has it, became very unpleasant on hot summer days as it served as an open sewer. Also visible in the same image are the wooden planks leading from the road to the properties, which, apparently, were the only means of access.

Although the route of the road has remained the same, obviously through the years many properties have been built or changed hands. By early 1920, numerous houses and businesses were established; personal reminiscences give us some idea of what it was like to live here, beginning with the site occupied, at the time of writing, by the garage.

One gentleman who is no longer with us recalled:

On the corner where the garage is now, there was a cottage and then a large garden. Next to this there was a ginger-beer shop that had been there for many years run by Mr Wilkins. Later the building became a private house owned by Mr and Mrs Sam Pitt. Adjoining this was another large house surrounded by a large garden. This was owned by Mrs Wall, who let out rooms, and when the Quakers had their meetings in the spring and the autumn, many of the relatives would stay there, so she was very busy.

Where Apple Tree Drive is now, there was a butcher's shop owned by the Chapman family, and the entrance to the garden was off this road. One lady remembers this business, because the Chapmans reared their own cattle and when they killed an animal, a portion could be selected, so that the customer would have a leg or the neck or perhaps the loin, and then it would be put back for them.

Woodborough Road from the bridge. Note the open drain and wooden planks on the right-hand side of the picture.

Left: *Mr Stephens' forge in Sidcot Lane. The family emigrated to Australia around 1900.*
Right: *The Old Post Office, Sidcot Lane.*

Another lady remembers Mr and Mrs Amesbury who lived up the road:

> *He lived there when he retired, together with his daughter, Hilda, who bred Angora rabbits. When one had to be killed, the butcher would always tell my mother, who made super rabbit casseroles, and she would always have one. Further up lived the Cook family. The front room of their house was the village chemist shop. In the windows they had large glass containers with the glowing bright-blue or green coloured liquids in them, which many of the youngsters found fascinating.*

The Salisbury family occupied the large house on the corner. Mr Salisbury was a cobbler and leather worker, and when his wife died his two daughters looked after him. Their house went right around the corner to the cottage next door, the home of monumental mason Mr Osbourne. He was very busy, as in those days most people had a memorial of some sort on their graves. The next property was Apple Tree Farm where Mrs Willis Hancock lived. After this one came to the forge owned by Joseph Stephens, whose family later emigrated to Australia. This was one of two forges, the other being owned by Mr John Mabbett on the corner of Church Road. The older men of the village still remember taking their broken hoops to the smithy as children and waiting for them to be mended for the princely sum of one penny.

Where the main road runs around the corner into Sidcot Lane there was another property which was used as a Post Office and owned by Mr Brooks. His sister, Hilda Amesbury, was his assistant. In the Post Office itself many 'odds and ends' could be bought, as testified by Theodore Compton who noted in *Winscombe Sketches* that the Post Office was the source of almost anything one might have needed in the early 1900s:

> *... in short, an inventory of all the articles the shop can supply would contain something for every letter in the alphabet. Let us try: Arrowroot, Boots and butter, Corduroy and comforters. Dips and dust-shovels, Eatables without end, Frills and frying-pans, Geese and Gridirons, Hams and Halters, Ink and Irons, Knives and Ketchup, Lemons and Lollypops, Medicines and Nutmegs, Oatmeal, Umbrellas and Vinegar, Wax and Xylographs, Youths' clothing, and Zoedone, with other articles too numerous to mention.*

This property was also the telephone exchange; thus anyone ringing up would get through to the Post Office, and when, in 1908, the National Telephone Company opened an exchange in the village, it was in this property. It held the distinguished telephone number of '1'. Many people remember those days:

> *... you then asked to be put through to the number you required, and you would be connected. Often, when making a call, every now and then you would hear a comment such as 'I didn't know that!' or 'You don't say!'*

No one appeared to think that these interruptions were unusual.

Around the corner in The Lynch was a sweet shop adjoining the 'Men's Institute'. As one story goes:

> *If you bought some humbugs, for instance, and, after they had been weighed, they were found to be a bit over-weight, the owner would cut one in half to make sure that the amount was exactly right. Her name was Miss Lou Chappell.*

The cottage where Miss Lou Chappell used to live, c.1910. She sold sweets and cigarettes to the Men's Institute.

It appears she had another side to her character, as another elderly gentleman who knew her well remarked:

She did an awful lot for soldiers in the First World War. She was not 'moneyed' in any way but she used to send parcels to the troops. She had a little dog called 'Spotty'. A lot of her trade came from the Men's Club next door e.g. cigarettes and lemonade.

BOOKSELLER & STATIONER.
RANSFORD'S CIRCULATING
MENDIP
BOOKS lent to read at 2d & 3d per week
LIBRARY.
WINSCOMBE.
NEWSPAPERS & MAGAZINES SUPPLIED.

His final comment was: 'I think she was an angel'!

On the corner on the other side of the road is The Green and next to this there was a little site owned by Mr Ransford, who had the paper shop, a library, and (as many of the old photographs show) also worked as the village photographer.

Next one arrived at a shoe shop, followed by Winslades, the ironmongers:

Mr Winslade was a dear old man. He sat at the back of the shop doing nothing much but greeting customers, and so on. Of course, the shop floors were at a different level from the pavements, so you walked down quite a slope. But the number of items you could get there was amazing – things wrapped up that hadn't seen the light of day for ages could be ferreted out. It really was surprising that such a small shop could provide quite so much.

The next building was the Gospel Hall, and then there was a grocer's shop kept by the Walters family. Adjoining this (where the bank is now) was just a garden with hens in it. The next property was 'The Red House' and the three shops that nowadays follow were at that time part of the vegetable garden belonging to the big house at the rear. The next shop was Anthony's stationery shop, and then there was a shoe shop run by Mr Urch.

Always recalled by those old enough to remember it was the fish and poultry shop called Wildridges which was later bought by the Cooper family:

When it came to Christmas time, there being no fridges or deep freezers, ice had to be sent from Weston. The display of turkey, chickens and rabbits and everything else you could imagine, was almost beyond belief because birds started as high up as they could – not quite to the apex – and it came down to

Above: *Cooper's Fish Shop, c.1930.*

Above left: *The building presented by Mr and Mrs Tanner, variously called Tanners Hall, the Temperance Hall, the Men's Institute, the Board School and Woodborough Hall.*

Left: *'Sniffer' Ransford's son Gordon – note the harness on the back of the car. The photograph was taken opposite Birds Shop.* COURTESY OF WESTON MUSEUM

Right: *The corner of The Green and Sidcot Lane, c.1920.*

Above: *Ernest Winslade at around 80 years of age.*

Right: Mr *Winslade in the doorway of his shop; note the advertisements in the windows, showing the varied contents of his shop.*

Right: *Winslades with Mr Uffindell, the manager, before he handed over to Lanes of Cheddar, pictured on 22 April 1979.*

Woodborough Road, c.1930, from a postcard.

Mary Kinsey, c.1970.

the bottom of the window level.

Mrs Maureen Winchester (née Cooper) explains how this display evolved:

My father would go to the market at 4.30 in the morning and open the shop at 7. On 3 December he would go to Winford and do a lot of judging for people. Then he would pick up all the turkeys and chickens he wanted himself. He used to bring all the birds to the back of the shop where he would kill them, truss and draw them and put them in the loft until everything was ready. There was never enough room to keep them at the back of the shop so he had to have a frame specially made to cover the front of the shop, and he would hang all the birds there. There was no 'shop front' as there is today; we just used to drop down a shutter at night. My father used to have a brazier and he would put two stools out on the pavement for Mr Clark and Mr Hemmens to sit on, and he would give them a bottle of whiskey – to keep them warm. This was in 1934. Most of these birds would go to the Wills tobacco factory in Bristol. The managers would have a turkey each and the rest of the staff would have a chicken. Later on, we had a slab at the front of the shop where we kept the fish.

One of the largest shops in the village was Kinsey's, a drapery on the corner of the Woodborough Road; the owner's daughter, Mary, remembers this shop in the early days.

The original shop was in Banwell, and after about four years was moved to Winscombe and occupied the shop next to the Co-op, but later my father built the shop on the corner where the Co-op now stands. He gave a big 'tea' on the day it was opened.

Kinsey's shop, c.1920.

Her father had a tremendous relationship with the farming community throughout the area, which was not surprising as he came from a farming family himself. Mary's grandfather farmed at Brent Knoll:

Edwin Eade's sawmill in Woodborough Road, c.1910.

... my father used to visit the farmers regularly, and, typically, they took their time in paying their bills! As he got more involved with community work he had a man who travelled around the district collecting orders, and another used to deliver parcels. We also had a manageress. She was fully trained and she then trained the apprentices. There were three or four girls in the shop, one of whom remarked that if she had not been so well trained, she would not have been able to get a job at Marshall & Snelgrove in London at a later date. She was very proud of this!

There was a complete men's outfitting department, and the shop sold a variety of goods: materials, haberdashery, clothing, etc. My father also used to sell 'lino' and even laid it out for people. In the shop there was an office where people paid their bills and my father had his own little office at the other end of the shop. The big shop was quite well filled really. It was on one floor, with a stockroom above.

There were very few cars in those days so people shopped locally. Our first car was a Ford, but we also had a van for the man who went travelling. Later my father had a 'De Dion Boniton' car. It had a fringe at the back, and a hood that could be pulled up. It had no windscreen wipers and, at night, the lighting consisted of acetylene lamps. We didn't go out a lot at night, but, if we did, we, as children, were told to be quiet and behave well as the lamps were very tricky to light and my dad was always 'edgy' until he got them properly lit.

Similar comments can probably be recalled by many other people who remember when 'starting handles' wouldn't work properly!

When Mr Kinsey retired in 1936, the business was sold

Thomas Milkins & Sons, coal merchants, c.1920.

Mr Milkins with coal cart and horse, c.1930.

Milkins' shire-horses, c.1920. Left to right: *A.B. Mitchell, Bill Milkins and Jack Milkins. Thomas Milkins and Gladys Milkins with the foal.*

A sketch of Browns Corner, c.1920.

to Messrs Brewer & Page, and they ran it until being bought up by the Co-op. At the time Mr Kinsey advertised a 'Great Transfer Sale', offering special bargains in menswear. For example: 'Men's Bib Overalls' for 1s.0d.; 'Youths' Sports Coats' for 6s.8d.; and men's black or brown shoes for 10s.9d.

Following on from the corner shop, where the butcher, bookshop and pharmacy can all be found in 2004, was a field, and a little further down there were two semi-detached houses. At one time this was the site of a sawmill owned by the Eade family. Unfortunately their business did not survive, and when the mill was shut down at the end of the century, the old steam-engine which was used for power was finally dumped in the old yard at the back of the pub and left to rust away.

Where the council-houses are now used to be a coal and taxi business run by Thomas and Rachael Milkins who lived in 'Hope House' ('Hope Cottage'). They had three sons, Jack, Bill and Ernie, and a daughter, Doris, who married Jack Pain, whose parents owned The Vinery. (In earlier days the coal used to be obtained from Mr A.G. Weeks' coal yard by horse and cart, but later it was collected in cwt coal bags from the station and delivered to the customers.) The Milkins family rented apple orchards to make cider, which was stored in huge barrels in outhouses off a yard where the weigh-bridge was. On Sunday mornings shire-horses were brought there by their owners who would 'sup the cider'.

Saturday, Oct. 29th, 1910.

THE OPENING MEET
OF THE
WESTON-SUPER-MARE HARRIERS
AT
Bird's Assembly Rooms,
WINSCOMBE.

BIRD & SONS,
CATERERS.

During the war they had German POWs working for them. Bill Milkins, who ran a taxi service, would collect them from Yatton in the car, then return them in the evening. He had a garage and workshop with its own petrol pump opposite The Myrtles. Bill used to drive various people to church, or take others, like Sir George Oakley, to catch trains to Bristol. In those days, there were some very wealthy people whom he would drive to different parts of the country for holidays. Most of them lived in Sidcot Lane. Eventually the business was sold to 'Prossers' who had already taken over the concern previously run by A.G. Weeks.

At the corner of Nippors Way there was a sweet shop. The owner, Mr Chapman, won a first prize at Olympia one year for his ice-cream. As Maureen Winchester remarked 'We were very proud of this', and she reliably confirms that he sold 'the most amazing 'gobstoppers' that could be found for the astonishing price of four for a penny.'

Opposite this shop there was a little hut, which may have been used as an abattoir by Mr Abram Bird when he first came to the village. He later bought land on the other side of the road and the Assembly Rooms, and Birds Hotel, Restaurant and Shop occupied the next sites. These hold particular memories for many residents – 'When the bread ovens were opened, the smell in our garden was wonderful.'

Following these buildings where there are now shops, there were two private houses; Mr Sully the cobbler lived in one and Miss Zelley in the other. (She died in 1965 and was, according to the Women's Institute, well known for her artistic and floral activities.) Then, on the corner, one came to Browns Grocery. The family lived on the premises and the corner is named after them.

The village pub was originally (from 1835) on the left-hand side of Woodborough Drive and was known as the Woodborough Inn, but was burned down in 1853. A new pub called the Railway Hotel was built on the same corner in 1927 and the landlord was Mr George Owen. Originally it had a cobbled pavement outside and a market was held there. It was replaced in the late 1930s where the present 'Woodborough Hotel' now stands.

The site of the Railway Hotel, 1927–1938.

Above: *Xanne Blythe, Winscombe's first female parish clerk, 2003.*

Above: *The waterworks between Banwell Road and Max.*

The drinking fountain built by George Thomas of Bristol, 1869.

Above, inset: *The well at Brookside.*

Above: *Fullers Pond in Fullers Lane.*

Left: *Max Mill, Barton.*

Four

Local Government

A meeting was held on 4 December 1894 in order that the parish could elect its Council following the implementation of the Local Government Act.

Chairmen of Winscombe (later Winscombe & Sandford) Parish Council

4 December 1894 Inaugural Parish Meeting to establish Council: Revd R.F. Follett in chair.

1894–96	*Mr W.H. Edmunds*
1896–1900	*Mr J.H.T. Evans*
1900– 07	*Mr C. Burcham*
1907–24	*Mr W. Yatman*
1924–47	*Mr G.J. Dyer*
1947–52	*Mr C.H. Haydon*
1952–53	*Mr R.G.H. Milligan*
1953–58	*Mr N.F. Bird*
1958–61	*Mr E.F. Winslade*
1961–67	*Mr F.G. Austin*
1967–82	*Mr W. Weeks*
1982–84	*Mr D.J. King*
1984–98	*Mr F. Westlake*
1998–2000	*Ms M.J. Ballard*
2000–	*Mr C.R. Sampson*

Clerks of Winscombe (later Winscombe & Sandford) Parish Council

1894–97	*Mr G. Seymour*
1897–1909	*Mr A.L. Newing*
1909–21	*Mr H. Weeks*
1921–22	*Mr H. Clark*
1922–45	*Mr F.J. Anthony*
1945–54	*Mr A.W. Brown*
1954–94	*Mr F.J. Higgins*
1994–99	*Mr R.W.J. Dew*
1999–2003	*Mrs X. Blythe*
2003–	*Mrs L. Rampton*

At this meeting 26 nominations were received for the post of councillor, of which six were declared invalid by the chairman – the Revd Follett. Votes were taken by 'a show of hands' and the seven with the most votes were declared 'duly elected'. (The number of members on the Parish Council was increased from seven to nine in 1929.)

After the election of councillors, the first meeting was held on 31 December. It was a brief affair, intended for little more than the election of officers: Mr W.H. Edmunds was elected chairman and Mrs M. Tanner vice-chairman, and the remaining members were Mr Burcham, Mr H.D. Card, Mr Kerton, Mr Park and Mr G. Seymour. The latter was unanimously elected clerk, at a salary of £5. It was decided that members of the public should not be admitted to their meetings – an exception being made for members of the press.

The Parish Council continues to hold regular meetings to the present day, but parishioners are now encouraged to attend, although it is only recently that they have been permitted to speak – at the time of writing the first ten minutes of a Parish Council meeting are given over to the public.

The duties of those first parish councillors were many and varied; they received and dealt with complaints regarding a whole range of issues, from the lateness of postal deliveries and the provision of letterboxes, to the question of fire hydrants and shooting rights. Yet, apart from these duties, they still managed to find two willing representatives to act as school managers to accord with the provisions of the new Education Act which was passed in 1902.

Motoring & Light

One nuisance that appears to have been with us for a long time is the speed at which motor cars go through the village. The first complaint regarding this appears in the Parish Council minutes of October 1908, although the Motor Bill of 1903 imposed several considerable restrictions on the freedoms of the motorist. Boroughs and counties still retained the right to apply to the Local Government Board to fix lower maximum limits of speed for corners, dangerous places, or for special reasons. All cars were to be registered and licensed by the County or Borough Council, and the first mention of 'Number Plates' was made. These numbers were to be visible at all times.

One specific comment may raise a smile: 'A licence will not be a test or guarantee of skill. It may be endorsed, suspended or forfeited on conviction.' The penalties for breach of these regulations appear quite strict in view of the early date: '£20 or three months imprisonment for first offence. £30 or six months for second offence.'

The inevitable result of the narrow roads was that, with the coming of the car and other large vehicles, accidents were bound to happen. One such event which occurred as early as June 1907 is described as follows in C. Gladwin's *Island in the Hills* (1998):

A motor accident occurred at the corner where Fullers Lane runs onto the Axbridge Road... probably due to reckless driving of a chauffeur alone in his master's very fine car. The driver evidently did not hear another motor coming round the corner in the opposite direction... and applied the brakes so quickly that he skidded across the road, ran up the bank and fell right over upside down... Luckily no appreciable injuries were sustained by the people or the cars...

Although this accident happened nearly a century ago, many similar ones have taken place on the same corner since.

The influence of the Parish Council spread throughout the locality. They arranged for the villagers to have lectures on subjects such as poultry care and orchard management with speakers supplied by the County Council. They also tried, in 1908 (and without immediate success), to arrange for the provision of allotments.

In 1911, the growing volume of traffic, together with its increased speed, necessitated consideration being given to the erection of street lights. The parish had originally been lit by oil-lamps, and it was decided to canvass the villagers regarding the provision of a proper lighting scheme. The Parish Council also decided to erect 'Danger' warnings at Browns Corner, Lewisham Corner and at the corner of The Lynch, but it was not until 1912 that these posts appeared, despite the fact that the Council had given a firm order for them in April 1911 and guaranteed the sum of £1.3.0d. towards the cost. A quotation was received from the Winscombe Electric Light and Power Company to erect 40 lights to be lit from 1 October to 31 March. This would result in the levy of a 3d. rate to which there was strong opposition. It was decided that no action was to be taken at that time. It was not until 1 October 1931 that the following note appeared in the Council minutes: 'The lighting of streets is now complete and will be available from the following Sunday.'

Refuse

Until July 1933 refuse had been tipped at the dump, in a somewhat haphazard manner. On examination the Parish Council found it to be in a very untidy state. A slope, which had been made to enable litter to be tipped on the top, had been filled in and part of an old motor car deposited on top of it. It was decided that the time had come for 'stringent measures' to be taken for the regulation of the site. It was proposed that a Mr Cox should be employed twice a week – on Mondays from 9a.m.–1p.m. and on Wednesdays from 2–6p.m. at a rate of 10d. per hour.

Further comments are to be found in the Council minutes dating from January 1935 to the effect that a further supply of poison was required for the destruction of rats at the dump, and the first mention of a weekly rubbish collection was also made.

On 1 September 1939 a request for a house-to-house collection was rejected. It was noted that such a service would involve imposing at least a 1d. rate. Permission was given for 'excrementary' matter to be deposited at the tip, provided that it was disinfected and buried in a trench not less than 2ft deep and covered with soil, this stipulation to be properly enforced. The situation was somewhat improved in April 1937 when it was announced that refuse would be collected daily at the dump. It appears that this change of mind was brought about due to the increase in the price of old iron – this was to be extracted by the caretaker and sold.

Water-Supply

In the days before the village had a proper water-supply, the local people had to depend on one of the several local wells. There were also two or three springs from which water could be fetched. In 1863 George Thomas of Bristol had a fountain built, which was supplied by the springs from Sidcot Combe. It proved a great benefit to the villagers. According to the Women's Institute:

A dry summer before 1900 recalls the rumbling of water-barrels wheeled, on dusty roads, to and from George Thomas' Fountain. From here many would fetch their water supply for the day.

The fountain gradually fell into disrepair, and only in 2003 was it reinstated. Unfortunately it was not possible to obtain an exact copy of the original pump, but a close likeness could be achieved.

Another villager reports how his father fetched water for domestic purposes from Winscombe Brook – which had never been known to dry up – and later from Hale Well. This he carried in barrels transported using a horse-drawn cart. Eventually a mains supply was laid from Blackdown to Shipham and across Old Down to Daffodil Valley and then Star.

Along the main road to Sidcot standpipes were erected, and later householders had the mains tapped and taken into their houses.

After considerable discussion the Parish Council decided that it would not be possible to form a water company due to the cost. Some members felt that 'if certain people wanted drinking water supplied to their houses, they should be prepared to pay for it themselves.' Eventually the Council received a petition from several residents in favour of the scheme so they decided to obtain reports regarding the cost and the best source of supply – little did they know what they were letting themselves in for.

Indeed, before the information regarding costs could be obtained, a counter-petition was received objecting to the supply of water. On examination, it was found that the petition in favour carried 111 signatures, and the petition against 110. Eight names appeared on both documents! The Council were told that this was easily explained: those who had signed in favour of the supply had changed their minds when they found out that it would have to be paid for out of the rates!

An outbreak of diphtheria put further pressure on the Council to organise a clean water-supply, and the fact that several of the wells in the centre of the village had become polluted added to the urgency of the situation.

The Council must have considered every well in the district, and visited most of them with the surveyor, but for one reason or another they were all rejected as an acceptable source. On 31 September 1901 a suitable scheme was finally put into operation with a supply being brought from Blackdown. This, however, was not the end of the story. The Council discovered that the new scheme did not include provision for Revd Yatman's house at Winterhead but felt that this state of affairs should be redressed because the rateable value of the property was so high. Finally, it was decided to try to find a water-supply on the other side of the parish, at or in the neighbourhood of Hale Well. This would avoid the need to pump water from the low side of the village to higher-level properties. In all it took the best part of five years to set up a satisfactory scheme.

Clockwise from top left: *The mill-pond sluice; the windmill pumping Five Springs; Five Springs in Eastwell Lane; Five Springs.*

Background picture: *Winscombe Church of St James the Great.*

Inset, left: *Winscombe Church interior.*

Left: *Lynch Chapel, c.1850.*
COURTESY OF WESTON MUSEUM

Left and above: *Lynch Chapel, 2003.*

Five

Religion Through the Ages

The following are extracts taken from Maria Forbes' *The Church in Winscombe* and Adrian Shephard's *The Lynch Chapel* – booklets produced as part of the *Millennium Series*, 2000:

The Parish Church of St James

This is a thirteenth-century building on the hill and can be seen from most of the village and the famous Yew tree is over 500 years old. Prior to the Modern times of District Councils, the Churchwardens were responsible for the education and the distribution of poor relief. One other, rather unusual responsibility was the control of vermin. In 1704 John Burges was paid 3/4d. for killing ten polecats. Today their duties include the collection of alms, the disposal of the communion alms, the allocation of seats, the parochial registers and the protection of church property.

In the nineteenth century the church was in need of restoration and this was completed in 1864 'using a donation of £500 from Reverend John Yatman. Resident at Winscombe Hall.' (Compton, 1882, p47)

By the twentieth century the Rev Richard Follett was the Vicar, and lived at the vicarage with his sister, Caroline Follett. In 1871, at the age of 42 he married 22 year old Mary Ann Rawlison and by 1886 they had three sons and seven daughters. When he retired in 1895 at the age of 67, he and his family joined his sister Mrs Fanny Lethbridge (née Yatman) at Winscombe Court.

Since the Rev Follett died there have been several incumbents – from the Rev John Alfred Dodd, who came in 1895 and after him, there have been six others. The present vicar – Rev Michael Slade, feels that the Church has an important role to play in the community, perhaps even more so now in our present age. Due to the ever-increasing secularism of British society, where anything goes so long as it does not hurt anybody, and people are working longer hours than most industrialised countries in the world, the family unit is under increasing pressure from debt and relationship-breakdown. Christianity and the message of the Gospels has never been more relevant.

Mike believes that the Church's role is to engage with people by making them think in new and refreshing ways. Communities and people can become very self-centred, and, by coming closer to God we can find new ways of living that will spill over into our daily lives and affect our relationship with our neighbours. It will also help us to get to know ourselves and love our character and so seek to be better people. He says:

The Church is often seen as the Community's front room. A place to go for special family occasions of celebration and at times of corporate sadness. The occasional Offices of Marriages, Baptisms and Funerals are examples of this, as are times of national concern. People know where to go at these times and recognise the special nature of God's house of prayer, where he is especially present in a mysterious way.

St James the Great continues to reach out to those in need, whether regular worshipper or not. Part of its mission is to respond to human need by loving service. This is achieved through ordinary Christian people going out into the community and showing their love by supporting and caring for their neighbour. All the time there is a Church on the Hill in Winscombe that will continue.

The Lynch Chapel

Prior to the purchase of land in 1827 a non-conformist group had been meeting in private houses in the village under the guidance of Rev Robert Hooppell. Once the Chapel was built there was also enough ground for burials. This was very important because, as dissenters, they would have not been allowed burial in the Parish Church graveyard. The ground contains several graves from early days, including that of a 'Navvy's Child' which was buried around the time of the building of the railway.

As is common in most non-conformist churches, reliance has always been placed on lay preachers, and this practice was continued in the local church. By the beginning of the twentieth century the chapel had become known as 'Winscombe Union Chapel', and was too small for the congregation. After much discussion, in September 1910 it was decided to erect a new building which would cost, at that time, £800. Eventually the new building was opened in July 1911 and at a Church meeting in 1912, Herbert Weeks was elected Church Secretary. He held this post for 48 years. The Church Anniversary was celebrated every Good Friday.

In 1932 Reginald H. Maliphant was appointed Minister, and was a 'well loved' Pastor who convinced the Church that the Sunday School project was viable, even in a period of financial depression. Mr Norman Wills laid the foundation stone in January 1933 and representatives of the other churches in Winscombe attended.

The church continued to flourish. Between 1938–1941 Rev. George Gear was Minister, and the Chapel hosted regular Sunday Services during the war for visiting G.I. soldiers. Miss Margaret Weeks played the organ on these occasions.

The present Associate Pastor Rev. Colin Speed comments:

We continue to meet each Sunday, as generations have done before us, thus guaranteeing a continuation of Christian influence for the present and the future. It is good to report a growing Sunday School, and the formation of a Crusaders Club, so that children and young people can be reminded of the basis of life, as well as having fun together. This enables us to be confident that another generation will continue the work and witness. Other activities take place during the week which include a prayer meeting, a 'drop in' coffee morning, an afternoon meeting and house groups. We are happy for our premises to be used for the benefit of the community and welcome their use by The Rainbow Nursery, Winscombe Orchestra and Winscombe Light Orchestra. Our Mission Statement is very simple yet very sincere. 'We are here to say that God is great and to tell others He loves them.'

The Friends Meeting House at Sidcot.

The Quakers

One of the main influences in the area has come from the Society of Friends, or Quakers. Quakers had already been meeting at a spot in Sidcot north of Woodborough (alongside today's A38) when, in 1699, William Jenkins was invited to open a school there – which is now known as Sidcot School.

A meeting of the Religious Society of Friends is held every Sunday at 10.30a.m. in the Meeting House attached to school and it is open to all those who feel at home in the atmosphere of living silence, when the clamour of daily life is stilled and God's voice can be heard. The basis of Quaker life and practice is a conviction that there is something of God's spirit in everyone; that all can have communion with Him. This involves an attempt to accept literally the command to love God and one another, and so rules out war. It recognises evil but meets it with that goodwill which outlasts it or transforms it.

Associated with the meetings are groups such as Sidcot Peace Action Group (a prayer and support group for those facing some form of crisis) and the sections working for Quaker work at home and abroad. The social side of the meeting is well catered for and every effort is made to ensure that members find true friendship and enjoyment.

The Gospel Hall (Later Plymouth Brethren)

This society no longer exists in the village, but the area occupied by the group's building can still be seen. The story of the Gospel Hall has been told by Mrs Ruth Uffindell, an inhabitant who knew it well; she writes:

Above: *The property that was formerly the Gospel Hall, pictured in 2003.*

Right: *The blue plaque on the Gospel Hall.*

Far right: *A concert at Sidcot School in 1904 for the Temperance Society.*

Winscombe & Sandford Parish Council
Gospel Hall
Built of Triassic conglomerate this and the two cottages behind were part of a cider factory. A place of worship from 1907 to 1976, it was bought in the 1950's by Plymouth Bretheren and called 'The Gospel Hall'. Inside were mobile benches, a small pulpit and a harmonium.

In The Green there were three cottages, believed to be owned by the Walters family – one of which was a Cider House, and was rented during the late 1920s by The Plymouth Brethren, who opened it as the Gospel Hall. They were known as The Assembly, and would have held a devotional service at 11a.m. – similar to The Quakers, with no set speaker and also the 'breaking of bread'. There may have been a Sunday School in the afternoon and a Gospel Service at 6.30p.m. with a set Speaker. During the week a Prayer Meeting was held.

Eventually, the building was purchased by the Brethren for £400. The idea to buy coming from Mr & Mrs Pitt, together with Mr Solly, who was a Boot and Shoe maker and repairer in the village. The money was raised through the Collection Plate, and no doubt some of the members and friends from the sister Assembly in Cheddar. No one had any idea what the other gave.

Preachers included several from the Cheddar area – some of them were Mr S. Pavey, Mr H. Harris and Mr Wade. The Hardridge and Holbrook family were all connected.

The seating was mobile benches. There was a central aisle, with a small pulpit and a table at the front for the serving of Communion. A Harmonium provided the music – Sankey's Hymn Books were usually used. A Conference was held every Good Friday at Birds Assembly Rooms, with possibly a tea, and special Speakers.

The Hall was later sold, the money from the sale being donated to charity. Some went to the Gideons, and, under the influence of leper specialists Brothers Dr Rendle and Latimore Short, some was also given to a leper hospital in India. This donation took the form of surgical equipment.

Winscombe Temperance Society: 1878-1960

Adapted from an unpublished report by Richard Dew

According to available records, this was possibly the earliest established 'society' in the parish. The first meeting took place on 28 November 1878, chaired by the Revd Richard Follett. Records include mention of the fact that this was a 'revival' of a previous Temperance Society, but no further information has come to light regarding this.

The object of the Temperance Society was to discourage the use of intoxicating beverages as being 'unnecessary, dangerous, and often injurious, and the cause of a large proportion of the drunkenness, disease, poverty and crime which afflicted and disgraced the country.' Over the next few months meetings became fortnightly and attendance varied from 20 to 30. Many contributed songs, recitations, or readings for the entertainment of their fellow members. One can only imagine the type of material chosen. The meetings were held in the hall donated to the village by Mr and Mrs Tanner (which at the time of writing is used by the Scout troop).

In 1880 the society was extended to include Sandford where a Band of Hope for the children was formed, and in September of that year the children walked in procession with the Banwell Juvenile Templars to Winscombe Court for a tea provided by Mrs Lethbridge – the Revd Follett's sister. As the meetings continued the number of 'No' pledges recorded increased. In 1890 it was agreed that the name of the group should be changed to the 'Winscombe, Woodborough and Sidcot Gospel Temperance Society'.

At the start of the twentieth century the organisation (by this time now known as 'The Winscombe Temperance Society') held more of their meetings at the Birds Assembly Rooms, presumably because the original venue had become too small. In 1901 a Winscombe Reading Room and Club was formed at Woodborough Hall, and some 70 members were enrolled. The notes left by the Women's Institute in 1933 record the fact that some visitors stayed at 'The Temperance Hotel, opposite the turnpike'. Whether this statement is correct has not yet been confirmed.

Throughout the coming years the society continued to spread its message. Christmas 1904 saw the delivery of 250 leaflets, counselling in a 'loving and earnest appeal' prevention against selfish indulgence, as this brought misery to many homes, and urging abstinence from putting temptation in the way of others. In 1912 an 'Open Air Temperance Fête' was held at The Down with a brass band and games. About 160 attended and the event was followed by a public meeting at which an 'earnest and telling address' was given. A resolution urging the Government to introduce a 'Measure of Temperance reform', as promised by the Prime Minister, was sent to all Cabinet ministers.

The First World War provided the society with the opportunity of spreading its views country-wide. It was felt that the conflict with drink was greater than the conflict with Germany. Apparently, this view was shared by Lord Kitchener who, in 1915, was quoted as saying that 'Germany was a great evil, but the drink evil was a still greater one.'

The outbreak of the war provided the society with a platform on which to place its views. There was concern about the supply of liquor to the Armed Forces and various resolutions were sent to Government ministers and to the local MP. According to a press cutting from 1915 over two million signatures were attached to a 'memorial' over 11 miles in length and weighing a ton which was presented to the Prime Minister urging the prohibition of the liquor trade during the war and for six months thereafter. In the local minutes it is not noted whether Winscombe contributed to this document.

Comforting letters were sent to about 20 society members serving in the Armed Forces, encouraging them to keep their pledge, and by the end of 1917 the society was giving thought to the men's demobilisation. Members were advised that gratitude and kindness should not justify returning servicemen to drink.

Following the war, the society went through a difficult time. Although the situation in the early twenties suggested that the membership was growing, by the middle of that decade it appears that instead of the large meetings of earlier days, the members (mainly women) were meeting in smaller groups in private houses. In 1927 only six members attended the annual meeting, but a public gathering in that year held at Sidcot School attracted a large audience. During 1930 public meetings were held in Sidcot School with talks being given on such subjects as 'The new Outlook in Temperance Reform' and 'Alcohol and the Brain'. Unfortunately, there is no mention of content.

In 1934 Parliament was promoting bills to standardise licensing hours and provide for intoxicating liquor in hotels and restaurants. These attracted strong opposition from the society which reminded the Government and the local MP that not only were these proposals not in the true interest and welfare of the nation, but were contrary to the recommendations of the Royal Commission on Licensing.

By 1937/8 protests were being made to the BBC about a number of programmes on drink, and drinking episodes in broadcast items. At the outbreak of war in 1939 the society was concerned about the unrestricted use of food in the brewing and distilling industries, although rationing had been applied to individual food consumption. Letters were sent to the Government, and in 1942 a letter from Lord Woolton's (Minister of Food) office explained that the Government had decided that beer production should be limited to the level of the year preceding the start of war, that distilling had been reduced, and that other economies in production had also been achieved.

When arrangements were being made for the 'Welcome Home', the society sent a representative who was instructed to make a strong protest again at the provision of a 'Wet Canteen', but the committee eventually upheld the decision of a public meeting held early in 1946 that such a canteen should be provided.

Gradually through the coming years, the membership of the society declined and in 1960 the committee were raising questions about the usefulness of the group. At a general meeting on 25 October 1960, following a long discussion, members agreed that continuation could not be justified. The society was therefore dissolved and the funds in hand (about £10) were sent to the Western Temperance League for the benefit of young persons. Local churches and Friends meetings were asked to use any influence at their disposal for the continuation of Temperance work.

Winscombe Temperance Society.

A

Social Meeting

WILL BE HELD IN THE

WOODBOROUGH HALL,

On FRIDAY, January 29, 1909.

MEMBERS' TEA

At 6 o'clock.

ANNUAL MEETING

(Open to the Public) at 7 o'clock.

At which the Reports of Secretary and Treasurer will be read, and Officers and Committee elected for the current year.

ADDRESSES BY

Mrs. J. WESTON PAULL

AND OTHERS.

Mrs. Bewes, Miss Bewes, Miss Phyllis Ashby, Dr. Lewis and Mr. Spencer Smith will render Songs and Solos during the Evening.

ADMISSION FREE.

Collection for the expenses of the Society.

Left and bottom left: *Examples of the Temperance Society notices regarding future meetings.*

WINSCOMBE

Temperance Society.

A

SOCIAL MEETING

WILL BE HELD IN THE

ASSEMBLY ROOM,

ON

TUESDAY, OCTOBER 24, 1905,

AT 7.30 P.M.

THERE WILL BE

Singing, Readings,

AND

Recitations.

Members are invited to bring their friends.

REFRESHMENTS AT MODERATE CHARGES.

Below: *This is presumably a booklet on the dangers of drink, especially for young people.*

HERE'S HEALTH TO YOU!

A Physiology for Boys and Girls with Special Reference to Alcohol.

BY

MARGARET BAKER

WITH FOREWORD BY

DR. COURTENAY C. WEEKS.

ILLUSTRATED BY THE AUTHOR
AND PUBLISHED BY HER AT
BEACON FIELD, WESTON ROAD, RUNCORN, CHESHIRE.
1927.

OBTAINABLE FROM
THE WORLD PROHIBITION FEDERATION,
LAWSON HOUSE, 190, VAUXHALL BRIDGE ROAD, WESTMINSTER,
S.W.1.

Stiff Paper Cover, 1/6; *Cloth*, 2/-.

Left: *Winscombe Primary School now the Community Centre in 2004.*

Below: *Winscombe School with Mr Scadding, headmaster, 1925.*

Bottom: *Winscombe School. Daisy White is in the second row with the white ribbon, c.1920.*

Six

School Days

Education has long played an important part in village life at Winscombe. The main village school was in Sandford Road and an extract from the Inspector's Report of 1904 indicates that the level of education expected in the village was surprisingly high. For example:

Work to be completed by February 28th 1904 and Approved by H.M.I.:

DIVISION I (Standards 1 and 2)

READING:
'Palmerston'; 'Work at Home' – St. 1
'New Graphic Atlas Readers' – St. 2

WRITING:
Copy Books. Transcription. Dictation.

ENGLISH:
Talkative lessons including Subject and Predicate ('naming' & 'telling') parts. Also to pick out nouns and verbs, all with a view to prepare for the work of Division II.

ARITHMETIC:
The First Four Rules. Concrete examples. Easy money sums to be introduced as the year advances.

ELEMENTARY SCIENCE, or OBJECT LESSONS:
Birds nests. Woodpeckers. Hen's egg. Leaves. Wild Flowers. The Poppy. Parts of a plant. Roots of plants and uses. Orange. Lemon. Cork. Gardening. Plough and Harrow. Haymaking. Hedgehogs. Moles. Bees. Squirrels. Spiders. Stone Fruits. Fruit. Berries. Butter. Cheese. Blacksmith's shop. Tea. Autumn. Paw and Claws with uses.

However, judging by the comments of HMI the school did not always meet the standards required:

The children range from 9–13 years of age inclusive. The scheme of instruction is meagre. It should be given in more detail and show a two years' course in

Winscombe School, Class 1, c.1910.

Reading, Geography, History and Nature Study for each class. Reading is fairly fluent and expression is good, but the Recitation is not well known. Few of the children could repeat poetry learnt a short time back. The Poetry was delivered without any animation and not very distinctly... The Composition exercises are not dated, and consist too much of reproduction [sic]. *The exercises appear to be done by the class, and not by the individual.*

Winscombe School, Class 3, 1925.

The school-leaving age was originally ten but in 1891 this was raised by two years. However, 'exemption' certificates could be obtained for children below this age who were needed to provide financial support for the family. Alternatively, a pupil could obtain a 'labour certificate' upon reaching a certain level of proficiency in reading and writing – although they might be under age. For some families it was more important for the children to get a job and earn a wage than to expand their minds. Two examples from the school registers confirm this. In 1915 ten-year-old Herbert Tucker left for 'work' and in 1915 Edward Wall, aged 13, left for 'war work'.

One elderly resident, Miss Margaret Weeks, who at the age of 15 taught the infants class prior to going to Cambridge for her full teacher training, has clear memories of those days. The school consisted of one large room, divided into three by curtains. The rooms were heated by 'tortoise' boilers, surrounded by a metal guard. In order to light the heater, one required a bit of wood, then a little coal and then the stove was kept going with coke. In wet weather most of the children's coats were hung on the railings to dry, as there were no waterproof macintoshes or wellington boots in those days.

There was no provision for exercise, but, considering that many of the children had a long way to walk to and from school, this was probably not necessary. Some of the children came from as far as Sandford, Barton, Shipham and Winscombe Hill, and the children whose mothers worked would bring something with them for lunch. Miss Weeks remembers on one particularly cold day that the teacher heated some milk and made the children a drink of cocoa, the cost of which she provided herself. The headmistress at this time was Miss Derrick.

Most of the children appear to have enjoyed their school days, but one elderly gentleman recalls his early education thus:

I hated going to school, and I remember getting a 'darned' good hiding for not wanting to go. I'd lay in the road and kick. I knew that when I turned the corner and the Master saw me, if he said 'Good morning Edward' – I knew he was cross, so I went in. If he said 'Good morning Ted' I knew he was in a good mood and I used to play him up a bit. I used to lay down and kick at him and he used to poke me with his stick now and then – mind you, I probably deserved it. One thing I always remember – I used to 'ply' a pin (Bend it up like this, so that the point would stand up) and then I would put it on his seat. Then he got into the habit of dusting his seat every morning, and strangely enough, every time he found a pin, he used to say 'Come here Ted Hares' and I'd get the stick round my bottom! He wasn't a bad Master.

The Chestnuts

There was also a private school in the village known as The Chestnuts. Joan Searle's description of the way that lessons were taught there suggests little difference between that and the main village school. There was no need for PE lessons at The Chestnuts either; Joan got plenty of 'exercise' in her daily life without doing any more at school:

I walked to school, back for lunch and then back again. I started at 8.45 and I didn't finish till gone four o'clock. We always had a lot of homework right from the beginning, and I also had to help on the farm. After I was twelve years old, I milked three cows before I went to school, then milked them again when I came home. We all had jobs allotted to us – my sister would bring the cows in from the field in the morning and take them out again at night. Someone would feed the hens and collect the eggs.

There were three teachers at the school – the Gadd family who lived at Towerhead, Banwell. Their names were Lucy, Ethel and Edith, and they came to school by pony and trap. One of their daughters, Dorothy, also went to the school. The school was on the first floor and underneath was a large open area. It had wooden battens with hooks attached all round, and we went in this way. We took off our coats and, in sun, rain or snow, we had to walk up the outside steps to the classroom.

This was a very big room... divided into three with curtains, so that if you weren't keen on your lesson you could sit there – looking attentive – and listen to

Miss Gadd, a teacher at The Chestnuts, c.1920.

Chestnuts School and a botany lesson in progress, 1930.

Chestnuts School pupils, 1920.

Winscombe Primary School, c.1925.

Chestnuts School, Sidcot Lane, c.1930.

Betty Kinsey in the uniform of Chestnuts School, 1920.

'We all went to The Chestnuts!' These are pupils from the 1920s, pictured in 2002. Left to right: *Joan Searle, Ruth Searle, Margaret Weeks, Mary Kinsey, M.G. (Bunty) Tracy.*

what was going on in the next room! But if you were found out, woe betide you!

An early example of the standard of work expected at this school can be gleaned from an 'essay' written by Ethel Weeks in approximately 1903.

A Public Gathering

On the 10th of this month a public entertainment was held in the Assembly Rooms. The Misses Edmunds and Follett had the arrangement of the programme which was composed of singing, recitations, readings, duets and Pianoforte pieces.

Mr Dodd (the Vicar) spoke very nicely to the audience, telling them when the bells were to be repaired, and other Church and parochial matters. Mr Jarman gave us a reading entitled 'A Devonshire Supper' which was very amusing. Mr Prideaux sang two songs, one was entitled 'Tomorrow will be Friday' which was very prettily arranged. One very interesting part of the programme was a dialogue by Miss Follett and Miss Nellie Edmunds. They wore wigs and were dressed to represent old maids. Miss Nellie Edmunds also recited a very pretty poem called 'The Evening Hymn'.

Miss Butterfield, a whistler, very ably whistled 'Home Sweet Home' and 'The Harmonious Blacksmith'. She was the only one that was really encored. Mr Robinson, a friend of Mr Dodds, sang a song called 'How Jem Found a Wife' which was most amusing. One verse told how he (Jem) chanced to kiss a Parson's wife. Mr Garaway sang 'I'm a True-born Englishman' in which all who knew the chorus joined. Miss Evans and Edith Mabel Thatcher played a very pretty (but rather long) duet. Mrs Prideaux's voice sounded very well in the song entitled 'A Quaker's Daughter'. Miss Hancock played a piano solo, 'Sleigh Bells'. She had bells tied on her arms so as to make a tinkling, like sleigh bells.

Mr Dodd at the close said he was sure everyone had spent a most enjoyable evening and thanked Miss Follett and Miss Edmunds for all the trouble they had gone to to benefit others.

This essay was written in the most perfect copperplate handwriting and shows not only the quality of the work of the school, but also conveys something of the social life at the time. Joan also recalls a special day when a large procession took place which, she thinks, was organised by the Quakers. As far as she remembers, it was referred to as 'Empire Day':

I remember we were all given a very wide band to go round our shoulders, and the names of different countries were written on each one, so that all the countries of the Empire were mentioned. One year, my father led the procession behind the band. He was dressed as John Bull. We all walked down the road, and finished up at Birds Assembly Rooms where tea was provided. I was asked to be Britannia because I had very fair hair, but as it was thought to be a bit short, I was given a wig made out of straw-coloured string that had been teased out and was very heavy. Then something was put round my shoulders to represent Britannia.

I had to sit at the end of the room where there was a platform, and on top of this there was a table with a chair on it. It looked a bit 'wobbly' to me but people seemed to think it was all right. I can't remember what was said or done after this, but eventually I was allowed to come down from my wobbly perch and we all tucked in to tea.

After their primary education, most of the children went straight to work. Joan had always wanted to be a nurse, but she had to wait until she was 18 before she could start. In the event, she became engaged at 17 and at 19 she married her husband, George. Many of the boys were in farming and the girls went either into 'service' or worked in one of the local shops. Further education took place either at Weston-super-Mare at the Grammar School, or in Wells at The Blue School.

Sidcot School

Taken from *The Island* by Christine Gladwin

There have been schools at Sidcot since 1699 on a site where the air was considered healthy, and there was the added bonus of a well-established Friends Meeting (see Chapter Five). Educational provision was much the same as in other schools of the period, but Quaker beliefs were a strong influence. A number of Quaker boarding-schools were founded in England throughout the nineteenth century, of which seven still exist. Local meetings approved the plan to educate 70 children and agreed to help with subscriptions. John Benwell was willing to sell his 14-acre estate to Sidcot for the purpose, and he and his wife carried on as superintendent and mistress until 1810. The new school opened on 1 September 1808 with nine pupils – six boys and three girls – on the roll.

By the early 1900s the curriculum had become more liberal – for example, art and music were introduced. Standards rose and more children of non-Friends were accepted. According to a report, in 1902 the school had 132 pupils, and this figure had greatly increased by 1908.

Through the years the participation of Sidcot School in local and national events has had a considerable influence within the parish and the connection between the school and the 'Friends' has been a constant feature.

With all the changes in technology during the following years, even school days were affected. Whilst pupils living only a few miles from Sidcot came as boarders in the early-twentieth century because even that short distance entailed two changes of train, the invention of the motor car completely changed all this. By the 1920s parents were beginning to bring their children to school by car, so the 'school run' is nothing new.

The headmaster in those days was Bevan Lean, and as he was there for such a long time he inevitably made a big impression, not only on the pupils, but also on the school itself. Major building projects and changes in policy regarding such issues as co-education and discipline needed time to be completed and the stability of his headship made this possible.

Left: *Sidcot School, 2003.*

Top picture: *Sidcot School; the art room, c.1920.*

Above: *Sidcot School and a painting class, 1920.*

Tanners Hall, 2003.

Tanners Hall

This building in the Lynch has been used for a variety of purposes through the years, including as a night-school for a short time. When the 'National School' was built in Sandford Road, the room was altered and enlarged, and was, for a while, the largest room in the area. According to the Women's Institute records:

> *Several activities took place there, including Spelling Bees. These were one of the first kinds of entertainment and the 'leading spirit' was a master from Sidcot School. Later, lectures were given and 'Penny Readings with Songs' instituted. These were probably the forerunner of the Choral Society that followed. This was a small mixed choir of men and women and they practised at the Vicarage.*

During the First World War, the Men's Club closed, presumably because most of the members who were not in the Forces combined with other village associations. In 1916 special window blinds were obtained due to lighting restrictions, and in 1918 electric light was installed. During this period, the building was used as part of the 'British School' until 1912 when this was discontinued. The Club reopened in 1917.

In the 1930s the Hall was used mainly in the winter for a Men's Club and Institute. Being that this was a strictly 'non-alcoholic' building, there are many tales of the early days when men would dash out, mount their horses and run off to the pub. Although card-playing was permitted, no gambling was allowed.

In 1921 the Hall was officially declared not to be a school building and a new group of trustees was formed. When the building was enlarged, billiards tables were put in and electric light was installed. No one was allowed to use the room on Sundays or on Good Friday. During the Second World War the building was used by the ARP authorities and after the war it was still in use as a billiards room. Finally, it was used regularly by the local Scouts, a situation which continues at the time of writing.

Above: *Sidcot School's workshop, c.1920.*

Right: *A cycle outing pictured at Sidcot School, c.1880.*

Seven

A Lively Village

By the early-twentieth century Winscombe was becoming well known locally. A newspaper report of 8 April 1908 included the comment that it had undoubtedly become one of the most go-ahead villages in the district, not so much due to its being a picturesque holiday destination, but because of the united spirit which prevailed among the residents, and which resulted in 'the organisation of quite a multiplicity of attractions.'

Despite the fact that most of the villagers worked hard, they still took every opportunity to enjoy themselves. One elderly gentleman recalls spending many happy childhood hours sailing on a pond in a small tub, which had to be handled carefully or it would capsize. Sometimes the boys also played 'Hare and Hounds', rounders or walking on stilts. Former villager Mr Orion Caple remembered an activity that was not at all unusual in the early part of the century:

> *My neighbours and I would go twice a week to Sandford Wood with lamps to shine into the trees to enable us to pick off all the birds that were roosting there. It was mostly starlings, but there were also the blackbirds and thrushes. Occasionally, there were pigeons and ring doves and the odd pheasant.*

The birds would be gathered and then taken home in sacks before being sent to Bristol by carter for food. Apparently, one would get a return of ½d. per sparrow, 1d. per starling, thrush or blackbird, and 2d. for a pigeon or a dove. A pheasant would bring in 5d. In total an average of 2s.6d. was 'good money in those days for a night's work.'

By 1908 Winscombe was also becoming well known as a holiday resort and visitors could come by train and then be taken around the nearby countryside by what were advertised as 'Attractive Rail and Coach Trips through the Mendip Hills' organised by A.G. Weeks. The trips were so arranged that when a train arrived at Winscombe or Cheddar, a charabanc or brake would be waiting to take passengers to the next village. There were options regarding the return journey for those who wished to remain longer. The return fares for the circular trips were decided according to the 'class' of seat, but varied from 5s. first class to 3s.6d. third class for Tour No. 1, and from 4s.6d. to 2s.9d. for Tour No. 2. Although tickets were available for first, second or third class, however, there was no classification given for Mr Weeks' charabanc or other vehicles.

The villagers were not only concerned with local events; they participated in occasions of national importance with equal enthusiasm. After considerable discussion the Parish Council decided to hold a meeting to decide the best way in which the village would commemorate King Edward VII's accession to the throne in 1902, and arrangements were made for a day of 'festivities' for the whole village. However, things did not go exactly to plan. As some people will remember, the arrangements had to be changed due to the fact that the King had appendicitis. In view of the seriousness of the illness, it was decided that the original programme should be cancelled. Instead, the Revd J.A. Dodd held a morning service in the church at which most of the villagers were present. In the afternoon, a tea party was given for about 120 children, and at six o'clock some 300–400 parishioners enjoyed a 'meat tea' in a marquee that had been specially obtained. The National Anthem was sung after both these events.

A.G. Weeks – coaches for hire, c.1920.

Apparently, these arrangements did not suit everybody, as a letter of protest printed in the local paper shows:

Left: *Winscombe Scouts and the Cub mistress, Miss Ramson, c.1930. The Scoutmaster is Herbert Weeks.*

Right: *A family picnic under a chestnut tree in Sidcot Lane, c.1920.*

Below: *Church Road and Barton Corner, c.1920.*

Left: *The corner of Sidcot Lane and Woodborough Road, c.1920.*

Below: *Hunt at the corner of Nippors Way, c.1920.*

Whilst the King was lying seriously ill, the residents should have not been encouraged to indulge in feasting... can you fancy Englishmen going in for enjoyment under the circumstances, especially in a civilised village like Winscombe. There must be some truth in the old saying, however, 'where there is no sense there is no feeling'... disgust largely prevails in the village at the fact of residents indulging in senseless amusement, while the King lay suffering.

The newspaper finished the article with the following comment regarding the unnamed complainant's letter – 'We have given our correspondent's remarks, not from any desire to endorse the same, but merely "for what they are worth".' The complaint does appear most unfair as the waste from tea for almost 500 people would have been unthinkable.

One might imagine that in 1912 a small village such as this would not have involved itself in a heated political argument. However, at a meeting in February of that year Revd Dodd appears to have upset certain people once again. A letter from Mr George Day the same month clearly conveyed very strong views on the subject, according to this extract from the *Weston Mercury*:

I should be glad of a little space in which to make one or two remarks in reference to the speech made by the Rev. J.A. Dodd at the Women's Suffrage Meeting held at Winscombe the other week.

Revd J.A. Dodd, c.1920.

Most of us may possibly agree with the main part of the speech, but there is one part of it that is so clearly hostile to any extension of the franchise in a democratic direction that no liberal can for a moment accept it. Personally I am very much surprised that he should have made any such remark after emphasising the non-party nature of the question they were to discuss.

The remark the Rev. gentleman is reported to have made is as follows 'He was sorry to say that in his opinion, a great many people had the vote who should not have it, and he should certainly take away the vote from any people who could not read or write...'

One would like to know who the 'many' are that he says should not have the vote. At any rate, the poor illiterates have come in for it. I am sorry our local vicar has not more sympathy with the illiterates... But, Sir, I am one of those that believe that education and refinement are not the only or even the chief things that qualify for the proper exercise of the vote. The grim struggle for existence, the keeping of homes, and the successful rearing of families on a few shillings per week, are things that bring people into contact with the hard facts of life. Yours etc...

Serious political issues were far from the minds of several people on a different morning in 1912. This was when the Round Britain Air Race took place and as the 'planes would actually pass over the village, it would prove to be very exciting, particularly in these very early days of flying.' One story of the event was given by Mr Orion Caple:

... my father took us kids, in the company of many others, up to the top of Callow at 3a.m. in July because we had learned overnight that the competitors in the 'Round Britain Air Race' had arrived in Bristol and would be leaving again at sunrise to continue their journey to Bristol. One of the girls who was there spotted them first and shouted 'here he is!' There were two planes approaching... coming over Shipham towards us. It was two Frenchmen by the names of Beaumont and Verdrines. We also spotted another plane which proved to be piloted by Col. Cody.

Slightly lower in the sky were the wires which had appeared the previous year when the Winscombe Electric Light and Power Company was established. A comment in Knight's *Heart of Mendip* reads as follows:

For some time there were only two overhead wires; but even these two proved fatal to many birds, especially landrails [or corncrakes], partridges, woodcocks and skylarks, which flew against them, no doubt chiefly in the dark. Dead birds are picked up under the telegraph wires still, but in much smaller numbers than was the case forty years ago. Whether it is a consequence or merely a coincidence, it is a fact that thunderstorms are less frequent and less severe in the district than they were before the erection of this long line of wires.

A coach outing pictured outside Browns Stores, c.1920.

Some older inhabitants remember corks being hung on the wires, presumably to try to prevent such occurrences.

Early Railway Days

According to the information provided for us by the Women's Institute, prior to the arrival of the railway the transportation of goods to another area could involve quite a difficult journey:

An uncle of one of our elderly neighbours used to take his harvest of teasels, by road, in his dilley, all the way from this parish to one of the cloth districts in Yorkshire. We are told that wax dolls and wax flowers were made by another villager from candles obtained from an Italian warehouse in Bristol. He not only attempted these items, but was ambitious enough to make a wax effigy of his wife, which resides on his mantel-piece.

There are also unconfirmed tales of a postman, many years ago, bringing letters from Bristol when he had only a horse and cart, and on arrival in the village one winter he was frozen stiff. Indeed, the whole question of travel was of interest to all:

It was a serious matter to go off on a train journey. The farmers and most of the gentry had their own conveyances to take them to Yatton or Banwell station, as Puxton was then called. Those who had no carriage or cart had to content themselves with one or other of the very few vehicles which could be borrowed. Of course, there was a carrier to Bristol, travelling in his covered cart by night to avoid a second toll, if he could pass through just after midnight. A tall man he was, and looked a fine figure dressed in his smock and drab gaiters. He was invaluable in doing all sorts of commissions in town, besides fetching and carrying packages of all sorts and sizes.

When Winscombe's station was first built, it was a little chalet built of wood for the sake of lightness as it was being placed on a newly-made embankment. In 1902 the embankment was widened to enable a 'loop' to be inserted for the goods wagons to carry stone from Sandford and Cheddar quarries. The stone was initially used to build the St Edwards dock at Avonmouth and later as ballast on the track.

In 1904 a new station was built and one of today's elderly residents notes that his first memories included watching his father, one Sunday morning, helping to drag the old wooden station from the yard up the main street. Later it was cut in half and used as a shop for many years. Like many changes in life, the railway gradually became accepted and was found to be very useful, and many people became quite attached to the whole idea. Locally, in the very early days of the line, it was not uncommon for the stationmaster to apologise to would-be passengers for having let the train go without them!

As early as 1908 – when Sidcot School held its centenary celebrations – train travel was part of everyday life, as testified by the information list carried at the end of the programme for the celebrations. Another comment which may raise a smile today is the final note regarding 'smoking'. An excerpt from the programme reads:

LUGGAGE: should be labelled with address of lodgings. G.W.R. Agent (Fry) will deliver luggage at 3d. per package (6d.) to outlying districts, e.g. Shipham, if a load can be made up; otherwise by arrangement.
WEEK'S LIVERY STABLES: close to Winscombe Station. The school is not quite a mile from the Station. Name Badges to be worn by all present, will be issued here. Visitors are requested to obtain badges promptly, and also to sign the visitor's book at the office. The wearing of the Badges is a necessary passport to the Loan Exhibition.
It is requested that there shall be NO SMOKING on the School premises (The 'Island') except in the Gymnasium, which, after Saturday evening, will be spent as a Smoking Room.

Eight

The First World War

Soldiers and nurses at 'Monkshaven', Winscombe. Mrs Yatman and Mrs Follett are shown at the front of the group.

One of the benefits of country life when it came to wartime is that food was, perhaps, not as scarce as it might have been in town. 'There was always the odd rabbit to be had' is an oft-quoted phrase and, as Orion Caple explained, catching birds could also be a means of getting money and providing food.

This practice was not forgotten during the war. A request was received from the Rural District Council by way of a letter regarding the destruction of rats and house sparrows. The problem was that these creatures were eating food and seed meant for people. Rewards were given for their destruction and bills were posted offering the following sums: 1s.0d. per dozen for rats' tails; 3d. per dozen for fully fledged sparrows' heads; 2d. per dozen for unfledged sparrows' heads; and 1d. per dozen for house sparrows' eggs.

Although there is very little locally recorded data regarding the First World War, there is no doubt that it impacted heavily upon the village. Many of the local men were in reserved occupations such as farming, but there is one record that shows even those who were unable to enlist were prepared to do whatever they could to help with the war effort. As early as August 1914, only ten days after the declaration of war, reference was made to a 'communication' from the Chief Constable of Somerset which resulted in a meeting in the Birds Assembly Rooms that evening. The aim was to find volunteers to guard the tunnels and bridges on the railway line through the village, together with the water-supply at Blackdown. Roughly 60 people put their names down.

The following day the committee appointed met at the Railway Hotel at 10a.m. Col W. Yatman was elected chairman and Mr W.R. Temple Bourne hon. sec. Mr F. Frost was appointed CO of the force, with full power to act in any way he thought fit. It was agreed that the volunteer group should be called The Winscombe and District Civil Defence Force (Somerset Record office, DD/X/TBW).

As the area to be covered was so large it was decided that it would be impossible to guard the potential targets by day, and that the best thing would be for a member of the committee to visit them occasionally. This was a considerable undertaking given that many of the volunteers had businesses to run or other duties to carry out – men such as Revd J. Dodd, A.G. Weeks, R. Kinsey and Mr K. Dunster. After carrying out their daily tasks, they were then prepared to go out at night to do their wartime duties.

Whilst the men of the village were prepared to continue for as long as was necessary, it transpired that their services were only required for a few months. On 10 September the Rural District Council decided that it was unnecessary for the railway bridges and tunnels to be guarded and on 24 September the force received a rather curt letter informing them that:

Right: *'Sunny' Brown in Army uniform.*

This picture: *Families saying goodbye at the station.*

Below: *Winscombe Reserves.* **The photograph includes:** *A. Bird, Mr Kinsey, Mr Mabbett, P. Weeks, K. Dunster, Mr Hemmens, Mr Amesbury.*

No more guard duties will... be fixed for the present and all those appointed to duty this week are relieved of their duties... [we] *wish the Force to remain in existence for future use in case any other local work should become necessary, or in case the necessity for guarding the Waterworks should arise again. The Force is therefore not disbanded although its activities cease for the time being.*

However, on 24 September Col Yatman received a letter from the Rural District Council:

... expressing the Council's warm appreciation and thanks to you and the organisers of the Winscombe Civil Defence Force, and the Volunteers for the prompt and efficient manner in which you have afforded and are continuing to render, such assistance in their guarding of the Water Works properties.

Sidcot School

Taken from *The Island* by Christine Gladwin

The outbreak of war changed the peaceful life of this school from its former daily routine. By 1915 64 old scholars were in the Armed Forces, 28 were in the Friends' Ambulance Unit, and six were in War Victims Relief Work. Some of these were older brothers and sisters of pupils still at the school, and consequently the dangers and dreadful conditions in the trenches were brought home much more forcibly.

At the school the main complaint appears to have been the food.

... sometimes we went to bed hungry. We had about one egg a term. Breakfast – rather lumpy porridge, bread and marge... Tea, bread and marge, perhaps jam. Tea on Sunday was cake instead of jam... sometimes burnt! Supper. Cold milk (very cold in winter) or so-called soup, more like washing-up water as we called it.

For the first few months of the war, a collection of between £5–6 was made by the pupils towards the relief of distressed Belgians and in aid of the Ambulance Unit. By Easter £450 had been raised, and a talk on the Unit's work gave not only the school, but also visitors from Winscombe, an insight into what was happening in Europe. By the end of April 1915 three ambulances had been provided which were to be used at Dunkirk on 5 May. Each contained four stretchers named after the local hills.

The number of old scholars on active service continued to grow and many more joined the Friends' Ambulance Unit. A report in 1916 included the comment that of the 89 men on active service, five had already been killed. By 1918, 130 old scholars had joined the Services and, of that number, 21 were

Ronald Weeks of the Somerset Yeomanry.

Below: *Sidcot School fire crew, 1913.*

A party for wives and families of servicemen in the grounds of Kildare, c.1914.

dead and 31 wounded. The final toll was 167. Thankfully, when the 'flu epidemic swept Europe at the end of 1918, there were no fatalities in the school, but eventually there were 137 cases, including some of the teaching staff and maids.

Winscombe Women at War

With regard to the majority of the women, there is very little material to be found referring to their day-to-day life, but from what little evidence there is, it seems that most people tried to do their best and to take enjoyment where it could be found. Naturally, parcels were prepared for the troops and photographs show families waving their men off from the station.

Several of the women with large houses gave tea parties for the families and children of the soldiers, and one house was used as a convalescent home – one photograph *(page 51)* shows the soldiers, their nurses and the local Scouts sitting out the front. The two elderly women in the front are Mrs Yatman and Mrs Follett. Another photograph *(page 54)* shows a group of village women working in what appears to be a 'supply depot' for the district in a hall in Winscombe.

There is one photograph *(page 54)* that has proved very difficult to explain. It clearly shows a column of men marching through the village, presumably on their way to the station, but, despite numerous enquiries, their presence has remained a mystery. One explanation is that they were stationed somewhere locally and were being moved to the Front, or perhaps they were taking part in a route march.

Wartime Stories

Of the many men who served their country from this parish little information has survived. Most of them appear to have been in either the 1st Somerset Light Infantry or the 1st Gloucesters. What follows is the outline story of just three of these brave young men.

Sgt James F. Bancroft was awarded the Croix de Guerre on behalf of the French Government. He was later reported to be slowly recovering from dangerous wounds in an English military hospital. Sgt Bancroft had previously been awarded the DCM on 5 May 1916. The citation reads:

> *For very great gallantry and leadership on the evening of the 14th April 1916 at RIEZ DU VINAGE. In the attack when the leading Companies were held up by M.G. fire, he went forward with Captain Osborne for support, reinforced the front line, and started his platoon in section rushes, himself going ahead. His gallantry was largely responsible for getting the whole line forward in a difficult situation. He again did good work in clearing the village. In the enemy counter-attack at noon on the 16th, he again shewed* [sic] *exceptional courage and ability in helping to repel it. Awarded. DISTINGUISHED CONDUCT MEDAL 5.5.16*

Right: *A column of troops marching through the village towards the station. The regiment and destination are unknown.*

Left: *Winscombe Ambulance Team, c.1914, in the grounds of 'Mooseheart'.*

Right: *Winscombe Hospital Supply Depot, 1916.*

Left: *Winscombe Red Cross, with Mrs Parry the Commissioner, c.1915.*

When he recovered from his wounds, Bancroft returned home on a few days' leave, and before returning to the Front he was given a silver watch from his friends, with their good wishes. He was the first man to receive these distinctions in the neighbourhood, although many other men from this area also served in the same campaigns. The presentation was organised by Corp. A.J. Tucker, who had also served in the Gloucesters.

James Edward (Ted) Bancroft was awarded the DSM and the Croix de Guerre.

Another man from the village who served in the war was Albert Nipper. According to information supplied by his family, William Nipper was born in 1738 and had a son, grandson, and great-grandson named after him, all of whom were born in Woodborough (now Winscombe) and were farmers. In c.1883 William, the great-grandson, married Sara Marshall and had a son; this was Albert.

Aged around 30 Albert joined up, enrolling in the 1st/14th Gloucester Regiment (The City of Bath TF) and was Private No.201971. The regiment went to the Western Front as part of the 105 Brigade, 35 Division, on 30 January 1916.

According to the Brigade War Diary, on 12 April 1917 the Battalion moved to Monchy Lagache in Divisional Reserve. The following morning the Companies were at the disposal of the Company officers. Several were trained under the 'Specialist' officers, who continued their training in the afternoon. The rest of the Battalion worked on the Monticourt–Trefcon Road. There is no indication of casualties, but something must have happened to Albert. He is remembered on the Thiepval Memorial, France, but has no known grave.

In the Roll of Honour in the Parish Church at Winscombe, Albert's surname is spelt incorrectly as NIPPOR, but on the war memorial in the churchyard it appears correctly. He is also remembered in the Book of Remembrance at Wells Cathedral (p.166).

It is easy to remember Albert's family thanks to the fact that there is a lane in the village known as 'Nippors Way' where the family lived for many years. The lane was originally called 'Beck Nippors Way' on old maps, but whether there is any link between the two families is not known.

Another young local boy did what so many others decided to do and joined up without telling anyone. His name was Frederick Conibeare. His great-aunt, Mrs Ruth Conibeare, tells how one morning his father, the local policeman, went into Weston to collect his orders as usual, when he met a friend who said 'I've just seen your son – he's at the station and is going to enlist.' Despite the pleading of his family, Frederick enlisted aged 17 and was one of the unfortunate ones who did not return. His name is recorded on the plaque in the Community Centre with those who attended the village school. He is also shown on the memorial of those who fell from Sandford.

Role of Honour

The names of those who had served in the First World War from Winscombe were listed on a 'Role of Honour and Role of Service' board. Initially, this was made of wood (thought to be taken from the timber of an old battleship) and could be viewed at the bottom of The Green. Later, however, it was replaced by a new one installed in the porch of the Parish Church.

The present war memorial stands on high ground in the churchyard, beyond the west door and overlooking the beautiful countryside for which these lives were given. The Sandford names were listed on a 'Roll of Honour' board near the church. Sadly, this seems to have disappeared when the garage was rebuilt. According to the list of servicemen in *From Parish Pump to Parish Present* by P. Cram four of the 37 Sandford men who fought in the conflict were lost.

Another memorial on the wall of Winscombe School listed the names of the scholars who died. This plaque is now in the Community Centre.

The pupils of Sidcot School converted an old swimming-pool into a Garden of Remembrance for those pupils who had served.

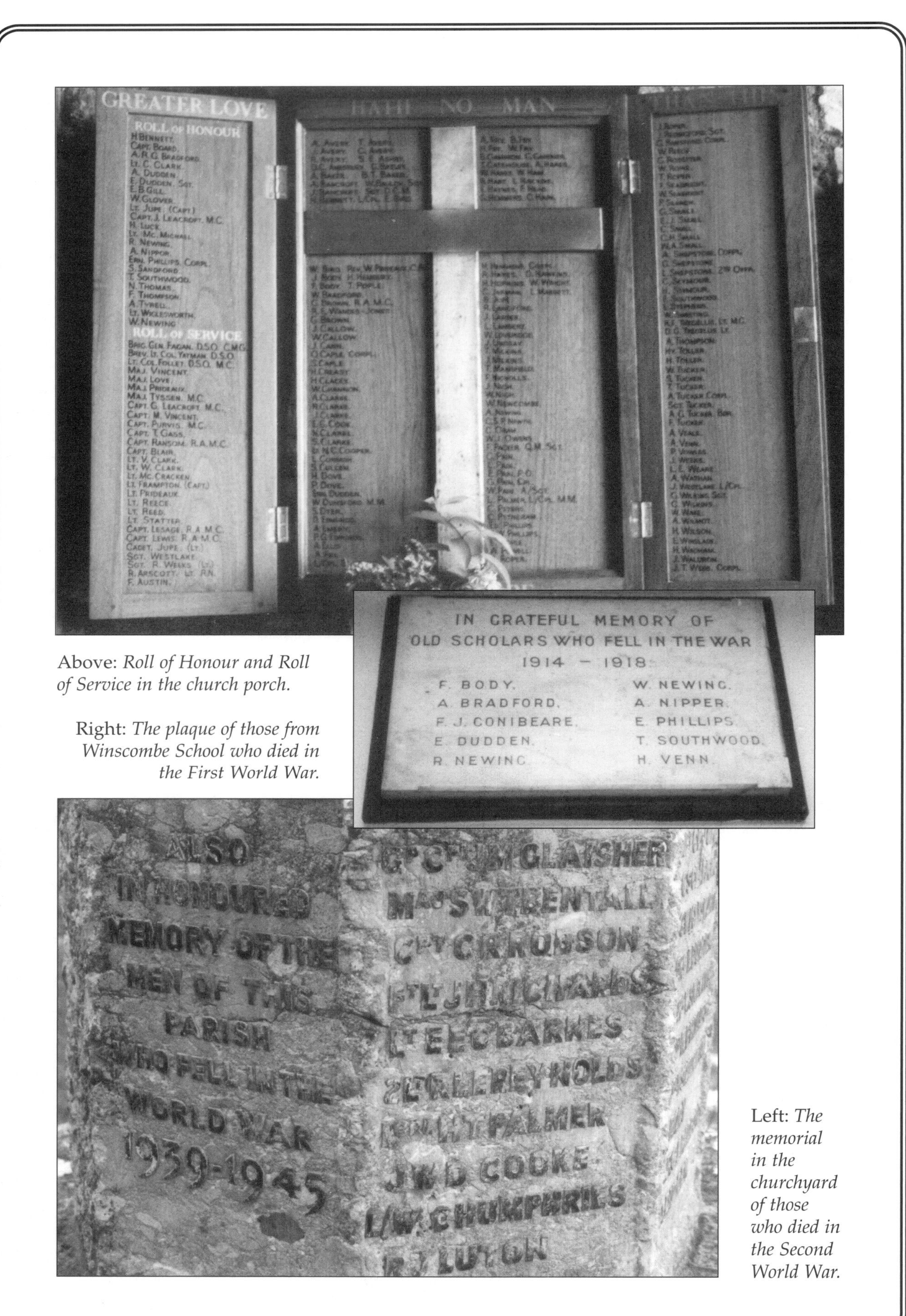

Above: *Roll of Honour and Roll of Service in the church porch.*

Right: *The plaque of those from Winscombe School who died in the First World War.*

Left: *The memorial in the churchyard of those who died in the Second World War.*

Peace Celebrations, 1919

In order to fund the celebrations for these events, the Council decided to allocate the proceeds of a 2d. rate to be divided between Winscombe and Sandford. The sum of £60 was allocated to Winscombe and £30 to Sandford. On the day itself, 19 July, the British weather played its usual game – it rained from morning to night. However, Winscombe was fortunate to have two large halls – the Drill Hall and Birds Assembly Rooms – and these were put to good use. As usual Winscombe people were used to making the best of a bad job and were not going to allow the weather to interrupt their arrangements. A full day of events was hastily organised and, apparently, a great time was had by all.

The day started with a long peal of the church bells and the villagers emerged to see a beautifully decorated village, thanks to a committee run by Mrs Bucker and her helpers. At lunchtime, a catering committee under the watchful eye of Mrs Bourne Clark, who had been at work since early morning, provided lunch in the Drill Hall at 1p.m. for 16 servicemen together with their wives or parents. The Revd J.A. Dodd said Grace and after the meal everyone was invited to a United service at 2p.m. in the Assembly Rooms. The choirs of both the Parish Church and the Union Chapel led the singing.

In the afternoon Mr Knight Dunster and Mrs Douglas Brown arranged an impromptu concert which kept everyone entertained until tea. This was held in the Drill Hall in two sessions: the first at 3.45 and the second at 4.45. Between 700 and 800 villagers were fed, and after the tea a programme of songs and duets took place for a couple of hours. After this, the people made their way to the Assembly Rooms where Mr Douglas Brown had arranged an entertaining programme at remarkably short notice.

During this time, Mr Moore and Mr Amesbury entertained the children with various games in the Drill Hall. Before leaving, each child was given a shilling and a bag of sweets. After this, dancing took place from 8–10p.m. The music was provided by Miss Gower and an impromptu orchestra. Messrs Bird and Son had provided the catering for the whole event, and were assisted at very short notice by their lady helpers. Sports and fireworks which had previously been arranged took place on a more suitable day. Sandford held a similar event, but they had decided to postpone this until August, hoping that more of the enlisted men would have returned home, and, of course, that the weather would improve.

Names in the churchyard of those who died in the First World War.

Stone cross in the churchyard.

Left: *Painters at The Court, c.1920.*

Right: *A poster advertising a Centenary Lantern Lecture by the Temperance Society, 1932.*

Below: *Farmers' market at the rear of the Railway Hotel, c.1920.*

Nine

The 1920s and '30s

As is well known, conditions following the First World War were socially and economically tough. One of the major local contributing factors was the 'winding-down' in the mining of calamine at Shipham prior to the war, which was made even worse by the conflict. The Shipham families were looking for work in Winscombe, but there was little enough for those living here. Farming had become more mechanised and fewer labourers were required. The large houses with their resident staff and large gardens were a shadow of what they had been before the war. This situation brought about a further and less obvious change. In the past, many of the labourers had been provided with accommodation as part of their wages. Now, even the 'upper classes' were no longer able to maintain staff at their previous level, and this only added to an already strained situation.

The villagers tried to unite in several ways, and to provide help for those who needed it. One area of support was provided by the Men's Institute at the Woodborough Hall; different types of events were staged there and members played billiards and provided boxing instruction for junior members. A gift of billiard balls had been received, together with some armchairs and periodicals for the members. The membership at that time was nearly 100 – the Institute undoubtedly supplied a real need, and was appreciated by the members.

The question of unemployment is mentioned time and time again in the pages of the Parish Council minutes. Early in the 1930s a circular letter was received from the clerk of the Axbridge Rural District Council giving 'Recommendations made by a Committee appointed, and since approved by

Girls' Friendly Society, c.1930. Known names include Mrs Chandler, Mrs Sydenham, Mrs Morris, Miss Miller and Renie Simms.

Winscombe Scouts, c.1930. Edward Pain is behind the poles. Harry Hopkins is sitting to the right of the picture.

British Legion Women's Section outing to 'Hosegood' Flour Mill, 1930.

that Council, for the alleviation of unemployment in the District.'

The Council had previously discussed the possibility of a sewerage scheme utilising a Government grant of 75 per cent, but when the amount was reduced to 25 per cent the clerk was asked to write to the District Council informing them that they deemed it inadvisable to proceed with the work in its entirety. The outcome, unfortunately, was that the work was not completed until 1938 when Axbridge District Council took up the scheme for the provision of sewerage systems in Winscombe and Worle. On 20 March 1939, the official works were opened at Max, near Barton.

Despite the large amount of work that the Council had to carry out, the clerk at least did not lose his sense of humour. He commented at the end of one of the meetings' minutes: 'Other matters were discussed, the purport of which the clerk did not hear.'

Locally, the Women's Institute, Mothers' Union and the Girls' Friendly Society had no difficulty in finding members. The two latter societies were connected with the church and the meetings were held at the Vicarage. In the case of the Girls' Friendly Society, they met once a week and the vicar and the policeman's wife made themselves responsible for organisation. The aims were partly to offer a little education – there were lectures on cooking and care in the home – but also to play sports, including tennis and rounders in the summer and 'party games' in the winter. In essence the object was to give the girls somewhere to go and something to do.

Fire Brigade

In the early 1920s the Council took the decision to purchase standpipes and hoses for use in case of fire, and to establish a brigade to use this equipment. Captain Wills was asked to be captain of the brigade, but he was unfortunately unable to carry out this task due to ill health, although he felt it possible to undertake the formation.

When it was found that the cost of such a project would result in a 3d. rate, the matter appears to have been deferred until the end of 1925 when the parish minutes record the setting up of fire hydrants; two at Shipham, one at Star, and five for Winscombe.

Later, in June 1930, the Chief Officer of the Banwell Fire Brigade wrote the following:

... having seen in the Weston paper that the Winscombe Parish Council were enquiring into the matter of a water supply in case of fire, Banwell Brigade has gone into the matter with the Axbridge Council and we have purchased two portable standpipes to fit Winscombe mains, and have tested same from Sandford to Winscombe square near the Church; also around Sidcot and Sidcot School to the extreme end at Churchill corner.

The main point of the letter was that Banwell could offer Winscombe full cover in the event of a fire and, most importantly:

... they were also on the 'phone at Banwell 22 and, in the event of not being able to contact the Brigade this way, the Post Office will always ring through by night or day!! As Axbridge was a voluntary Brigade, and Winscombe had always supported it since it was started in 1888, it was hoped that Winscombe would continue to do so.

Upon receipt of this, the local Council decided to defer the matter once again.

A note in a report on the work of the Banwell Fire Brigade provides interesting reading:

Before 1928 another cause of delay was the horses to pull the pump. They had to be caught, brought to the Fire Station and harnessed before anything could happen. It was known for firemen, on hearing the warning bell, to put on the kettle at home to make a cup of tea before reporting to the station, because they knew full well that the horses were being grazed some distance away on the Moor and would take some time to collect.

(BANWELL SOCIETY OF ARCHAEOLOGY 'SEARCH', NO. 16)

The British Legion

Although the British Legion was formed in 1921 it was not until 11 May 1933 that a meeting was held in the Club Room at the Railway Hotel when it was decided to start a branch which would include all the adjoining areas of the village. The first branch meeting was on 18 May of that year. In these minutes the following was noted:

As a means of helping with the Benevolent Fund and insuring punctualness [sic] *of members at all meetings, the Chairman proposed that late arrivals should pay money into a box, unless an excuse be accepted.*

It was also agreed that a branch Standard would be purchased and later in that year the branch received an offer to lay a skittle alley for members in the Drill Hall, and this offer was gratefully accepted. This alley was to play an important role in the life of the branch. They held many matches, and later, when troops were billeted in the village during the war, they too used the alley and held inter-group competitions. In the course of the first year, the treasurer reported a balance of £181.5s.5d.

On the first Armistice Sunday on 12 November 1933, services were held both at St James Church at 10.15a.m. and at Shipham Church at 6.30p.m. This was a period when poverty and sickness were common, and there were many who could not work due to illness or lack of opportunity; the branch tried in many ways to provide some relief. In the first year a Christmas treat was organised for the members' children and a whist drive and dance was held to defray expenses. Additionally, several local children were given tickets to a pantomime.

This is where the Women's Section came into its own. Throughout the period, they helped to arrange many such activities. They were also asked to organise the Poppy Day collection and this continues to the present day. The amount collected in 1933 from collection boxes and church services is recorded to have been £63.10s.11d.

Throughout the years, the branch continued to use their Benevolent Fund where it was thought to be appropriate. They also started a 'Thrift Club' using the branch savings cards, and continued to give support to those in ill health and to arrange a holiday scheme for members' children.

A list of 'jobs vacant' was kept, together with a list of employers for which there were suitable men on the register, and these were placed on the noticeboard. By November 1934 the branch had between 250 and 300 members. In 1936 the Benevolent Fund was registered under the War Charities Act.

At Christmas 1937, the branch provided entertainment for the children at Birds Hotel. There was also tea for 210 children and parents plus the 25 helpers. The cost of this was £9.15s.10d. The hotel also gave a quote of 2s.6d. per head for the annual dinner.

The branch were awarded the Wills Memorial Cup for being the most efficient in Somerset during that year.

It is in the area of support of the sick that the work of the British Legion can best be demonstrated. The local branch provided assistance and support by means of grocery or clothing vouchers and sometimes a weekly delivery of coal. Apart from those men who were still suffering from their wounds, there were a number of cases of tuberculosis in the area and many local families were helped – not only with money for travelling to visit those in hospital, but also with daily pints of milk which were provided. Eggs and the occasional bottle of brandy are noted as having been given, and regular visits were made to those who were ill. Besides this, a local 'employment officer' voluntarily kept a note of those jobs that were available, and these were offered to those out of work. This support continued for a considerable time.

The branch arranged many events in order to raise money for the Benevolent Fund, which it was hoped could alleviate the distress, particularly in the mining areas. A suggestion was made that a 'Walls Ice Cream van' should be present at these events, as Walls were employing disabled ex-servicemen. The Walls tricycles were very different from the modern vans with their 'jingles' and their huge variety of ice-creams. These men rode a small tricycle with a basket on the back and a notice on the front which read 'STOP ME AND BUY ONE'. Those who could afford it usually had a penny 'fruit triangle' – a water ice about 5in long, wrapped in a cardboard paper. The 'wafers' were too expensive for most children.

Enjoying Home Life

During this period when money was short and not many had the means to travel, the villagers still maintained their resolve to enjoy life as far as it was possible, and ensure that life was not all sad or hard work. Families did not have holidays as we know them today. A trip to Weston was quite an adventure; for the most part the local people made their own enjoyment. Joan Searle remarked:

We just realised that you had to be careful and that you had to go without – especially in the farming community. Things were pretty much in the doldrums. Father often had to sell a bullock to be able to pay the butcher for the meat, or the grocer, or something like that. No help was available for bringing up five children.

A local dance band held regular dances at the Drill Hall, whist drives were also popular, and much of the housewives' entertainment centred around the church. Mrs Florence Brown recalls how she and her husband:

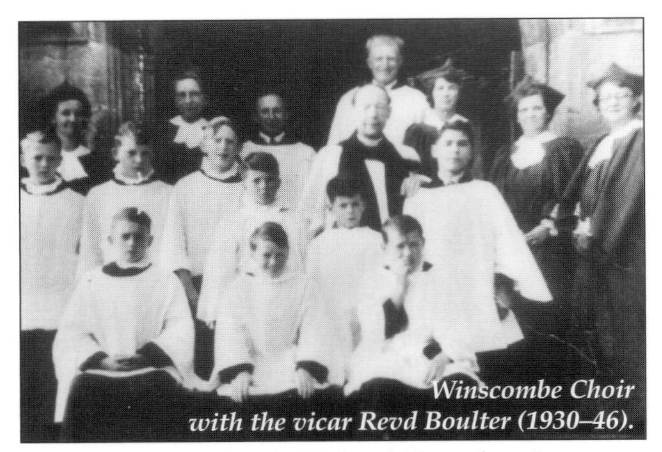
Winscombe Choir with the vicar Revd Boulter (1930–46).

... were in the Church Choir, which at that time, was very good. Miss Thomas was the organist and Dr. Le Sage was the choir master. We used to sing such pieces as 'Olivet to Calvary' and 'The Crucifixion' and give 'productions' in the Assembly Rooms. We had great enjoyment from both the Sunday School Outings to Weston – sometimes to Clevedon or Burnham – but the Choir Outings were very special. They would go to the South coast – Weymouth, Paignton or Torquay, and, like most such outings, we would sing all the way home!

Another early memory is that Christmases were always very happy. The house was constantly open to others. Many did not have a Christmas tree, it was too expensive, but they would choose a bough and make things to hang on it. There was no 'special lunch' – usually one had beef. The stockings had a few nuts and perhaps a bar of chocolate in them – little more than that. Joan remembers hearing that some children hung up pillowcases and thought that was dreadful – they were expecting too much.

Holidays, if any, usually took the form of staying with a relative. A day in Weston was quite a treat, something out of the blue! Most people stayed in the village, mainly due to the expense of travelling.

Another early memory is of the time when the primroses were out, and the children used to go to gather them in bunches of 20, with four leaves to each bunch, which were then sent to London and sold for charity. One inhabitant admits that even now when picking primroses she still counts to 20!

A different form of entertainment was 'home-made' by the children themselves. Mary Kinsey remembers that her two brothers and the 'Dunster', boys who went to the same school – 'Kingsholm' at Weston – would get together and arrange an 'entertainment' during the summer holidays. They would write little plays and perform them in front of their parents and also did a 'sketch or two' and acrobatics – cartwheels and handstands, etc:

We also used to sing, and sometimes, I did a recitation. We usually put these events on in the garden and our parents would sit patiently through it all. Sometimes we put on the entertainment in aid of a charity, it was all to do with the 'PIP, SQUEAK & WILFRED' Cartoon in the Daily Mirror.

Alternatively, families got together to entertain each other with songs and music. One story tells how this ability could sometimes be used as an advantage:

We all had piano lessons, but never followed it up. My sister could play by ear – she only had to hear something once and she could play it. In fact, she got out of quite a lot of 'chores' that way. My Mother used to say 'you go and play us a tune, and we'll do so-and-so.' Two or three families used to get together round a piano and have quite an evening. Also several groups would meet at each other's houses and play whist. It was very popular.

The parish ran a Village Moot (this was originally a sum bequeathed in 1842 by Francis Taylor Doolan, plus another bequest from Miss Charlotte Knollys in 1853). Initially, these sums were to provide warm clothing and coal for the poor, but the trusts proved to be a bad investment and the sum produced was very small. At the request of the trustees the original scheme was altered and the vicar, the churchwardens and two members of the Council now administer the funds. One recent comment on this was:

This was to help families with children who had ability, with their schooling or training. This was always a bit secretive – my Mother was on the Committee, but no one used to know who was being helped.

Apart from this, most wives took in paying guests to supplement the farming. It really was a necessity. The alternative was to provide accommodation for the parents and children visiting Sidcot School.

The atmosphere that emerges from this period of difficulty is not one of sadness. Speaking of her own family, one elderly lady, when asked how her mother relaxed, replied:

She always seemed to consider herself 'one of the girls' and used to relax with us. She entered into what we were doing. I can never remember her saying 'I can't' or 'I need a rest'. It just seemed she was always there. Her one highlight was to play badminton, so there must have been a club quite early on – probably at Birds Hall.

Whatever the situation it seems that Winscombe folk always found a way to enjoy themselves.

Another woman who spent her childhood here remembers roaming through the fields, which have long since been developed. There was a pond at the top of 'Hillyfields' that used to freeze in the winter and the children would skate on it. Another favourite pastime was to have a toboggan, or something similar, and slide down the hill on the grass. She thinks that they had a 'fine start' to their young lives.

Royal Celebrations

In 1935 arrangements were made to celebrate the silver jubilee of King George V. The entire afternoon and evening were spent in various activities. At two o'clock the procession, together with other villagers, assembled in the Drill Hall field and at 2.30 they marched, preceded by the British Sports Military Band, to a field in Sandford Road where the 'salute the flag' ceremony took place. They then walked down the road 'marshalled' by the British Legion. There were representatives from every organisation in the village and these can be seen in photographs taken at the time. A dozen groups were mentioned on the official list of those taking part. Banners were hung across the street, painted with lines from the National Anthem.

At three o'clock a United thanksgiving service was held, followed by children's sports, a balloon race and the fancy-dress competition. At five o'clock tea was provided for parishioners in a marquee and, as Phyllis Cram comments in *From Parish Pump to Parish Present*, the tent must have been very large, because there were 1,000 people at the meal. The children were given presentation beakers.

At six o'clock in the evening there was a general sports event and at eight there was a broadcast of the King's speech. The evening concluded with a dance in the marquee which was free for everyone, and the day ended at 9.15p.m. with the lighting of a bonfire on Sandford Hill.

It was generally accepted that the event had been very successful, but also expensive, a fact which was to be reflected in the rates at 3d. in the pound. The total expense was £172.5s.0d. The parish donated the £19 that was left to the King's Jubilee Trust Fund and the following winter a commemorative oak tree was planted in the war memorial recreation-ground. Many other groups organised 'outings' for themselves; for example, the British Legion Women's Section went on a tour of the Hosegood Flour Mill.

The main event of the period was the coronation of George VI. A large procession marched through the village and various prizes were awarded for the best costumes. There was a children's fancy-dress event and a display of Victorian women's costume. A concert was held in Birds Assembly Rooms and there was a dinner in the hotel. After the procession – when banners once again decorated with lines from the National Anthem were hung across the streets – there followed the usual sports and tea. In retrospect, it would appear that much of the restraint of the previous years was forgotten, at least for this one day.

Above: *An unused calendar for Edward VIII, 1937.*

Left: *Silver jubilee programme, 1935.*

Above: *Birds Assembly Rooms, silver jubilee, 1935.*

Right: *Silver jubilee procession, 1935.*

Left: *Silver jubilee mug.*

Below: *Dinner at Birds Assembly Rooms, George VI's coronation, 1937.*

Right: *Coronation march, 1937.*

Above: *Children's fancy dress, 1937. Note the coronation cracker.*

Right: *Birds Shop decorated in 1937.*

Below: *Women through the ages, 1937.*

The camping coach, June 1958. COURTESY OF R. GRIFFITHS

Holiday Experiences

Although Doris Cook had been born in Bristol, she had lived in Winscombe for many years. Her parents would take the family to Clevedon for a summer holiday. After her mother had got the children ready – three boys and four girls – they then had to sit, quite still, with their hats and coats on, and even wearing gloves, until everyone was ready to go.

When the 'conveyance' arrived, the luggage was loaded and then they all got into the horse-drawn coach. The problem was that the road from Bristol to Clevedon is very hilly and when they approached a slope, the family (with the exception of mother) had to get out and walk so that the horse could get to the top!

They always stayed at the same house and had what was called 'Rooms and Attendance'. This rather strange arrangement involved the landlady providing the accommodation, but only cooking (rather than planning and shopping for) the meals. Thus it gave her mother very little by way of a 'break' as she still had much to think about. Nevertheless, the memory remained a happy one – of days on the 'Prom' and so on. Apparently, not many families could afford even this type of holiday, and Doris said that it made her feel 'rather superior', although she did not think her own family would have enjoyed it these days.

There was one other, rather unusual way of spending a holiday in the village. At the station, there was a coach that had been converted into a 'camping coach'. This was parked on a siding, and visitors would stay for a week or two and visit the surrounding areas. The coach was well equipped, with a full set of cutlery, crockery, teapot, glass tumblers and eggcups, and the essential tin opener and corkscrew were provided. In the kitchen there was a frying pan, saucepan and a steamer, together with water buckets, a refuse bucket and a sanitary bucket.

The sleeping cubicles had a full set of blankets, sheets, pillowcases and pillow slips. Also in the inventory were a pair of tablecloths, a dishcloth, three tea cloths, dusters and a variety of towels and an oven cloth. Under 'miscellaneous' were listed such items as oil-lamps for the bedrooms, a duplex lamp for the sitting-room, a hurricane lamp, a paraffin jug with a funnel, and a mirror. Deckchairs were also included along with four chamber pots. Laundry was sent to the GWR laundry at Swindon Works and new linen was returned from there.

By this period, despite the lack of financial resources, the Parish Council was working hard to make improvements. In March 1939 a sewage works was opened at Max, and the streets were lit until late evening. Although some residents complained that they were unable to read their mail until 10.30 in the morning, this appears to be fairly insignificant compared with the tremendous advantage of the installation of an electricity supply to the village. John Westlake remembers coming home from school day after day, and asking 'Is it on yet?' One day, it was, and he says he still remembers how exciting he found this revolution.

Ten

Winscombe at Work

From the middle of the twentieth century Winscombe had become known not only for its holiday attractions but also for the excellence of its shops. One of these, Kinsey's, has already been described, but several of the newcomers to the area at the beginning of the century also started businesses that would survive for many years to come.

Birds Hotel, Restaurant & Shop

This institution has stood in the village for over a century. The grandfather of the present owner, Abram Bird, who had been a butler at 'The Hall', brought his wife Ann to Woodborough hamlet in c.1895. He opened a business in a small shop near the bridge and just opposite Nippors Way. (Apparently, Mrs Yatman took an active interest in the bakery business in its early days, arranging for staff to provide teas for various families.) Later, Mr Bird bought land on the opposite side of the road and built a successful bakery and catering business. He had a large family of eight children – five girls and four boys. He also built an adjoining hotel where visitors from many places used to stay – some of them being the parents of scholars at Sidcot School. Mr Bird kept a visitors' book, from which we learn that people came from as far away as China, America and Switzerland, to name but a few.

Abram Bird, c.1890.

Apparently, the bread was found to be so good that, on several occasions, it was taken back to London, and elsewhere, for the visitors' friends or relatives. The shop windows were also beautifully dressed with bunches of well-starched fine muslin, with a multitude of confections, possibly even a wedding or Christmas cake, perched in the dips of fabric. As one resident recalls:

> *In about 1940 you could buy a bun or a rock-cake for 1d. Alternatively, two small scones could be bought for the same price. A 2l. loaf (a really big one) was 4d. and a 'super' lardy cake cost 4½d. Initially, bread was delivered by horse and cart, and the delivery man would have a large basket which would be covered with a cloth, and inside there would be a lovely selection of bread. In fact, the horse knew the round so well that he didn't need telling where to stop.*

Besides running the hotel and bakery, the family used to undertake a great deal of outside catering, for occasions large and small. Some of the events were quite a distance away, sometimes as far afield as Wells, and a way had to be found to keep the food hot until the meal was served. The answer was to line a 'truck' with straw to cover the food until it was required. This proved to be a very efficient method of insulation. The firm had a number of local women who used to work for them on such occasions, and one picture shows them at a Harvest Home *(see page 69)*.

Above: *The oven in the bakery, c.1900.*

Left: *Abram Bird with son Arthur, c.1903.*

Right: *Ann Bird with Arthur, c.1903.*

Right: *Birds Bakery, c.1920.*

Below: *Birds horse and cart, c.1920.*

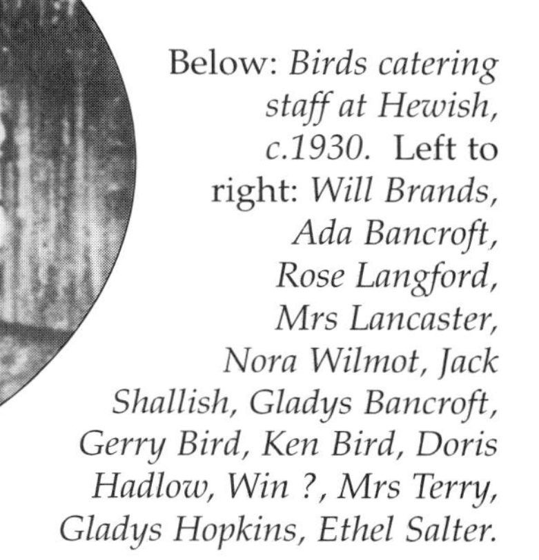

Below: *Birds catering staff at Hewish, c.1930.* Left to right: *Will Brands, Ada Bancroft, Rose Langford, Mrs Lancaster, Nora Wilmot, Jack Shallish, Gladys Bancroft, Gerry Bird, Ken Bird, Doris Hadlow, Win ?, Mrs Terry, Gladys Hopkins, Ethel Salter.*

Birds Shop window, c.1940.

Ordinary meals could be obtained at the hotel at a reasonable cost. Lunch in the restaurant cost 2s.6d. for three courses. Coffee was 2d. extra.

Attached to the shop and hotel were the Assembly Rooms. These were built in c.1899 and constituted the largest covered area in the district. They were used for concerts, dances, meetings and almost any other function that required a room large enough to hold a great number of people. Sometimes, a company would advertise that a film was to be shown there – the only chance for many villagers to see one – and, of course, nearly everyone in the village went along to see it. Going to the pictures was a great occasion.

The Vinery

Yet another, and quite a different, type of business was also started at this time. George and Mary Pain bought some land from a Mr Ash, a local landowner, who, when the railway ran through the village, had 'small' pieces of land to be sold. George built a vinery at the corner of The Lynch and, unlikely though it may seem, he would load up his cart and drive to Bristol where his customers would pay £1 per pound for his black grapes – which was quite a lot of money for those days! George and Mary had three sons, William, Henry and Charles, and when George died in 1899, William, who at some time

Birds Assembly Rooms.

George and Mary Pain, c.1900.

Top right: *The front of the house before the shop (which replaced the original greenhouse) was added, c.1928.*

Above, inset: *Cattle in the field at the end of The Vinery.*

Above: *Inside The Vinery before c.1928.*

Right: *Aerial view of The Vinery, c.1980.*

Left: *The first greenhouse.*

Right: *Demolition of the shop, 1985.*

previously had worked as a gardener at Chatsworth, returned to take care of The Vinery with his wife Jane and their son, Wilfred.

Over the years the business expanded, and was taken over by various family members who sold the apples, pears and plums, etc. locally. The first greenhouses were extended so that seeds and flowers could also be sold. Wilfred, who before joining the Army had worked at Kildare, took over the running of the business on his return in 1924. When he died it passed into the hands of his brother Edward and his wife, Maud. By 1936 The Vinery had grown into a large concern with seven greenhouses. Coldframes were added to 'harden off' seedlings and bulbs were bought from Holland, either to be grown or sold. Daily trips to Bristol Central Market were made by van and sometimes unusual plants were brought back from abroad. The cucumbers and tomatoes became so popular that further greenhouses were built just for them.

The last owner, Norman Pain, ran the business with his wife Betty until his retirement in 1985. She would take care of the shop that had been added, and also worked on the land looking after the plants. As well as vegetables, there was an orchard, and, at one time, even a few pigs and other animals were kept at the bottom of the plot. Gradually, as well as their own produce, they added a small quantity of groceries and potting compost, also potted plants such as chrysanthemums and cyclamen.

At one time, the entire water-supply for The Vinery was by means of a two-inch pipe, which, considering the amount of work to be done, was somewhat inadequate. Early in 1960 Norman decided to sink a borehole. To his amazement he only had to go to 102 feet. Then he built a pumping house with a 500-gallon tank, and never went short of water again – which was just as well because when the trains came through the tunnel, the railway track, which ran along the edge of their property, allowed the firemen to throw out their cinders on the bank. Many a time Betty has had to rush out with a bucket of water to put out a fire. Apparently this was not unusual; other people who lived in this area had similar experiences.

Brown Bros

Another business which flourished at this time was the grocery firm Brown Bros. Many villagers have memories of this shop:

The shop was on the corner and the Brown family lived there. In the shop there were counters down each side, and in front of the counters there were tins of biscuits with glass lids, and you could lift up the lid – if asked – and take out a biscuit and taste it. What fascinated me as a child, was the way the goods were paid for. There was an arrangement where part of a wooden cup was taken off the wire, which ran overhead, and your money was screwed in. A handle was pulled and it went over to the cashier's desk. [Browns was the first shop to install electricity.] *I was very tall as a child and my one aim when I was in the shop with my Mother, was to get on my toes to see if I could bang my head against the container – much to her annoyance! The assistants there were always so ready to help you. You could give your order in, and if you hadn't mentioned – say, butter –*

Brown Bros Stores with staff and cart, c.1920s.

Right: *Brown Bros staff with the Railway Hotel in the background, c.1930.*

they would ask 'Now did you want any butter or cheese or anything?' So different from today. Having given your order in, it would be sent to you and then you could pay the bill the next time you went in the shop.

Alex Brown was the manager and his nephew William, who was always known as 'Sunny', remarks:

I remember that the shop had always to be made to look attractive for the customers when they came in. There was a provision counter on the left as you entered the door, and a counter with biscuit tins and a show case for chocolates. There were two parallel counters further down the shop where the customers' orders were packed. At the back was the old office with the 'cash railway'. My wife worked in the shop from the day she left school, and that is how we met. By that time I was driving a van to deliver the orders. In the shop we had a hand coffee mill, and I can still remember the smell of the freshly ground coffee. Things like currants and sultanas used to arrive in bulk in wooden boxes with about 56lbs in each. Then we used to fill up the drawers from these boxes. The cheeses came wrapped in cloth and had to be skinned.

Browns killed their own pigs and cured their own bacon and ham.

The shop was always known as Browns and now the corner is named after it. After Sunny left school he worked in the shop and married Florence in 1937. He then went to work as a chauffeur/gardener to Miss Carwardine, who lived in a large house on the main road, as there was not enough money generated from the shop. The couple earned £2.50 per week but their accommodation was free. Three years later Sunny was called up and spent five years in the Army. After the war he had to return to the shop where his uncle, Alec Brown, was the manager. Later the business was taken over by Brown Bros of Weston (no connection). In the original business they had a butchery department, and they used to buy a pig and cut it up at the back of the shop.

'Sunny' Brown and Florence at their wedding.

Village Families

Not all of the early families went into the service businesses. One family, whose influence spread throughout the village, started when Mr William Weeks came into the area. He had children from both of his two marriages and they joined other local families to start their own businesses. His son, Alfred, married Ellen Mabbett and he started a coal yard and travel businesses called A.G. Weeks. He also ran the quarry at Sandford and was the owner of the woods at Knightstone, Weston-super-Mare. Various other members of the family became property owners. Alfred's son Ronald owned land in Knapps Drive and built there. His brother, Hubert, owned Mill Pond Cottage, and together they helped in the coal business. One of Ronald's daughters, Edith, went to Australia, and another, Ethel, married Ronald Kinsey when his first wife died. As mentioned, he owned the drapery business on the corner of Woodborough Road.

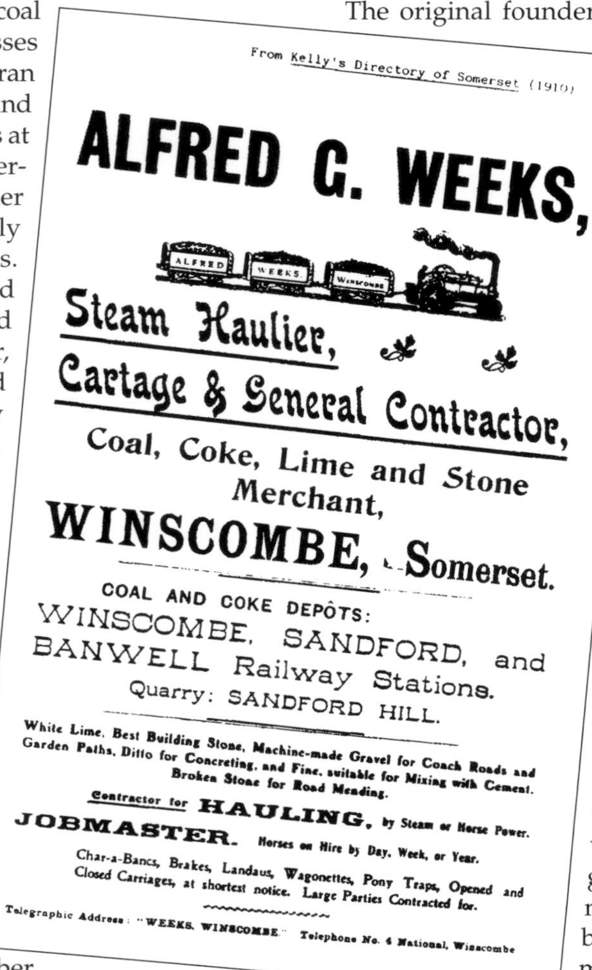

Herbert Weeks, who so kindly left records of his childhood farming days at Hillcrest Farm, was one of three sons of William Weeks by his second marriage, and he was also an active member of the Lynch Chapel as well as being a Scoutmaster. Another son from the same marriage was Arnold, who became a vicar, whilst the third son, Percy, married Eva and farmed at Sidcot. Their daughter, Margaret, played the organ at the chapel and also became a schoolteacher.

The more recent members of the family continue to play an active part in village life. Wilfred Weeks, always known as 'Digger' due to his active participation in cricket, was the chairman of the Parish Council for 12 years, and captain of the local cricket side for 20 years.

In his working life he was a representative for a firm of lead manufacturers in Bristol. He was so attached to his sport that he bought some land near the disused railway track on which he built his bungalow and from where he could see the cricket ground. He was also a regular participant in the local drama groups. His wife 'Mickie' – christened with a name she hated, 'Florence' – is an active participant in all things rural. Sadly, Digger Weeks died unexpectedly on his way to a Parish Council meeting on the evening of 21 October 1982.

Several other families who first came to Winscombe around the beginning of the twentieth century are still flourishing in 2004, one of these on a decidedly different course to that taken by his father. The original founder of Nut Tree Farm was Henry John Mabbett, who was the son of John Mabbett, the blacksmith who started a forge in 1842 on the corner of Church Road. In about 1890 Henry, his son, decided not to follow in his father's footsteps and he bought some land almost opposite. Together with his wife, Ellen Counsell, he started a farm that is still very much alive at the time of writing.

Henry and Ellen had two sons, Edgar who died in 1898 at the age of 16, and Fred who married Alice Bird – the daughter of Abram Bird, the baker. Together, Henry and Ellen expanded the business with an emphasis on dairy cattle, two breeds of which were necessary to provide an adequate supply of milk – Guernseys produce better milk which is particularly good for general use, but Ayrshires give milk better suited to making butter and cheese. Eventually, more milk was being produced than could be sold from the farm gate, so Alice took over the control of a number of daily milk rounds in the area.

In the 1930s there were no purpose-built tractors on the market, so the Mabbetts adapted a Ford car for towing carts, and, for mowing, they attached a mower to a Bull-nose Morris. Although purpose-built tractors were available later, horses were worked on the farm right up until 1951, when they purchased two Ferguson tractors, with all the necessary equipment, for the sum of £375 each.

The coming of the Second World War led to many changes having to be made. Most of the farm workforce were enlisted, but Fred managed to continue with the help of his son, Ron, and two villagers, Frank Larder and Lennie Tucker. Additional help was provided by three members of the Land Army – Fluffy, Marie and Vera.

In those days, Guernsey bulls, not surprisingly,

Left: *Mr A. Weeks and Mrs Kinsey, c.1920.*

Below: *Arthur, Effie, Ronald and Margaret Mabbett, c.1910.*

Miss Margaret Weeks, c.1970.

Wilfred 'Digger' Weeks, c.1960.

Left: *The first Mabbett family at The Forge, c.1842.*

Below: *Ellen Counsell going to Nut Tree Farm, c.1930.*

Fred Mabbett, c.1930.

Henry John Mabbett, c.1930.

Noted for Clean Milk Production

F. J. MABBETT & SON

NUTTREE DAIRY

WINSCOMBE

Guernsey Milk, Clotted and Raw Cream, Eggs and Butter delivered to all parts of Winscombe and Sandford daily.

MILK DELIVERED IN BOTTLES

We specialise in DEVONSHIRE CREAM and post it to all parts

Phone: WINSCOMBE 59

Top picture: *The Forge just before it was demolished, c.1980.*

Above: *Ron Mabbett, c.1975.*

Harvesting at Nut Tree Farm, 2002.

came from Guernsey. A rather unusual story relates to the arrival of such an animal in 1945. Fred's grandson remembers travelling to the island to buy the bull, although how it was brought back to Winscombe remains a mystery to this day. In any event, the choice of animal proved to be worth the trouble. The herd began to expand and totalled about 45 head of cattle, mostly Guernseys. Fred's proud boast was that his herd was one of the eight in Somerset who were 'tuberculin tested' and that his milk was safe, and was thus much sought after.

Fred Mabbett retired in 1946, and his son, Ron, who had previously helped organise his father's milk rounds, was able to take over Nut Tree Farm which by now stood at 114 acres. His first major development was the construction of one of the first Somerset milking parlours, which, together with his son John, made possible the expansion of the herd to about 180 Guernseys, of which 110 were milkers.

John Mabbett's son, Phillip, runs the 232-acre farm at the time of writing. A comparison with past times is interesting. With the help of much machinery, including three tractors, one still a Ferguson, Phillip works the farm with just a little help from his father. Even so, they still need the support of a bull called Humphrey, for a herd of about 70 milkers that produce 'organic' milk.

Nut Tree Farm, c.2002.

Housewives' Tales

Many of the local housewives have described their lives in the early part of the twentieth century, telling of housework, school life and the various other activities that formed part of everyday life in these difficult times.

An outstanding event was the way in which labour-saving devices changed the running of the home, especially when combined with the arrival of electricity and gas. One lady recalls:

> *I particularly remember... the flapping of sheets on the line on village washing day. The wash really did take all day. The whites had to be 'dolly-blued' and starched... We had an outhouse part to the kitchen where the oil stove was, and also in here was a boiler with a little fire underneath and a wooden lid on top. This contained the water supply for the washing day... then there were three huge zinc baths. Our 'household aids' consisted of a washing machine with a thick wooden exterior and cogs and wheels to move the central agitator... The mangle originally had thick wooden rollers before the rubber ones came in.*
>
> *Before this most people cooked on coal fires and it took many years for a proper supply of electricity to be available... the gas was put in the houses free! It really was quite amusing to see everyone dashing out to buy their first cooker.*

The arrival of gas, whilst being of great benefit, particularly to the housewife, was not without its problems, as the following story by Orion Caple shows:

> *I well remember when the trench was being dug for the mains, and the blasting operations close to The Avenue. After blasting had taken place, the men returned to their work in the trench. I stood there talking to a friend, the late Charlie Shepstone, when, adjoining them in the trench was a Mr Lawrence and Mr Ernest Ellis. When they started boring again with a bar and sledge hammer they put the bar into the hole where, apparently, the charge had not gone off, and yet the explosions were supposed to have been counted correctly... as Mr Lawrence struck the bar with the hammer... a large explosion occurred, I was only 6ft away at the time, but the striker and his mate were badly injured. Mr Lawrence losing an eye as well as* [sustaining] *injuries to his body. Mr Ellis was not seriously injured. The sledge hammer was found later up The Avenue.*

Another incident recalled from this period by 'Bunty' Tracy gives a clear example of the changes new technology brought:

> *We had a range, and in the summer it was terribly hot. I had to learn to use it when I was about fourteen, so that I could cook dinners and cakes etc. (My Mother had a very bad heart attack)... It was always a*

mystery to me how you kept the fire big enough to boil the pans, yet not so big that the cakes got scorched. Then we had a three-burner Valor gas stove in the outhouse – it was wonderful... the temperature remained constant and you didn't have to put coal on. We also had a 'suction' carpet sweeper. It consisted of a thick concertina bag with a handle which you pumped up and down to make the suction pick up bits – I doubt if it picked up much dust.

Nowadays a lot is heard about 'insulation', but the following story from Joan Searle reveals how different the job of keeping warm used to be:

I don't remember any insulation in the loft or around the pipes, and in the wash-house the pipe came right against the wall and through into the scullery. The wash-house had very thin walls so it was nothing to find the pipes frozen. My sister and I would get the blow lamp and run it up and down the pipe until it was thawed (the thought terrifies me now!). We used to boil the kettle on the Primus stove. It had 'meths' in the little central bowl, and you lit it, waited a few seconds and pumped it up. This is another thing I wouldn't dream of doing now!

These stories also remind us of the way in which the term 'wash day' meant something entirely different for some of the village people. It was not merely one day of the week, but was a way of life for some – particularly those who were compelled by poverty to 'take in' washing as a means of increasing the family income. The following story illustrates this:

We had an elderly 'help' who was with us for twenty-five years, and she told us how her mother used to take in washing from other householders. Her family lived in Quarry Road in a cottage on the left-hand side which is now demolished, and her mother had a kind of 'truck' on wheels and walked to the people's houses to collect the washing... She then put it on the truck and pushed it back home where she washed it, ironed it, and then took it back in the same way.

Mr Tracy's New Technology

In many ways Winscombe was happy to accept the new technologies. The village was fortunate to have Mr J.W. Tracy living here as he was the local representative of the Marconiphone Company, and so Winscombe was chosen to be one of the 135 places in the UK to hear the King speaking live at the opening ceremony of the Wembley Exhibition 1924/5. His daughter, Mary Gertrude, always known as 'Bunty', has fond memories of that day:

Dad was very thrilled to be offered the chance to relay this service and to introduce people to the wireless and, when the very high aerial was erected in the garden, the postman told me he had never seen such a high clothes line like that! The Company lent the necessary apparatus to enable us to hear the opening of the Wembley Exhibition, and long before the proceedings were to start our large garden and drive were packed with people – even standing on the vegetable garden! I remember that we listened to the music from the massed bands, as well as the speeches and we clearly heard the prayers by the Bishop of London. I particularly remember when he said 'Let us Pray'. Everyone in the garden knelt down, even those on the vegetable garden or on the paved drive. I shall always remember the sight as I was in the tree so couldn't kneel down – I felt very, very out of place!

She also explained:

When wireless sets first came in, you had to have batteries which had to be charged, and my Father had quite a business in the 'battery-charging' side of his work. People were very upset, of course, if they forgot to fetch them when they should have done. You see, you had to have one battery in the set and then you had a spare one, and many a time people would arrive late on Saturday night or Sunday morning because their battery had run out and they couldn't listen to anything! My sister and I used to 'bless them' because my Dad used to decide that we could help by going and getting them!

The radio caused great excitement:

I remember going out to Barton to old Mr Body. He was terribly keen on those old 'whisker things'. We went out one evening because he had been able to get America! Mind you, you couldn't tell what it really was, it was just a noise. Nevertheless, it was America! We had a wind-up gramophone.

Mr Tracy was not only a representative of Marconiphone, but also a very clever inventor. One invention solved the problem that the local baker encountered when it came to manufacturing pastries of uniform size. His answer was 'The Tracy Pastry Cutter'. This had 12 wheeled cutters arranged so that items of the same size could be cut out without the necessity of measuring each one. Two cuts, one vertical and one horizontal, would result in 144 equally sized pastries. It cost £12 and must have been very popular, as the advert in *The British Baker* claimed it to be 'Indispensable to all Bakers and Confectioners'.

Bunty, however, has very different memories of this part in her father's life. Apparently, the pastry cutter was very intricate to set up, as the baker did not want the cutter to give the pastries 'curled' edges, so, in testing out the cutter she had to bake several lots of pastry, and cut out 144 squares to see if the edges curled! She remembers her somewhat impatient father asking 'Isn't it ready yet?'

Another 'Tracy' experiment involved a bed warmer and airer called the 'kantBEDamp' which worked with an ordinary electric light bulb. From an advert it would appear that he sold this item himself, as he states that, as he was a small manufacturer, there was no purchase tax. This experiment was completed on an old settee in the dining-room, where heaters of various shapes, sizes and strengths were covered and tested to measure their effectiveness and whether they would overheat. The final bed warmer sold in many parts of the world, although it was never nationally advertised. It appears that visitors would take one back home and orders would arrive from America, Canada, Australia and New Zealand. Many hundreds sold in this country. The only problem for the family was that they all had to be sent off from their home! Apparently these bed warmers were designed to last a long time, for another lady tells me that her sister has one of these in her house at the time of writing, and that she used it only a few years ago to air a bed.

THE TRACY PASTRY CUTTER

(Patent No. 556030)

So Speedy! So Simple!

Above: *The Tracy Pastry Cutter advertisement, 1941.*

Left: *The Pastry Cutter.*

Right: *Tracy 'kantBEDamp' Bedwarmer.*

Eleven

The Second World War

Before the outbreak of war the Parish Council were already making preparations. Arrangements were made with the Weston-super-Mare Gas Co. to ensure that lights could be extinguished quickly if necessary. Also, Winscombe was thoroughly immersed in an increasing amount of Government legislation. A respirator census was taken and arrangements made for a canvass of the district in connection with the Government's evacuation scheme, the area organisers of which were Mr Shearmur and Mr B. Gardiner.

Food rationing started in January 1940 and in the spring the Home Guard was formed. Air Raid Wardens had started work on a voluntary basis, but later in the war their duties became compulsory. The first mention of Air Raid Precautions in the parish records dates from 1938. The method arranged to relay the report of any raid appears, in retrospect, to be more reminiscent of the 'Mad Hatter's Tea Party' than the transmission of what may have been warnings concerning a serious situation. However, it obviously worked well enough. The routine, which is explained by the daughter of an ARP warden, was as follows:

> *... during the war a siren would go off in Weston to signify that enemy 'planes were about. It was then decided that all the villages must have their own systems – apart from the sirens. So people in different roads were asked to take responsibility for letting perhaps half-a-dozen people know that there was a Warning. My father did it for a radius of about half-a-mile... I remember that one of his contacts was in The Lynch. The wardens would ring you from Weston to tell you that there was a 'warning' and then you would ring your six or nine houses. In the interim, you might hear the 'All Clear' but you could do no other than continue your round. When the 'All Clear' message came through you had to repeat the whole process.*

One thing that perhaps affected the village people, in particular, was that church bells were to be rung only to warn of invasion, and the sound of the Sunday call to worship was greatly missed.

An agreement was signed to take over the Drill Hall from the Somerset Territorial Army (rent free) to be used as a communal centre for evacuees. A committee was elected – its members being drawn from the various organisations – and they were responsible for the cleaning of the premises. They became known as the Winscombe Welfare Committee, the secretary being Dr Johnson. Happily, after an inspection by two ladies from the Ministry of Health, it was decided that no financial responsibility for this amenity would be placed on either the parish or the district in connection with its use.

In the parish, preparations were made to prevent damage from incendiary bombs. The Rural District Council had been instructed to provide sand at a central place for distribution to villagers who were to have a bucketful each in the event of a bomb falling on their property. The Council discussed the

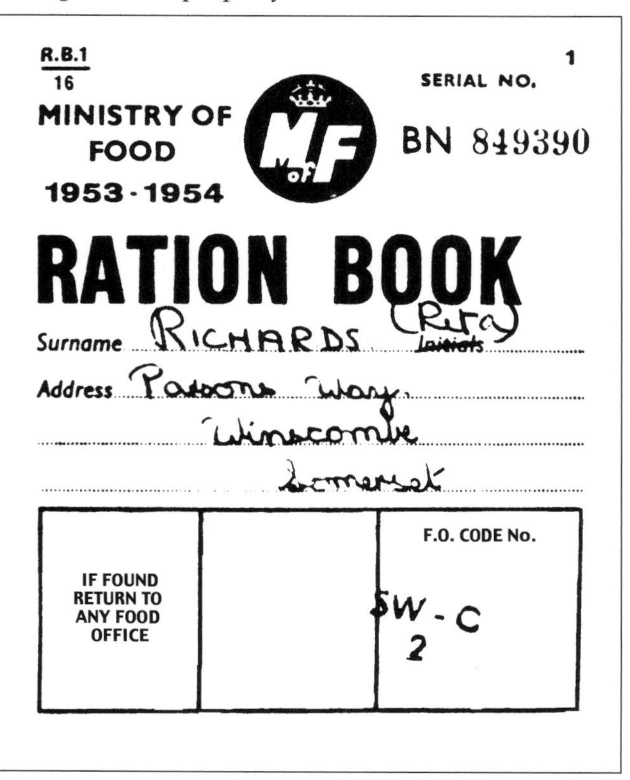
R.B.1
16
MINISTRY OF FOOD
1953-1954
1
SERIAL NO.
BN 849390
RATION BOOK
Surname RICHARDS (Rita) Initials
Address Parsons Way.
Winscombe
Somerset
IF FOUND RETURN TO ANY FOOD OFFICE
F.O. CODE No.
SW-C 2

Ration book, 1953.

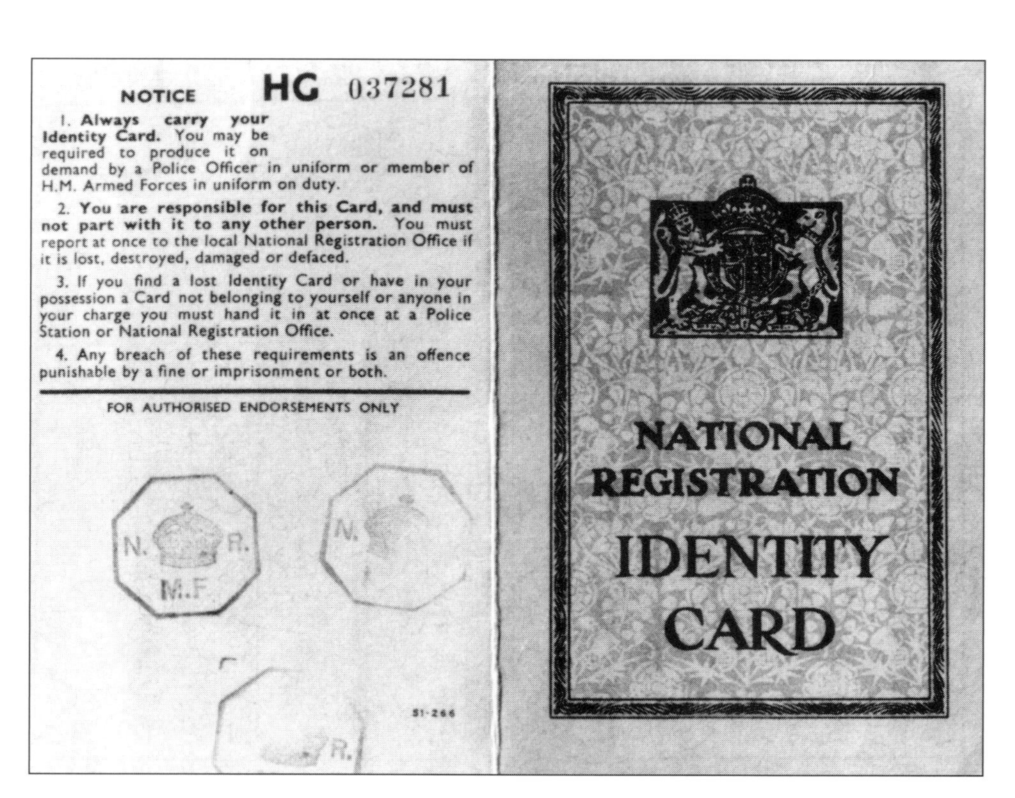

NOTICE HG 037281

1. **Always carry your Identity Card.** You may be required to produce it on demand by a Police Officer in uniform or member of H.M. Armed Forces in uniform on duty.

2. **You are responsible for this Card, and must not part with it to any other person.** You must report at once to the local National Registration Office if it is lost, destroyed, damaged or defaced.

3. If you find a lost Identity Card or have in your possession a Card not belonging to yourself or anyone in your charge you must hand it in at once at a Police Station or National Registration Office.

4. Any breach of these requirements is an offence punishable by a fine or imprisonment or both.

FOR AUTHORISED ENDORSEMENTS ONLY

N. R. M.F.

N.

R.

51-266

NATIONAL REGISTRATION IDENTITY CARD

Left: *Identity card, belonging to Miss Rita Richards.*

Below: *Post Office Savings Book.*

THIS BOOK BELONGS TO :—

Signature of owner: Rita Richards

N.B. In the case of a young child, a parent or guardian may sign, adding "For (child's name)"

Full Address: ~~Parsons~~ Parsons Way
Winscombe
Weston-S-Mare, Som

SIXPENNY NATIONAL SAVINGS STAMPS, which can be bought at any Post Office, or through a National Savings Group, should be affixed in this book by the owner in the order shown.

Stamps must not be detached except at a Post Office.

(For further information see inside of back cover)

The owner should insert his name and address above and should take great care of this book, as the value of lost stamps cannot be made good.

STAMPS MAY ONLY BE DETACHED AT A POST OFFICE.

31 6d. Savings Stamp to be affixed here
32 6d. Savings Stamp to be affixed here
33 6d. Savings Stamp to be affixed here
34 6d. Savings Stamp to be affixed here
15 6d. Savings Stamp to be affixed here
FOR VICTORY NATIONAL SAVINGS 6d
17 6d. Savings Stamp to be affixed here
18 6d. Savings Stamp to be affixed here
19 6d. Savings Stamp to be affixed here
20 6d. Savings Stamp to be affixed here

possibility of delivering this sand to those who could not collect it themselves. The decision arrived at was that this would not really be possible. However, most people had gardens and it was felt that a bucket of dry earth would be just as good as sand!

On 2 September 1939, although so early in the war, Winscombe was already making arrangements for the arrival of evacuees. However, as the reception officer at the time reports, things did not go exactly to plan. She has left a written account of that day, an extract of which is given below:

> *I don't suppose that any who were helping in the Government Scheme of evacuation will ever forget this date as long as they live...* [We] *had spent several days deciding exactly the sort of children we should put in exactly the right homes, and had, as we thought, everything beautifully planned. 150 children on the first day and 50 mothers and children on the next. The day arrived... and all the homes had been notified, the rations made up, the billeting officers all waiting at the Council School to receive the children.*
>
> *Out of the blue came shock number one! Fifty mothers and children, not expected until Monday, arrived tired and bewildered, clutching children and bundles indiscriminately. With the willing help of our local Scouts, they were all brought into the schoolroom. (The ices we had provided seemed thoroughly unsuitable, and there was no time to prepare the tea for which the mothers were all longing.) None of the householders were expecting their guests until Monday, but they were drafted to their destination as best we could. Meanwhile, the rain had started and another message came stating that only boys were on their way to us... this was shock number two... They came out of the charabancs – hundreds of them!... all large... not the small boys we had been expecting. They were taken into the School to be out of the rain.*

Eventually it was decided that each billeting officer with one or two small boys on her list should try to find homes for a large boy instead! Another problem was that instead of the half-a-dozen schoolmistresses from a London school that had been expected, 27 masters arrived. Eventually, 127 boys and 27 adults had been found accommodation – at least for the weekend. The report continues:

> *... then came the adjustments and re-arrangements. There was dissatisfaction on both sides to be smoothed*

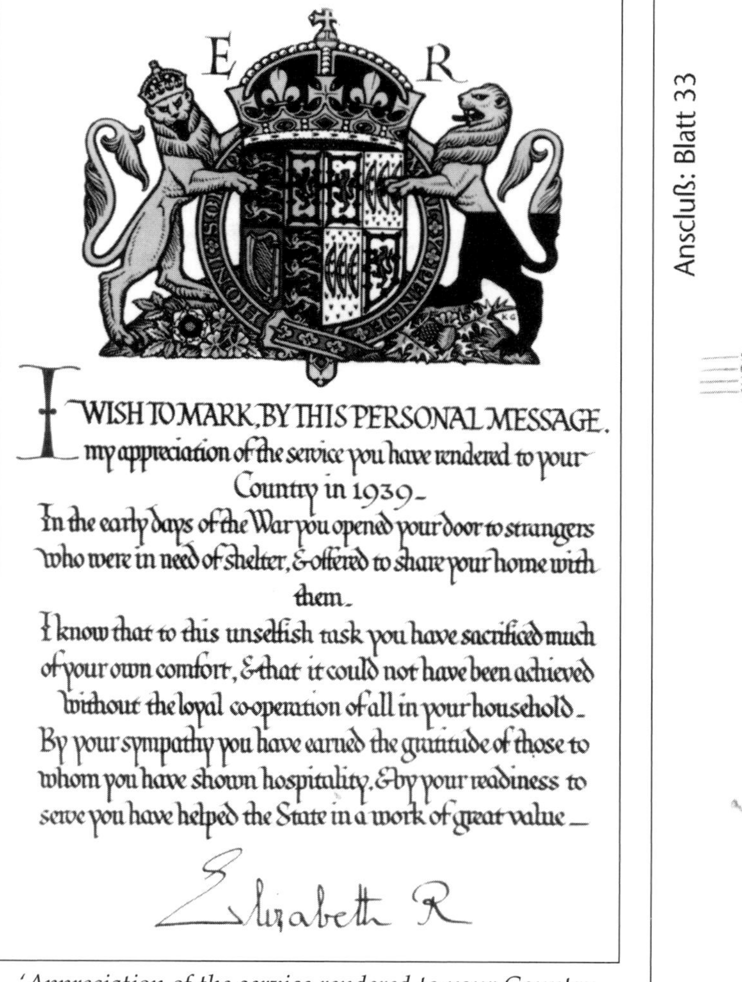

E R

I WISH TO MARK, BY THIS PERSONAL MESSAGE, my appreciation of the service you have rendered to your Country in 1939.

In the early days of the War you opened your door to strangers who were in need of shelter, & offered to share your home with them.

I know that to this unselfish task you have sacrificed much of your own comfort, & that it could not have been achieved without the loyal co-operation of all in your household.

By your sympathy you have earned the gratitude of those to whom you have shown hospitality, & by your readiness to serve you have helped the State in a work of great value.

Elizabeth R

'Appreciation of the service rendered to your Country in 1939, Elizabeth R.', c.1945.

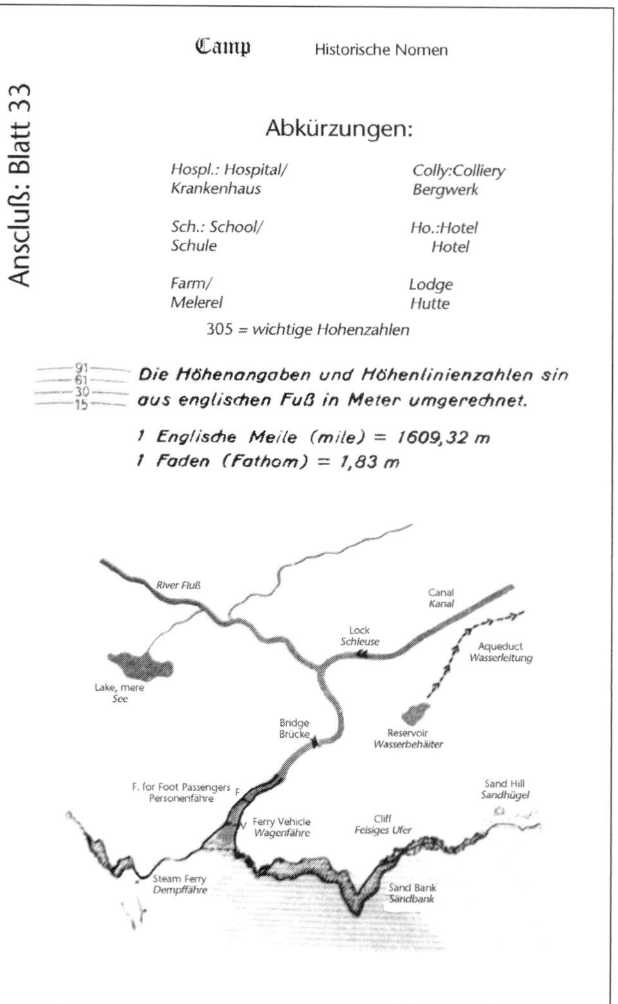

Directions in German, 1939.

Left: *National Fire Service. Winscombe W. 6, 1940.* Left to right, back row: *H. Henbury, L. Hadlow, F. Body, J. Watts;* middle row: *?, G. Lily, A. Weeks, G. Bird, J. Bell, ?;* front row: *W. Hares, J. Lovell, S.L., W.J. Egan (CO), H.G. Stephens (LF), ?.*

Left: *Winscombe Observatory, used during the Second World War by the Home Guard, c.1920.*

Winscombe and Sandford Home Guard, 1939.

out, and the gradual return home of the mothers and children had to be arranged... Billeting work was still not over, for batches came down at intervals until there were 158 boys and 47 adults, including wives and school masters. [These came from the London Polytechnic Craft School – see page 88.]

The report ends at Christmas when most of the evacuees went home for the holiday, as it was thought that this would provide a well-needed rest for all concerned. For those who were staying in the village some festivities were arranged, and a plea was made for invitations to tea, or a day out, to enable householders to have a break. The arrival of these young evacuees put great pressure on the local school, and, during the period when most of the evacuees remained in the parish, the school day was split in two – one set of children attending in the morning and the other in the afternoon. Gradually, some families returned home, disliking 'country life' and preferring to risk city conditions, including the bombing, in order to remain with their families.

The village was fortunate in that it was not affected by the air raids suffered by so many cities. There is an occasional record of a 'bomb crater' at Weare, and there was a 'direct hit' on Compton Bishop School in September. There are many cases of Molotov 'cocktail' bombs being dropped on the local hills, and some bombs were dropped in fields during Good Friday 1941, probably when the pilot was getting rid of them, but there were no local casualties at this time. One girl remembers seeing a dogfight overhead when the planes were caught in the searchlights. Her father insisted that she get back indoors in order to avoid being hit by falling shrapnel. Banwell, however, was not so fortunate and suffered quite a bit of damage when, in September 1940, they were caught by the end of a stick of bombs. Five people were killed and 15 injured.

Col William Yatman.

Fire!

At the outbreak of war it was decided that a new fire station was to be built in the village to serve as HQ for the whole district (this was the small building on the opposite side of the road where the fire station stands at the time of writing). The Parish Council were instructed to put in hand the recruitment of men to service the station. Men between the ages of 31 and 50 who were interested were asked to contact the clerk. They were to be provided with a uniform on completion of their training and would be paid for attendance at fires. The fire brigade personnel wore brown overalls, and the auxiliary service blue. They also had tin hats and gas masks. The story of the brigade has been told by ex-station officer Mabbett and leading fire officer Hares.

The man in charge was Jack Lovell, who owned the garage, and the brigade was now called the National Fire Service. Initially there were 16 members and they were housed at the old coal yard, which is The Rockeries in 2003. This was a tin shed and very cold in winter. Four of the station officers would report for duty in the early evening and stay there all night. As they had no radios, local Scouts and boys from the London Polytechnic Craft School were used as runners. Each watch was on duty every fourth night from 10p.m. to 6.30a.m.

Their equipment was a Vanguard car with a trailer pump and some suction hose and delivery hose, with various nozzles. They also had a standpipe key and bar to get water from the hydrants. In time the car was replaced by an ATV (auxiliary transport vehicle), which was a small lorry with a cabin on the back for the crew. The first raid they attended was at Banwell on 4 September 1940 and from then on raids at Bristol, Bath and Weston-super-Mare, and several others locally.

If there was any danger of a raid on Bristol, the men would be called to The Downs on the outskirts of the city, and wait until they could be sent to the most urgent situation.

Some of the other duties carried out by the local men were completely unknown at the time. Many of the Home Guard did far more than might be realised. Their story is told by Donald Brown in his book *Somerset v Hitler*. An extract reads:

> *... apart from these, preparations were being made for a new 'covert agency' called the British Resistance Operation whose job it was to carry out a guerrilla war of sabotage and attack. In Somerset 50 secret bases were established in caves, old mines and underground bunkers 12ft x 10ft dug into the hills.*

Much of the work was carried out at night, and in some bunkers supplies of food and water were stored, in case the men had to stay hidden for a while. Col W. Yatman was in charge of the 8th and 13th Battalions of the Somerset Home Guard. He was presented with a silver salver 'to mark the occasion of his relinquishing command of the Battalions which he formed and commanded, and to show the appreciation of all ranks.'

Winscombe Women at War

Feeding and clothing one's family, and simply making ends meet, was a challenge for many women during the war years. One story from this time was the 'Choose a Pig' scheme. If several families got together and bought a pig and then collected all their scraps in order to feed it, when it was time for it to be killed the families could share the meat between them. One group, however, became so fond of their pig, Mabel, that they could not bring themselves to eat her!

The Government published books on how to feed the family. Some of these volumes included instruction for better-off families with servants, making such suggestions as not to allow the latter to eat the scraps if these could be incorporated into other dishes. It was also mentioned that, as bread was the staple food of the poor, those who could afford it should eat as little as possible. This comment may seem of little importance these days, but it was obviously felt to be a serious matter during the early days of the war.

One more practical method of providing assistance during this time was the collection of (sometimes graded) paper and cardboard. Later the Men's and Women's Institutes joined together and introduced a fortnightly collection. Winscombe Scouts and the girls at Sidcot School undertook to do the collecting. Other changes were made, including the removal of iron railings to be turned into tanks and munitions, along with old pots and pans. Signposts were removed from road junctions to deter 'spies' from getting about. However, after the war, a member of one village family brought home several copies of local maps, with the necessary words translated into German! On reflection, it appears obvious that anyone travelling in Europe prior to 1939 could easily have picked up a copy of any map in a local shop!

Although some of the women became members of the WVS, many others just got together to do what they could, not only for their families, but also for the village as a whole. Mickie Weeks has many memories of those days and of the way in which people coped:

> *The main thing we did was fruit canning and jam making, this was organised by Mrs Helen Wills, a qualified domestic science teacher. The sugar was supplied by the Government, but we were not allowed to have any of this. However, as the jam was made in the Gas show rooms, near the bridge, we used to scrape off the scum and dash to Birds for some hot crusty bread and dip it in this – it was lovely! Of course, we all used to 'Dig for Victory' as we had gardens and we used to share what we grew between us. In this respect, perhaps we did not find rationing quite so difficult as those living in towns. Other things we did included the collection of rosehips (for vitamin C) and 'Valerian' which was used in medicine.*

Plays and pantomimes were organised to entertain the soldiers billeted in the village, and the women were greatly helped in this by Sidcot School, as when Birds Hall was taken over for the soldiers, the school let them use their room and stage. They also lent their costumes that they had collected over the years. This worked out quite well for everyone. When the play was finished, the WI used to repair and clean the costumes so that they would be ready for the next time.

There were many other activities. Classes were held in canvas and leatherwork, and the choir and drama group flourished. The choir continued for several years and was lead by Rosemary Bloomfield who was music teacher at Sidcot School. The drama groups were very popular – they used to entertain the villagers and those from nearby used to come as well. When the soldiers came, plays and other forms of entertainment were organised. The teachers from the London Polytechnic School were very useful in these cases as most of the local men were not available. Eventually, they became friends and were a great help with the pantomimes! Some of the plays are shown in the accompanying photographs, and were given titles such as *A Victorian Evening*, or *We are not amused!* Mickie writes:

> *We would take extracts from a Shakespearean tale and make up short plays. Sometimes we would perform pantomimes such as 'Cinderella', 'Alice in Wonderland' or a pageant of 'Famous Women'. Most of the parts were played by members of the Institute, but, occasionally, when we had the wives of members of the forces staying here, we would ask them if they would like to take part.*

Although acting was great fun, this was not the only activity undertaken; Mickie also recalls:

> *Another thing we did during the war was to knit balaclava helmets for the soldiers and socks for the Merchant Navy – the wool was awful – rough and oily, and made our hands sore! There were also things like Coffee Mornings for 'Salute the Soldier Week' and many others, some for the blitzed cities. It seems that we were a very 'combined' village and everyone did what they could. On one occasion we held 'A Midsummer Night's Dream' in the garden of 'Coombe House' at Sidcot. In fact, we did a lot of Shakespeare because most of the costumes that were available from Sidcot School were of this type! When the Americans left, they provided an 'American Meal' for us – Maryland chicken and 'Up-side-down Pie'.*

The villagers often remarked that they had been very lucky with their doctor and chemist. Dr Cooper, although a senior surgeon at Weston hospital, always had time to stop for a chat and was wonderful with children. He used to carry a small piece of plasticine with him and make lovely little animals.

Above: Shakespearean Women, *1942.* Left to right: *Belle Thompson, Mickie Weeks, Dolly Hunn, ? Sanders, Jan Grey, Rosie Baden-Baker.*

Left: Famous Women, *1942, with Mickie Weeks, Phyllis Cram, Dorothy Jones, Joyce Lindley, Dora Goddard, Irene Stubbs, Thelma Neal, Rosie Baden-Baker and visiting wives.*

Below: We Are Not Amused, *c.1945.*

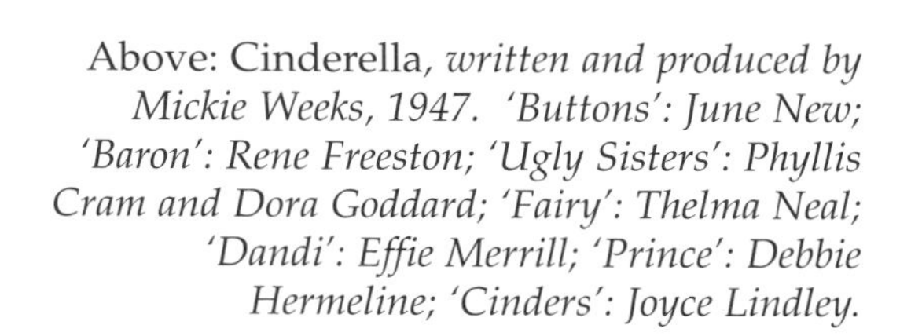

Above: Cinderella, *written and produced by Mickie Weeks, 1947. 'Buttons': June New; 'Baron': Rene Freeston; 'Ugly Sisters': Phyllis Cram and Dora Goddard; 'Fairy': Thelma Neal; 'Dandi': Effie Merrill; 'Prince': Debbie Hermeline; 'Cinders': Joyce Lindley.*

Mickie remarks: 'I also remember that sometimes he forgot to send a bill.' When he was free, he would help out at the various drama activities. Mr Smith was the chemist, and he was always prepared to deliver anything at any time.

One final note that Mickie Weeks makes reads:

After the war, when we all took down our black-out curtains, we wondered what to do with all this material. In the end we had a children's event, and we dressed them up as 'Pearly Kings and Queens'. Of course, we couldn't get pearl buttons, so we cut out little circles in white paper and sewed these on instead.

Throughout the war, mention was made in the Parish Council minutes regarding the various appeals for money to assist with the war effort. It appears that Winscombe nearly always raised more than their 'target' and the village was often the major contributor in the district. Some examples from 1942 onwards illustrate this point.

The Air Raid Distress Fund throughout the parish raised £327.8s.9d. In that same year a Warships Campaign Week was held from 15–22 May. As usual a committee was arranged to organise the week. The total amount raised by Axbridge RDC was £260. A certificate from the Lords Commissioners of the Admiralty was given to commemorate the local participation. The Rural District Council adopted HMS *Goatland**, and no doubt the ship's complement was well catered for during their service days. Winscombe's 'objective' was to raise £25,000. The final figure was £28,360.

* *HMS* Goatland *was a Type III Hunt Class Destroyer launched in 1942. She completed convoy escort duties in the English Channel, the Atlantic, and the North Sea and Mediterranean. In June 1942 she was a headquarters ship at the Normandy invasion, and remained just off 'Sword' Beach until the beachhead was established. [M. Jordon,* The story of Compton Bishop and Cross, *1944, p.86]*

Women's Institute planting a tree after the war, c.1946.

Mooseheart

In September 1939 47 boys and two masters from the London Polytechnic Craft School were evacuated to this house. The gym master was the father of the well-known film star Jean Simmons who went to the village school for a brief period and, later in the war, together with her sister, took part in concerts for the soldiers. According to one of the boys who stayed at 'Mooseheart', John Neesham, who now lives in the village:

Mooseheart in Winscombe threw its doors open to the Poly boys, having, at times, anything between 50 and 60 boys staying there. Some were boarded in the main house, and others in the Annexe which had rooms over the old stables. There were no horses in those days.

The kitchen was organised by Doris, Bronwyn and Olive, and cooking was done on a coal range supplemented by a gas cooker. The boys were responsible for making their own beds and sweeping the floors of their bedrooms. They also took turns in carrying food to the dining tables, but all the washing-up was done by the staff. The wartime meals were amazing. There was a well-varied menu to ensure that everyone got their full weekly quota of rationed items, and there was always a cooked breakfast.

Lessons were not taught at Mooseheart; it was purely residential. But the 'Motor and Craft' section did have a building in the grounds. The village school had the local children in the morning and the 'Poly boys' in the afternoons. A lady in Knapps Drive allowed Mr Stacey and Mr C. Ball, who taught hairdressing, to let the boys from the Polytechnic turn her garage into a room for the ladies' hairdressing training. All the local girls wanted to volunteer to have theirs cut into the latest styles! Weeks, the coal merchants, had a building near the railway bridge and allowed them to have their two upper rooms for the men's hairdressing. Sidcot School allowed the use of their sports field and some of their rooms for various subjects. There was also a large Drill Hall near the old Railway Hotel (as it was then called). This had four rooms as well as the hall, so they were made into classrooms.

John Neesham writes:

Amongst the Poly boys in those days we had a number of young Jews who were sent to England by their parents in Europe, just before the war was declared. Thus they avoided Hitler's gas chambers. Mooseheart and Winscombe gave them the stability and security that they so desperately needed as homeless refugees. One of them, now living in an Israel Kibbutz, recently mentioned in a letter how happy his days at Mooseheart and Winscombe were. My own treasured memory was when we said 'Grace' before meals. Then in perfect peace, all the boys of various nationalities and different religions could be as one to give thanks.

It was not only the young men who left the village to join the Forces. Several of our young unmarried women were equally anxious to 'do their bit'. One family of three sisters all joined the ATS. They ended up at Fuggleston Camp, Wilton, in a property that had belonged to the Pembroke family. This was during the time of 'Operation Overlord' prior to the invasion of Dunkirk. They remember that, despite having numerous inoculations, they never left this country. In fact, Betty was so ill that her arm was in a sling for ages. Because of this, on one occasion during exercises on Salisbury Plain, she was told the best thing she could do would be to lie down and pretend to be dead!

Another young woman, Mary Kinsey, was a nurse with the Queen Alexandra's Royal Nursing Service. She recorded her life in London when she was in Bart's Hospital during the Blitz from 1940–41. Then she was sent abroad to serve on a hospital ship. The full story of her adventures is too long to be told here, but she does make several interesting remarks about life at sea and the effect of modern medicines. After the introduction of the new medicines – 'Penicillin' and the sulphonamides – the methods of dealing with diseases changed dramatically.

She remarks that she never had a tidy ward, and some of the different races behaved unusually – the Gurkhas for instance tended to be very childlike in their behaviour; when they were beginning to feel better, they would walk around and pick up the counterpanes and start to dress up in them. Despite this, Mary says they had very little cross-infection. The Germans, on the other hand, were very good patients and well disciplined. Mary arrived safely home in time to celebrate the end of the war.

As well as the evacuees, the villagers were also visited by various members of the Armed Forces. Men from the Suffolk Regiment were the first to arrive and these were followed by the Green Howards. It was thought they were gathering before being sent to the South Coast prior to the Normandy Landings. Later some Americans arrived with their luxuries such as 'gum' and nylon stockings! After having seen our men with so little, the girls were somewhat overcome with the generosity of some of the Americans. One of the lasting impressions of their arrival was the fact that most of them were very homesick. They used to sit and talk about their homes and families and show photographs of their wives and children. However, they did learn to play cricket!

In the village, Mrs Doris Rendall started the local branch of the Women's Royal Voluntary Service and organised local 'meals on wheels'. These were originally prepared in a member's kitchen and, later, at the Community Centre. (At the time of writing they are prepared and cooked in Bristol and delivered frozen to the local volunteers.) Mrs Worsley also arranged for the distribution of parcels to the troops.

By 1942, due to rationing and other restrictions, most women became experts at 'make-do-and-mend', and when the soldiers were billeted in the village, the Toc H Hut (established by soldiers after the First World War in memory of those who served, it later became the Drill Hall) was used as a venue for entertainment and refreshment. Due to the lack of provisions and the rationing, there was not a lot that could be provided, so the story of the famous 'beetroot sandwiches' came into being. Apparently, these were extremely popular with the men, as was the opportunity for a 'chat'.

It was not only the local women whose lives were changed by the war. Ted Hares, the stationmaster, found that he never knew when he would be home and recalls that many a time 'my misses would come up to the station to see if I was dead or alive – or coming home.' Many things might affect his timetable. He might have to go out at any time of night to check the line when someone reported a suspected bomb, only to find when he returned that someone would have rung up to apologise for having a bonfire! When this happened he would have to ring Axbridge and Sandford stations to hold the train until he checked. He remembered that on one occasion he waited from 9p.m. to 2a.m. to be sure that everything was clear. He could not have a fire because of showing flames in the blackout, and he still has a hand lamp as a souvenir of those times at the station.

One thing of which he was particularly proud was that his wife kept him in good food. 'I was as well fed as any man in Winscombe. The wife would buy a bit here and then go into Weston.' The butcher knew he was on all night, and he never went without a meal. Whenever he arrived home, no matter what time it was, there was always a meal waiting for him. The fact that he grew his own vegetables was a great help. Ted and his wife, Florence, were both keen gardeners and won several first prizes in local shows *(see page 133)*.

Throughout the war the Drill Hall became the place for regular entertainment. Each Saturday there was a dance, the music provided by the 'Meritors Five Piece Dance Band' from Weston-super-Mare. The entry fee was 2s.0d. 'Uncle Ernie' (Winslade) used to collect the money at the door. Maureen tells how her father and Mr Clarke built a stage and decorated the hall. Usually, a notice would be sent to the nearby airforce camp at Locking, and the lads came in two lorries. When they all tumbled out, the village girls would be enveloped in a swarm of young airmen – at a favourable ratio of about 12:1. So, as someone remarked: 'We danced all night – really we had a wonderful time.'

On other occasions dances were held in Birds Assembly Rooms when some of the local men made up a band: Edward Hewlett and Mr Chivers, who owned the sweet shop on the corner, were two of the names recalled, including the fact that there were always 'trumpets'! One of the girls said that her father was not quite sure if this was the kind of thing she should be doing. He gave in when she took her elder sister with her – although she still suspects that her father had a 'quiet word' with one of his friends to keep an eye on her. At other times, there would be some stalls in the hall in aid of various charities and Birds Bakery used to provide the teas.

British Legion

At the outbreak of war the Legion received a letter from the County Committee advising branches to carry on as far as possible with their benevolent functions. One point mentioned in the minutes is that it was decided to hold their annual dinner as soon as possible 'in view of rationing' and a provisional date was fixed for 2 November. Nevertheless, at Christmas that year several members or their dependants were given gifts of money or grocery vouchers. The Women's Section prepared a tea and social event for the children.

The local branches took their job seriously, and on some occasions worked hard for men who had been discharged without means of subsistence. One member had been sent home pending discharge on 2 January, and, as his discharge papers did not arrive until 6 February, during this time neither he nor his wife received a penny from the Army Paymaster. The Labour Exchange had refused to pay out as he was still in the Army. It turned out that there had been five such cases in the county, and all were being taken up by headquarters.

In 1940 Toc H raised funds to entertain any troops billeted here for Christmas. On one day (unrecorded) during the festive period at 2.45p.m. there was a football match, and a cold dinner was served at 6.30, followed by a concert. All local servicemen home on leave were also invited.

From the provision of occasional financial help, to the supply of coal, the branch helped in many and various ways in the following years. Every case that came to their attention was considered. On one occasion a member of the Legion was in hospital, and his wife was obviously in need. The branch decided to supply the wife and child with 4cwt of coal during the cold weather and advanced 2s.3d. for her bus fare to the hospital so that she could take him a change of clothing. Additionally, if the weather continued to be cold a further cwt of coal was to be provided. It was decided to make further enquiries and that steps should be taken when the man returned to work.

It is apparent that, whilst the Legion was anxious to help those members in need, they did not casually hand out money to everyone. One long-standing case records that the member was being allowed 6s. weekly, on the condition that his son kept the war memorial in the parish churchyard in good order. Another entry mentions that the Services Welfare Committee had despatched between 40 and 50 parcels of comforts of various sorts to those men who replied to the committee letter.

It has to be remembered, of course, that many of the activities proposed by the Legion would not have been possible without the co-operation of their wives. The social events, parties and concerts all involved the Women's Section and they were entirely responsible for the Poppy Day collections, and in 1942 the sum raised was £150.5s.11d. – the largest amount to that date.

In Memory

The names of those who served and died in the Second World War are listed on the board in the church porch and on the stone cross in the churchyard.

Winscombe bell-ringers who rang the victory peal, 1945. Clockwise from bottom right: *John Vincent, Mrs Lily, Mr George Lily, Terry Golding, Alfred Wilmot, Walter Hancock, Fred Hancock, Mrs Rowett, Michael Lily. The ringer in the centre has not been named.*

Twelve

Wartime Memories

Although there are many stories of the way in which the war affected everyday life for the villagers, there are those who have looked back on their wartime experiences from a different angle. Two of the stories are from young boys who were evacuated here, or lived here at the time. Another explains the way in which the war completely changed the life of one of our 'village boys' and opened up a new world for him.

The first story comes from Peter Alletson who was a pupil at Sidcot School and was 11 years old at the time:

Aircraft seemed to be in the air much of the time and I became an enthusiastic 'plane spotter'. The planes I remember were (in no particular order) Avro Ansons, Spitfires, Hurricanes, Lancasters, Havard trainers, Tiger Moth trainers, Miles Majestic trainers, Westland Lysanders, Wellington Bombers, Sterlings, Halifaxes, Whitleys and, later on, the American B18 Flying Fortresses, Liberators, Mustangs and DC3 Dakotas.

A great excitement one day was the arrival of a Miles Majestic trainer which landed on the playing-field and scholars were allowed to go to the field to see it. A tanker came from somewhere to refuel it, and we saw it take off from the Sidcot Gate corner of the field in the direction of the church, only just clearing the fence at the other side of the field.

There was a searchlight stationed behind the pub at Star and at times of enemy air activity in the area we could see its bright white beam probing the sky with other searchlights around to catch the enemy planes so that the ack-ack guns could knock them out. There were guns nearer to Weston and Bristol... they could be heard firing and you could hear the shells exploding with the typical 'woof-woof' sound... At around the time of the 'Blitz' the National Fire Service and Auxiliary Fire Service held weekly training courses at the school. They used to arrive on Fridays in their green or grey fire tenders towing trailer pumps. The men used to sleep in the old gym which used to be in the Science block... they brought a large mobile canteen which had a large tall chimney. Most of the drill was with hosepipes – running them out and coiling them up again.

On one Saturday night there was an air-raid alert. The men and tenders were all there when we went to bed but next morning they had all gone – to fight the fires caused by a Blitz on one of the cities – Bristol, Bath or (someone said) Exeter.

There was a decoy city laid out on Blackdown to trick enemy raiders into thinking it was Bristol, and apparently it worked. They dumped quite a lot of bombs on it and, just after the war, you could see the remains of it and some can be seen now.

There were large convoys of six-wheeled American trucks taking stores down the A38 to their invasion embarkation places in Devon and Cornwall during the build-up to D-Day in 1944. It went on day and night and seemed to be endless. We used to watch them go by from the old swimming bath at the top of the boys' playground and, of course, at other times when we were out of school walking in the area. One of the spin-offs from this was the refuse thrown from the trucks – used ration packs, etc. If one was lucky one might find some unopened candy or gum, which was an absolute treasure in those days of strict rationing and austerity. Traffic consisted of tank-transporters with their tanks, and other armoured vehicles.

On the morning of 6 June 1944 I awoke to the sound of many heavy planes, and looking out of the window saw the sky full of formations of four-engined planes towing gliders. We realised that it must be D-Day and this was confirmed when we heard the news on the radio.

Peter's memory of the fake town is not an unusual one. There are many such stories of shadow factories or cities which were supposedly set up in the area. Rumours have suggested Brean Down and Hutton as well as the one mentioned above. Whether they are true or not has, to the author's knowledge, never been confirmed.

John Neesham was one of the young boys who arrived as an evacuee from the London Polytechnic School:

When we, the Poly boys, arrived in Winscombe on the second of September 1939, we were all found billets by a very efficient local billeting committee. They handed out ice-cream cones to refresh us, and we were all given a brown paper carrier bag containing 24-hour emergency food rations. These consisted of: ½lb cream biscuits; tin of corned beef; 1 large tin of Nestles unsweetened milk; 1 tin of sweetened condensed milk and ½lb bar of Cadbury's milk chocolate.

Walter Powell and Jim Bridger and I were taken to stay with Miss Edith Forden who lived in Harbury Batch, Sidcot, near the traffic lights that are now installed there. I remember that we all used to 'get the giggles' sometimes at meals, and Miss Forden used to join in and yet none of us knew why we were laughing or what started it off. They were very happy days. I kept in touch and visited her sometimes even when she eventually left Winscombe to live in Burnham-on-Sea after the war.

After about six to nine months we moved nearer to the village and stayed with Mr Henry Rolson and his wife, Dr Hilda Rolson. They had a large house in Knapps Drive. It was here that Walter Powell fell out of the bedroom window while trying to follow the instructions from the fire officer on how to leave a burning building.

According to earlier information from John, the fire officer came to give a talk to the boys. He started off by telling them why they had to resist and not let Hitler get to our shores, and he continued to paint a very bleak picture of England were Hitler ever to win the war. Then, he went on to talk about dealing with the incendiary bombs that were falling on the cities and towns. Most of the boys had tried out the 'stirrup pumps' and they all found it fun playing around with jets and sprays of water. At this stage, they secretly thought the grown-ups were making a fuss about what could be quite a laugh.

Then the fire officer came on to the subject of what to do if the house was on fire, and one could not put it out but had to abandon the premises:

'Now!' he said, 'you must never just stand on the windowsill and just jump. It is far better to lower yourself out of the window and hold on to the windowsill. That way you shorten the drop and there is less chance of doing any damage to yourself.' 'Or,' he said, 'you can tie the bed sheets together to make a rope and climb out of the window.'

Suddenly, the talk turned from boring to interesting. Walter and I thought that was a really good idea.

Walter, Jim and I resolved to put this into practice as soon as possible – which meant when our foster-parents were out. The day eventually arrived. As I had a small bedroom and Jim and Walter had a large one, it was here that we took off the sheets from the beds and tied them into a rope. Then we carefully tied the sheets onto the leg of one of the iron beds, as we had been instructed to do. Jim had been in the Scouts so we left all knot-tying to him as we knew from experience that his knots never came undone at the wrong moment. We threw the sheet-rope out of the window, saw with satisfaction that it reached the ground and we all moved towards the window to be the first to go. We each wanted to be first, but since Walter had already got hold of the sheets and was determined not to let go, Jim and I had to give way on this point. We both sat on the edge of the bed to watch Walter descend.

We watched him climb onto a chair, then onto the windowsill and out onto the outside windowsill. Holding the edge of the sill with both hands, plus the sheet, we watched until only the top of his head showed. We both said the daftest thing – 'Don't let go of the sheets'. Yet we both knew that this was the last thing he intended to do. Walter said he was ready and – Here Goes! At precisely the same moment Jim and I jumped up off the bed with the idea of going over to the window to watch Walter's gradual descent to the ground.

However, our getting off the bed stopped us acting as anchors, with the result that the bed flew across the room and was only stopped from flying out of the window as well by the wall underneath... Jim and I were horrified. One minute we had all been talking. Then there was the noise of the bed across the floor and now there was nothing. No sound at all and no cries of 'I've done it!' from outside. Just nothing. Jim and I looked over the windowsill – there was Walter, lying in a very mixed-up position on the concrete below. He did not move. He did not make a sound. Jim and I did not speak, we seemed frightened to express our fears in case they came true. Instead we both went to the top of the stairs and, without really noticing it, our feet took us to Walter, who was laying in the same position, huddled up on the concrete, still clutching the sheets. When we spoke his name there was no answer. It was all so quiet and still. Then, such a relief to see, he opened his eyes, but still lay there. We waited. Gradually he moved all his limbs and we realised he was all in one piece. We did not really know how we felt about the whole thing. All Walter said was that he had not let go of the rope so could not really understand what happened.

When we all went back to the bedroom, Walter seemed to think it would be a good idea if someone else went down the rope so that he could watch their descent. However, Jim and I were suddenly not interested any more. In the end, Walter knew his task was hopeless and he kept watch while we gathered up the sheets, untied the knots and then we all remade the beds.

It became known later that quite a few houses were complaining that their boys had inexplicably torn the

Right: *Arthur Langford on his 80th birthday flight aboard a Chipmunk, 2003.*

Below: *Arthur Langford's cattle, c.1950.*

sheets on their beds, so obviously they were not the only ones to try out the fire officer's idea. John says that they enjoyed their stay with the Rolsons as their sons had already grown up, leaving them enough time to be able to cope with the new influx. However, the bombing in towns and cities was getting serious and so the boys had to leave when members of their family arrived.

Walter now lives in Australia, and is married with a grown-up family, but still likes to keep in touch with news of Winscombe.

The Second World War changed the lives, not only for the many city children who came here, but also for some of the 'village boys' in a way that they could never have envisaged. Arthur Langford is but one of the many that could be mentioned. Together with his brother Dennis, Arthur attended the village school, which, like most of the local children, he left aged 14 – going to work for a well-known firm of cabinet makers – Wake & Dean, at Yatton. (In fact, this had not been Arthur's ambition as he actually wanted to become a farmer, having helped his uncle many a time with the cattle on his own farm.)

In 1941 Arthur left Wake & Dean and joined the Air Force, and two years later married his wife, Joan. The pair had known each other since attending the village school, but they were unable to be together long during the war as Joan managed to spend just a short spell with Arthur when he was sent briefly to the Isle of Man.

Later he sailed to Cape Town aboard HMS *Tamora* (a meat boat), before being sent to an officers' training camp in Rhodesia – apparently many British airmen were trained in a Commonwealth country, mainly due to the good weather conditions. Whilst in South Africa, Arthur visited many towns, including Mount Hampden near Salisbury, Heany near Bulawayo, and Gwelo near Pulsmoor, Cape Town.

Arthur trained for 12 months, first on Tiger Moths and then on Oxfords, before being promoted to Sgt Pilot in 1942 after having spent some 252 hours in the air. His career, in Training Command, gained him experience flying a great variety of planes, and over the next few years he also flew Martinets – carrying a drogue for trainee gunners to hit – followed by a time on Ansons carrying the gunners.

Later, he joined No. 12 Operational Training Unit at Chipping Warden as he prepared to join a squadron, and by this time he had clocked over 1,000 hours' flying time. He moved to various camps flying larger and larger planes – among them Wellingtons and Lancasters. When he joined Bomber Command, Arthur was 'kitted out' to fly to Japan, but fortunately the dropping of the atom bomb prevented this. He returned to England aboard HMS *Britannic* and in 1945 joined Transport Command at Pockington, York, from whence he carried anything that needed to be taken from A to B, whether it was machinery, food parcels or men. In June 1946 Arthur left the RAF, but he did not want to give up his flying, so he joined the Voluntary Reserve at Filton. He was then recalled to Oakington where he flew Harvards and Spitfires. And on moving to North Luffenham, he flew his first jet plane – the Vampire! Of all the planes he had flown, however, Arthur has always favoured the Lancaster, noting that he always felt 'right' when he was in one.

When he left the Air Force, Arthur worked as an agricultural representative for SWEB, for, although he still would have liked to have gone into farming, he was unable to buy any land. However, he did manage to rent a half-acre plot at the rear of the present council-houses near the bridge; this being opposite Arthur and his wife's home at The Myrtles which they shared with their daughter Sue. Arthur built some sheds on his plot and began pig farming, with ten pigs, being helped in this venture by Ben Durk, another well-known Winscombe lad and a great friend, and also his brother Dennis (who, despite also joining the RAF – as a wireless operator – never flew in the same aircraft as Arthur).

By ploughing every spare penny back into the farm, Arthur managed to save enough to buy some land on the hill and built a house there. He gradually increased his stock until he had nearly 800 pigs and 25 sows, a project which took some four or five years. (The gestation period for sows is about 16 weeks and some litters were as large as eight to twelve piglets. One boar would look after 20 sows.) Joan also kept about 500 pullets on deep litter in a couple of old Nissen huts which they had bought.

Arthur and Ben used to collect the food for the swill and cook it themselves on the hill with a steam boiler, and, as Arthur was also still working for the Electricity Board in order to keep the farm going, he and Ben would often have to get up at 4.30a.m. to do the feeding. At weekends, rather than put his feet up, Arthur also used to go flying – just to keep his hand in!

It is a well-known fact that pigs are not the easiest animals to move. Apparently, the best way is to use some corrugated-iron sheeting in order to shield the animal so that it does not know where it is going. However, on one particular occasion Dennis did not deem this to be necessary. So, with Arthur holding one ear, Den holding the other and Ben holding the tail, they set off to put the animal in a pen. All went well until the sow shook her head violently – Arthur went one way and Dennis the other, and Ben was left hanging on to the tail trying not to let go.

Den's hair-brained plans were not unusual; one day they were moving a pig from one field to another when he decided once again that no props were necessary. The pig had other ideas and set off at a great pace with Arthur, Dennis and Ben dashing after it for more than a mile before the animal decided that continuing wasn't worth the effort.

Arthur was fortunate in that he had a contract with Walls, the sausage company, and one benefit of this was that once a year he and Joan were invited to London for a 'grand weekend'. The were put up at a first-class hotel and enjoyed lunch at The Grosvenor House Hotel where they had the opportunity of meeting up to 100 other farmers and their wives. Joan still recalls these occasions with a big smile on her face! Unfortunately, the Government soon decided that entertainment could no longer be written off as a 'tax loss' and, apart from two such occasions, there were no more.

When the market for pig farming declined, Arthur decided to change to milk production and bought some Friesian cows. Initially, there were just ten animals, and he was milking into buckets and churns, but gradually the herd was built up to 150. By this time the family was living at Laurel Farm, in The Square, and unfortunately the first winter's milking coincided with one of the coldest spells in the area for many years. The snow was still to be seen under the hedges on top of the Mendips in June and the only way that the milk could be taken to the station at Puxton was to put the churns on the back of a Land Rover.

Although Arthur has officially retired he still walks around the farm every day, and his flying days are not over. For his 80th birthday in September 2003 his family arranged for him to fly once again, and he described the experience as 'wonderful'. He flew a Chipmunk from a field in Devon and was in the air for about half an hour. Just to prove that he hadn't forgotten his old skills, he even did a 'loop-the-loop' and it is an event which neither Arthur nor his family will ever forget.

He still finds it incredible that a village boy from a place as small as Winscombe once was, should ever have had the opportunity of gaining so much responsibility and having so many different experiences. The war, which brought such tragedy to so many, completely opened up the world to a boy who might otherwise have spent all his life within the confines of the Mendips.

Thirteen

The Postwar Era

After the war, a fund was set up for the 'welcome home' celebrations. There was enough money to present scrolls to the 210 villagers who had served in the conflict, together with a cheque for £7. The balance from the fund was distributed between Winscombe and Sandford Schools. The programme for the victory carnival week was largely arranged by the British Legion and, as well as preparing for a week of entertainment, it was proposed that the proceeds of the festivities would go towards the cost of the provision of a new convalescent home at Weston-super-Mare. The proposed target was £1,000 and, as the Government had decreed that 8 June should be Victory Day, this was to be the focus of local activities.

Victory Carnival Week

The programme was ambitious and varied, commencing on Saturday 1 June 1946 with a garden fête. On Saturday, a United memorial service was held at the Parish Church and, on the following Sunday, 9 June, an evening United Drumhead service at Sandford Church was to be led by Weston-super-Mare St John Ambulance Brigade Silver Band.

A 'gay nineties ball' was held from 8p.m.–1a.m., and on Monday 3rd there was a drama festival at the Legion Hall, where there were three 'grand' plays presented by local drama groups – *The Curse of Cairo* by WI Drama Club, *Mystery Cottage* by Nailsea Youth Club and *The Friends*

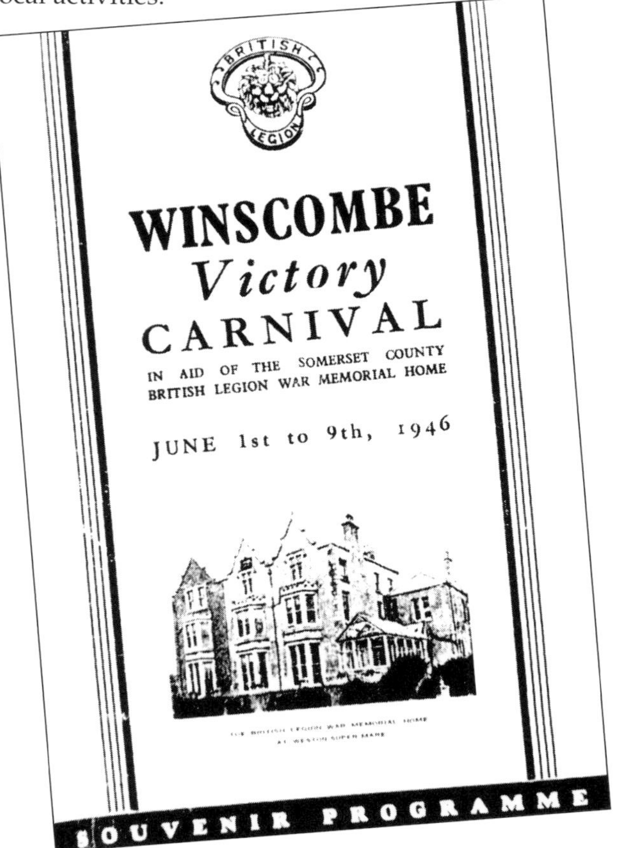

WINSCOMBE VICTORY CARNIVAL, JUNE 1st—9th, 1946

SATURDAY, JUNE 1st, 1946

Garden Fete

AT MONK'S HAVEN, WINSCOMBE
(by kind permission of Dr. and Mrs. W. W. Veale).

Fete to be Opened at 3 p.m. by Mr. W. L. Barnett, Secretary Somerset County British Legion.

BABY SHOW open to Winscombe, Sandford and District.

Various Competitions.

Numerous Side Shows and other Attractions.

Flower and Vegetable Stalls.

Auction Sale at 6 o'clock of Surplus Articles given by Friends.

Admission 1/-. Children 6d. Teas 1/-. *If wet to be held in Legion Hall.*

Grand Carnival Dance

AT LEGION HALL, WINSCOMBE.

Dancing - 8 to 11.45 p.m. to the Music of "The Meritors."

Competitions and Novelties. Admission 2/6 (Forces 2/-).

TIME CARDS on Sale for Stop Watch Competition at all functions

Programmes of celebration, 1946.

of Valerie Lane by the Winscombe Players.

A Victorian Ball was to take place on Wednesday evening, followed by a 'monster whist drive' and a prize draw at Birds Hall on Thursday. Friday saw a sports carnival and fun fair at the recreation ground which included three comic football matches – Home Guard v National Fire Service, The Specials v The Rogues, and Men v Women. A note at the foot of the programme reads 'Be sure to visit Ali Baba and the crystal reader.'

Saturday 8 June was the day of the grand victory carnival and events were planned from 2p.m. when there was a children's fancy-dress parade, and other sports continued until 5 o'clock when all the schoolchildren were invited to tea in Birds Assembly Rooms. At six o'clock there was a grand carnival procession with decorated cars and cycles. There were also various tableaux mounted on lorries and carts, and there were horses with riders in fancy dress.

At 7 o'clock in the evening there was a presentation to the men and women who served in the Forces during the war, and who were resident in the parish on 3 September 1939. The cheques – the gifts of the inhabitants of the parish – were presented by the chairman of the Parish Council, Mr J.C. Dyer, JP.

The village exceeded its target by a large amount, and the first war memorial Home was opened in Weston. Since then, another home at Knightstone has been used for many years, but this is not really suitable for all residents, and a new home, on the sea front and on one level, is to be opened as soon as possible.

Following the carnival week, it was decided at a meeting of the Children's Empire Tea Committee not to give a tea to the children that year as they would have one on Victory Day. Instead, they would be asked to 'give' and a collection was made at the school on Empire Day in aid of the British Leprosy Fund. The sum of £3.0s.6d. was collected and school sports were held in the recreation field in the evening. As a permanent memorial the Tea Committee offered to provide an oak tree to be planted by the children in the field when the Parish Council had given their permission.

Getting Back to Normal

With many of the difficulties of the war behind them, the villagers tried to regain some semblance of normality. This did not happen without some problems along the way. It was obvious that with the changing circumstances there would be a great deal of work for the Parish Council to cope with, and the number of councillors was increased to 15.

During the previous years the villagers had not forgotten their generosity. By 1946 it was possible to provide the final figure for Axbridge's Rural Pennies Scheme, which had been running from 1941. The total was an amazing £12,423.16s.2d., a sum which surely helped Somerset to become fifth in a fund-raising league of England and Wales' counties. The national figure reached was £107,409.13s.6d.

Although most people agreed that 'normality' was all they really wanted, it actually took far longer for this to be achieved than most of them had envisaged. Rationing, for example, was to remain for several years, and as late as 1953 certain basic items were still limited. At this time, grocery lists always began with the words – Rations – i.e. meat, butter and sugar (in particular), then the additional items. Even as late as this, the Ministry of Food was still issuing booklets on food and nutrition, and these clearly illustrate the emphasis which was by this time being given to the importance of vitamins and balanced meals. Vitamins were supplied to young children and expectant and nursing mothers, and extra milk was sent to schools where handicapped children attended. Cod-liver oil, which contained a considerable amount of vitamin C, was available for babies and young children, and from 1946 school milk was issued free to all schoolchildren.

New products gradually became part of our diet. Everyone remembers 'Smash' which first took the place of fresh potatoes and 'reconstituted eggs' which were used for cooking and for making scrambled eggs. Another item that appeared on the menu at that time was 'snook'. We never knew quite what it was but we all supposed it was whale meat and it was not popular. Another import – Spam – was eagerly accepted. It is difficult to realise that something that is so common today was a new experience at this time. Another item, which probably radically reduced the amount of tea that we drank, was Nescafé. At first it came in tiny tins about 2ins high and we gingerly tried it out in small spoonfuls at a time. Anyone who remembers the old 'Camp Coffee' will understand the great impact this single item made. Rationing was abolished in 1954.

There was one other 'new' product on the market, the washing powder 'Tide'. Having previously been used to washing up by 'swishing old bits of soap in the bowl' – unless the dishes were very greasy and called for a little soda to be added – 'Tide' was wonderful. It was used for everything, not just washing up dishes or clothes. It was used in baths and even for washing hair!

It is probably true to say that, five years after the end of the war, although food was not available in as many varieties as before, on the whole, the health of the population had improved considerably.

One change that took place immediately after the war was the complete reorganisation of the National Fire Service, and the present county system was born. When the old section leader, Jack Lovell, resigned, Mr Harold Hembery took over as the station officer and a siren was fixed to the tower on the opposite side of Sandford Road. The call-out system for the area was still 'dial O' and ask for the brigade. Even when the village had a new 'phone system they still had to ring Harold, and either he or his wife, Grace, would run over the road to operate the siren. One can't help but feel that it must have been difficult for them at times, as someone always had to be at home throughout the 24 hours.

In April 1946 a gorse fire above Shute Shelf was followed by the burning of thousands of acres of bracken on Blackdown. There was another huge blaze on the Sunday night when the dry gorse and bracken caught fire again. The fire started close to the village of Shipham at about 6p.m. but it was not until 7.30 the next morning that the flames were finally extinguished, and by this time they had destroyed hundreds of acres of brushwood. More than 70 firemen were engaged in fighting the flames, and they were assisted by volunteers. Many of the local firemen would have been involved, of course, as Blackdown is the highest point on the Mendips, and the glow from the fire could be seen for miles around.

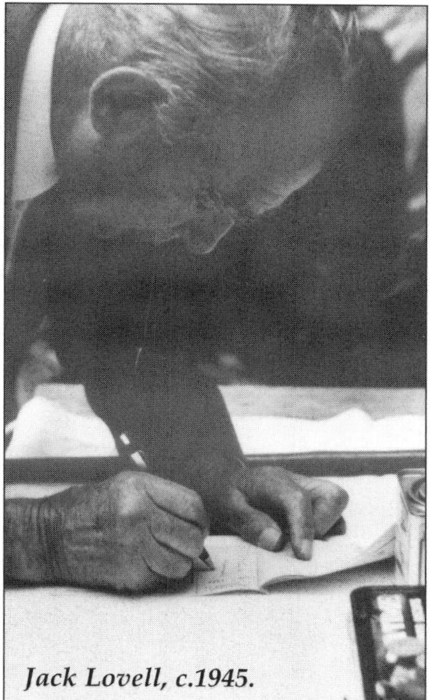
Jack Lovell, c.1945.

The brigade continued with gradual updating of equipment: a radio transmitter in 1947 and a featherweight pump stowed on the appliance, replaced by a Bedford TK which had a high-pressure hose.

The Community Centre & More

It was also during this period that perhaps one of the most important and unsettling local events was about to take place. It concerned the question of the setting up of a Community Centre in Winscombe. This issue arose when it was first decided that a new school was needed for the village, and it was suggested that the present school in Sandford Road would be ideal for the purpose. One main cause of disagreement was whether or not the centre would be licensed.

At this time there were grants available from the Carnegie Trust, via the National Council of Social Services, and they would make available a sum of £1,000 together with an interest-free loan of £3,000 for seven years. There then followed many years of discussion, after which it was decided that the only way to resolve the matter was to hold a vote. In 1947 polling-stations were provided so that the villagers could finally decide. One of the three stations provided was at Sandford where only 36 votes were recorded, and one of these was spoilt! When the result of the poll was declared on Saturday evening in Winscombe School, the general public 'were conspicuous by their absence'. The vote was 210 'against' and 100 'for'. Consequently the vote was lost. This was only a temporary setback, and later things changed dramatically.

It was felt that the absence of police was affecting the tone of the village. The Parish Council decided to write to the superintendent registering the disapproval of the village at having no police and asking that this state of affairs might soon be remedied. At a Council meeting the clerk repeated a complaint he had received regarding:

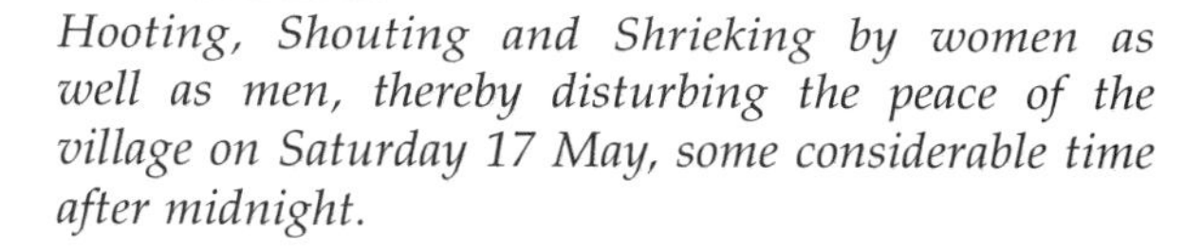
Hooting, Shouting and Shrieking by women as well as men, thereby disturbing the peace of the village on Saturday 17 May, some considerable time after midnight.

In 1952 two events took place which gave the villagers an opportunity to demonstrate the helpful side of their nature and their ability to really enjoy themselves when the occasion arose.

In the wake of the 'disastrous storm' (which only later became known as the 'Lynmouth disaster') a special meeting was held to consider what appropriate action could be taken by the Council to assist the victims. One money-raising event was a house-to-house collection and a dance was held at the Assembly Rooms, which was the first event to take

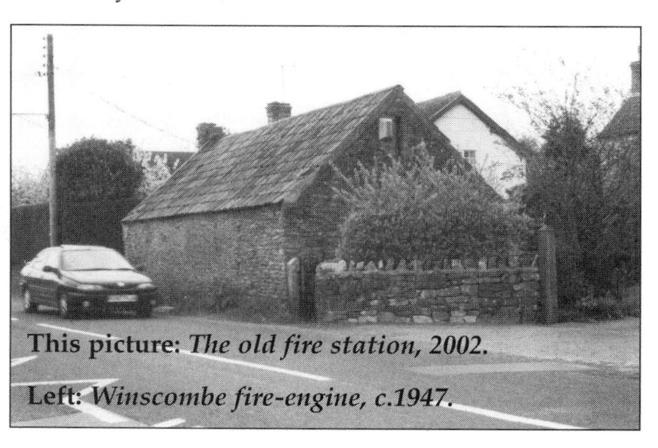
This picture: *The old fire station, 2002.*

Left: *Winscombe fire-engine, c.1947.*

place on the newly laid floor that had been replaced after the building had been used during the war. Another function was held at the Legion Hall and the total amount raised was £179.9s.5d.

Additional assistance for the villages concerned was provided by the WRVS. Several members, including Mrs Doris Rendall, went to the area and helped with the provision of temporary accommodation. They also gave support to the other organisations that arrived to help. Some unfortunate families had lost everything but what they stood in, and they needed not only tea and sympathy, but also clothing and towels, etc. The village was delighted to learn much later that Mrs Rendall had received the BEM 'for services rendered'.

In the year 1951 one very important comment was noted in the Council minutes: 'For the first time since records were taken there are no names on the unemployment register list at Axbridge.'

Coronation of Elizabeth, 1953

After considerable discussion between the Council and the villagers, it was decided that a 2d. rate towards the cost of these events would only raise the sum of £120, which would not be sufficient, and voluntary contributions were to be sought where possible. Both Winscombe and Sandford representatives of the British Legion offered their support and agreed to help with the raising of any money that might be needed. The idea of a bonfire was discussed, with the hope that all the villages would join in a chain of bonfires through the Mendips.

The Council had hoped that Winscombe and Sandford would make joint arrangements, but they decided to hold separate events. This being the case, the rates were split – Sandford £40, Winscombe £80.

The programme arranged by Sandford was as follows:

SATURDAY
Evening entertainment for the old people
at Legion Hall, Winscombe.

SUNDAY
Combined Service
at St James Church, Winscombe.

TUESDAY
Tea for all school children under 15 years.
Presentation of Souvenir Beaker.
Sports and Community Singing in
Winscombe Recreation Ground.
Comic Football Match.
Coronation Ball
at Birds Assembly Rooms.

WEDNESDAY
Children's Musical Festival.

Although Sandford prepared this programme, many of the events took place in Winscombe and doubtless a similar list of events was prepared for this village. One lady remembers seeing the marquee set up with a great deal of red, white and blue rosettes. The Parish Council also rented a colour television set and placed it in the Community Centre so that people who wished to do so could watch the spectacle from there.

After such a 'grand' occasion, Axbridge Rural District Council received what may be considered a rather 'petty' complaint regarding the 'vivid and contrasting colour scheme of the redecorated council houses.' The local Council wrote to Axbridge asking them if they would consult the parish before any further decorations were started. The reply stated that 'We have now appointed a ladies committee to go into the question of any future colour scheme.' As no further complaints are noted, it can only be assumed that this was deemed satisfactory.

The 1960s

The era of the '60s appears to have brought about a new spirit of determination, on the part of people, to retain their peaceful village. Perhaps, after the uncertainties of the previous decades, the reassurance of permanence was needed. This mood is almost tangible when looking through papers and minutes of the period, when there are constant signs of unease concerning any proposed change.

For instance, when a planning development for eight properties in Well Close was made, the Council agreed, provided that there would be an average of six houses per acre, and that they would have control of the removal of trees during the development. They also insisted that the type of property should be in keeping with existing dwellings and that plans should be given to them at every stage for their approval. There were complaints regarding the use of portable radios in the street, and the first mention of the proposed closure of the railway line was noted.

The year 1960 was World Refugee Year, a fund was organised and the sum of £436.11s.9d. was raised. In 1961 a unique event occurred when Winscombe came fifth in the 'Tidy Village' competition. It is unlikely that we could achieve the same result in 2004. Of more lasting importance is the fact that in 1966 the new library opened, with a considerably increased number of books and the introduction of a 'mobile' library for the surrounding villages.

Fourteen

The Changing Years

In 1965 the Women's Institute celebrated its golden anniversary, and the members described in their own way how the recent years had affected the life of the village. One of the main concerns was the effect of the ever-increasing movement of folk from the city. But, as they noted, 'Winscombe was still an agricultural district, surrounded by fields, woods and hills,' adding, 'The greatest change in agriculture was a move from mainly dairy to arable farming – the cause being the unprofitability of milk.'

This was the beginning of the period when a great deal of building was to take place in the village, most of it in the form of 'in-filling', with the original part of Winscombe on the hill remaining largely untouched. It was in the area 'Hillyfields' in the old 'Woodborough' that most of the new development took place and where two large estates had been built. The Institute passed comment on 'the influx of new blood [which] provided a considerable stimulus to the cultural life of the community.'

At this time the Parish Council decided to build seven one-bedroom bungalows for the elderly at the modest rental of 28s.0d. A bell connected them with the central warden's dwelling so that assistance in emergencies was readily available. When the Council were trying to find a name for this development, it was suggested it would be a suitable way of remembering one of our district nurses who had worked in the area for a long time, Alice Bignell, remembered by many for cycling through the village on her 'sit-up-and-beg' cycle with a basket on the front. The development was named 'Bignell Close'.

It was not only the Council who were concerned with housing of the elderly. The Quakers, or 'Friends', who had had an interest and influence in the village on numerous occasions, decided that it was time to provide a home for the elderly in Winscombe. This became the property known as Sewell House.

Sewell House

It appears that the idea of a home to provide for the elderly in Winscombe came from Marguerite Sewell late in 1964. She had become very concerned for the welfare of an elderly friend who, after spending most of her active life in the district, was living as a life tenant in a house belonging to her former employers. In her very old age she was unable to maintain the house and garden and had no other accommodation to which she could go. Marguerite spoke to her husband Arnold Sewell, expressing her wish that Sidcot Friends should do something, perhaps in the way of providing independent flatlets to help others who might find themselves in a similar dilemma.

In December 1969 the House Committee decided to adopt the name of 'Sewell House' for the building, in memory of its first chairman, Arnold E. Sewell, who had died in March of that year. The most important work of the committee was the appointment of the warden upon whom would fall the difficult task of making a home out of a house, and of setting the pattern of working for the future. In 1969 Mrs Joan Voysey was offered the post, and the warden at the time of writing is Mrs Sue Chandler.

As a result of a preliminary enquiry over 50 applications were received. There was, and is, no restriction of entry on account of age. Of the 23 tenants admitted in the first year, 1970, one lady was in her sixties at the time of admission and another was in her nineties. The average age was a little over 79. (On admission there has to be an undertaking by a relative or friend to accept 'some degree of responsibility for the applicant in case of serious ill-health or decreasing ability.')

It was hoped to achieve a balanced community of Friends and non-Friends, men and women, and it was the intention that the two double flats should be let to married couples. The weekly rental for a single flat in May 1970 was £8.10s.0d. In 1972 this was raised to £9.25p, and after this rentals were raised almost every year by about £1.50p. More recently, generally in line with inflation, the rents have had to be raised to a greater extent. Rent covers the cost of heating, electricity, rates, TV licence and a home-cooked lunch each day. There are also provisions for simple cooking arrangements in each flat, so that the tenant can prepare his/her breakfast, or make a cup of tea, etc.

It is hoped that a communal lounge will not be long coming. At the time of writing the dining-room fulfils this role when required. Whilst this is perfectly suitable for activities such as a game of cards or a chat amongst friends, there is no one area where all the residents can be seated at the same time, without a great deal of moving of furniture. Needless to say, there is always a waiting-list for accommodation.

Winscombe Club

After the war the British Legion continued to meet in the Drill Hall until, in 1962, it was sold. In order to secure a meeting-place, they purchased two old cottages in Nippors Way from Mr Bird for £1,500. These had previously been let by him to some of his workers. The Legion spent about £1,000 on alterations, creating a skittle alley and bar, and turning a little lean-to shed abutting Mr Brown's house into a cellar. To get to the club, one had to walk down a long path from Sandford Road – which is now the front of the building.

By 1963 a problem had arisen. In order to retain the club, at least 55 per cent of the members had to be Legionnaires. With a membership of only about 100 there was no way that this ratio could be maintained. On 12 February a formation meeting was held, the object of which was to create a club that was not only for Legion members, but also for any families that lived in the village.

At this meeting, Mr R.S. Brewer was appointed chairman and Mr G. Uffindell secretary/treasurer. An entrance fee of 5s.0d. and a 5s.0d. subscription payable by non-Legion members was agreed. Some 40 applications for membership had already been received, but as there was an urgent need for funds, it was decided to take the extra step of approaching other skittles league teams who might want to use their alley.

When the club was extended into the building we know today, at a cost of £25,000 (but consisting of one floor only), many of the members helped out with getting it ready for the opening on 9 August. In order to provide a little capital for the initial expenses (beer!), several members gave the club a loan of £5 each.

Initially the entertainment provided included not only the skittle alley for men and women, but also darts, bingo, fruit machines and a piano in the lounge. The bar sold wines, spirits, liqueurs, beer, cider, cigarettes and tobacco. At a count made on 16 August at the club there were 100 members and their friends. By 10 September the British Legion and the Winscombe Club became two completely separate organisations and the membership increased to 200.

The club grew in strength through the 1970s. The women members of the Legion were also involved in the running of the club, particularly in the realm of entertainment, and their names appear regularly in the minutes. By March 1974 the premises were finally complete, with an upper floor being added above the original building.

Education

Mr Burrows, the previous headmaster of the village school, retired in 1969. He was the last to have lived in the house attached to the school. He was

Winscombe Station at the end of school term.
Note the cases and bicycles. Ted Hares is in uniform, c.1950.

succeeded by Mr Abrahams. By this time the village school was very overcrowded and two new huts were added to be used as classrooms. This meant that there was no hall for assembly, and the children had to go to Birds Assembly Rooms for dinner in two relays. It was in this year that the 'Cuisenarie' system of numbers was started and the Initial Teaching Alphabet introduced in the infants class.

The private school – The Chestnuts – was still providing a good education for a limited number of children, their policy being that the school wanted to give as much individual attention as possible. Although only a small school, The Chestnuts held two open days for parents in 1969 and also a sports day in June. The children had collection boxes for Dr Barnado's Homes and they had great fun when they opened them. Each child opened his own box, and the older children made piles of the various coins. That year they collected £60.

At Sidcot School, although a few local children went there as day-scholars, most of the youngsters either came from further afield, or from another country. A foundation-stone for the new study block was laid, and a new laundry was installed, the old one, which had given decades of use, being placed in the Folk Museum at St Fagans, Cardiff.

One very important event took place in that year. The railway station closed, and all the lines were taken up and the bridges removed. With the going of the railway it is understandable that some parishioners were afraid that the tearing out of this lifeline would ruin their businesses, and greatly affect their lives. However, when one door closes, as the saying goes, another one opens... Another major project begun in this period was the building of the M5 motorway (which passes through the Mendips), which opened on 15 July 1967.

The sight of our beautiful area being torn up by huge machinery and bulldozers moving great amounts of soil made the future appear somewhat bleak. As time went by, however, the verges and slopes became green with grass, and in many places wild flowers could be seen. The red poppies, white daisies, bulrushes, thistles and many other wild flowers can now grow untrampled. Several small copses have been planted, and the lines of taller trees edge the motorway in many places.

One unforeseen result is the return of many of the small wild animals that had left the area when the original disturbance occurred, and they can now be found hiding in the undergrowth. Large birds such as crows or magpies are not afraid to dart down for their prey. Even small hawks can be seen hovering above the banks and waiting to catch some of the small mammals that have made their home there. Of course, these banks are perfect for wildlife, in that only very rarely will anyone walk along this part of the roadside.

Most people will agree that whilst they were very much against the coming of the motorway, the result has been better than was first thought.

Many other forms of local produce, thought at first to have been put at risk due to modernisation and the speed of transportation, have either survived, or been replaced in order to meet the new conditions. Strawberries are grown under large tunnels of plastic to encourage them to ripen early and so be ready for sale before those grown on the Continent. Instead of streams of local 'pickers' in the fields, 'PICK YOUR OWN' signs are everywhere. Whilst the volume grown may not compare with that of 'earlier days', the local strawberries are genuinely thought to be the best, and to have a structure and taste far ahead of those coming into the shops from Spain or Italy.

New markets have been found to supplement those fed by some of the forms of agriculture previously carried out in the area. Vines can be seen planted on the slopes of the hills and English wines are beginning to hold their own. Various other types of farming have taken place, for example Mendip snails are exported to France and elvers, always a local favourite, have become a delicacy in some restaurants. One of the best-known products of the area, cider, has blossomed. In early times most farms would have had their own 'press' and made their own, for cider was the main drink of the farm workers (see Chapter Two).

St James Church Hall

The story of the building of this hall began in 1942. On 6 September that year Miss Florence Maud Schacht ('shot') died. She had come to live in Winscombe after leaving Bristol, and made her home at The Myrtles in Woodborough Road. She had been born in Germany, and in April 1937 she bequeathed her land and adjoining property to the church for a church room. She had always attended services, despite the fact that she had to take a taxi for the journey.

The grand opening of the hall took place on 15 July 1967, and was led by the Right Revd Edward Henderson, Bishop of Bath and Wells. Mrs Hilary Mabbett became the caretaker and cleaner, and her deputy was Mrs Nigh. The cost of hiring the hall was £1 per hour, and the first autumn bazaar made £280. Badminton, whist drives and coffee mornings were all enjoyed on a regular basis in the early days of the venue.

Given the growth in both accommodation and population, the building became used for many and varied activities, from baby clinics to 'Friendly Hand' gatherings for the elderly, and Mothers' Union. The building is also used for numerous children's activities: a 'Friday Club' for the 5–11-year-olds meets after school until 4.30p.m.; for the older children 'Signposts' (11–14-year-olds) meet on

Left: *The opening of St James Church Hall, 1967, with Bishop Jock Henderson, the vicar Revd Jones, David King and Stanley Benbow.*

Below: *The 25th anniversary of St James Hall, 1992.* Left to right: *Joan Searle, David King, ?, Revd Ian Hubbard, Chris Sampson, Ann Bishop, Robert Easton, Geoff Norton (Chair).*

Below: *St James Church Hall, 2002.*

Left: *Winscombe Nursery School's end-of-term picnic, July 2003.* Those enjoying the day include: *Reuben, Jack, Nieve, Charlie, Louis, Bethany and Paige.*

Sundays from 7.15–8.45p.m. A weekly market which used to be held here for the sale of dairy and garden produce has since transferred to the Community Centre.

The Great Flood

On 12 July 1968 what became known as 'The Great Flood' took place. A quantity of water that had collected in a basin at Priddy on the Mendips broke through a retaining bank and poured straight down through the village. One gentleman who has very vivid memories of that evening is John Matthews, as he was a fireman at that time. He writes:

The rain started at approximately 11–12 o'clock in the morning. At first this was welcomed as we had a dry spell previously. As I went home at 5.30 in the evening, the wife said that if the rain continued, we would have trouble. I said – don't be silly (or words to that effect).

We were initially called out at 20.20 hrs, this was to the shop where the video shop is now. This was a very minor affair, but before we finished we had a second call to Moorham Road. This was opposite the school entrance where we piled the furniture on top of tables etc. At that time, the calls were coming in thick and fast. At that point, we ignored the property and concentrated on people. With the help of an ambulance we took approximately 50–60 to Sidcot School where they stayed in the teachers' common room, and the school supplied cups of tea, etc.

I personally went home at about 2 o'clock to put on dry clothes. At that point the water under the bridge was about 12–15ins deep. This rose to 24ins at its high point. One action we had was to rescue a chap who was rather elderly from the cottages opposite the entrance to Moorham Road and carry him to a house a bit further up the road. In doing this, we went through about 3ft of water. I did not go home to change again, but let the clothes dry on me. There was nothing we could do about the level of the water as the volume was too great.

The main problem was the railway embankment as there were only four places it could get through – 1. The main road bridge; 2. The bridge in Homefield Close; 3. The gout [an escape route for water] *at Greenfield Avenue; and 4. The gout at the bottom of Woodborough Crescent. This had its comical effect as a man in the bottom corner of the Crescent came down stairs and walked into 2ft of water – then he woke up.*

The rain eventually stopped at about three in the morning. At this time, there were about 8 or 10 drivers who had come to the fire station for shelter as the A38 was blocked at Hale Coombe and Paddingham Corner with stone and debris washed down on to it. The most damaged properties in Winscombe were those opposite the Community Centre and the properties in Woodborough Crescent. Greenfield Avenue was flooded by mainly static water that was unable to find a way out.

At the height [of the deluge], *Weston Fire Brigade were called to rescue an elderly woman at Sidcot as, at that point, the continuous rain made our radios useless so we went from one call to another, and then returned to the station for a further list of calls. We finally booked off duty at 20.20 hrs – a full 24 hrs on duty. We did very little pumping out, but instead, we carried furniture and carpets outside to dry. And, finally, the gouts at the Crescent and Greenfield were cleared out and we were promised that they would be kept clear. They are now back to their old state.*

One incident permanently etched on the author's memory during that evening was the sight of a man wearing bathing trunks, wellington boots and carrying an umbrella, walking down the road through the torrent of water pouring down the hill. It was never discovered who he was.

Left: *Floods in Church Road, 1968.*

Right: *Flooded recreation-ground, 1968.*

Below: *Winscombe bowling green with Mr Nuttycombe the groundsman, 1968.*

Fifteen

The Modern Era

By the early 1970s Winscombe had taken on its 'modern' appearance. Much had changed over the previous century, and the beginning of this new decade seemed to give the village a chance to pause and consider the future.

Medicine

Since the early days when the village doctors visited their patients at home, or hired a room in a house once a week for a surgery, Winscombe has developed a modern and efficient medical practice. Not only does it deal with everyday patient ills, but it also carries out regular reviews of such things as asthma and diabetes and the monitoring of blood pressure. A child health clinic is held twice a month and the doctors can carry out minor surgical procedures on the premises. Twice a week a physiotherapist can been seen at the practice.

The modern surgery has a staff of five doctors, two practice nurses, and a nurse practitioner who is trained to see and treat many acute problems, thus saving time for patients who might otherwise have to wait to be seen. There are also secretarial assistants. The district nurses, however, provide one of the main points of contact for the villagers, sometimes making daily visits. As with most practices in the early-twenty-first century, in order to be able to provide a 24-hour service, it has paired with another surgery, that at Banwell; together they are known as 'The Wavering Down Medical Centre'.

Dr David John and Dr Kathy Ruddell have been at the practice for many years and were later joined by Dr John Jackson, Dr Matthew Paul and Dr Wendy Fletcher. They prefer the country life to that of the big city practices, with their many doctors and specialised areas of concern. The rapid increase in the population of the village has been absorbed by the centre, and does not appear to be causing any difficulties at the time of writing.

In addition to the surgery, Winscombe also has two dentists and two osteopaths to take care of parishioners, together with a visiting chiropodist who comes to the Village Hall once a month. We also have a well-equipped optometrist who occupies the building which, many years ago, housed the gas showrooms. The chemist is conveniently situated in the main street, so we appear to be well looked after in every respect. Even our animals are well cared for – we have a good veterinary service.

The increase in population has led to increased pressures elsewhere and the Parish Council had to consider the provision of an additional burial-ground for the parish when a crisis point was reached and there were only seven spaces left in Winscombe churchyard. In December 1970 the Parish Council was authorised to purchase and provide this extra facility by means of a loan not exceeding £4,000. Eventually, land at the junction of the Sandford/ Winscombe boundary was chosen, and the approach was named 'Ilex Lane'.

Avon

The year 1971 is unlikely ever to be forgotten by the local people as this is the year that they became part of Avon. This Parliamentary decision affected everyone in the parish when the reorganisation of local government took place, and Winscombe came under the control of the brand-new county. It was a move greatly opposed by most villagers, who made plain their wish to remain in Somerset and continued their opposition undaunted for many years. Part of the problem lay in the fact that under the new tertiary system Parish Councils were in the unenviable position of having to answer to two 'masters'. Earlier, they had accepted the point of view of Axbridge or Somerset Councils. The new reference points of Woodspring and Avon were resented – particularly as it was felt that Avon was far more 'in tune' with, say, Bristol, than with any of the 'country' areas.

Of course, it was not just the unpopularity of the name that gave rise to the problem. For the District Council, there was the considerable stress involved in coming to terms with a new system. In the 'good old days', as one chairman of the Parish Council said:

If we had a problem we would ring Axbridge, and it would be dealt with. Now, it went from one committee to another, and the amount of paper work was amazing.

There was great disagreement over this decision, and all the villagers protested whenever the possibility arose. Perhaps one of the major concerns was the loss of our famous 'Shire' association. True, the river in the area is the Avon, but this did not smooth feelings. A great 'Back to Somerset' campaign was started which continued to the very end. In 1993, the reorganisation of local government and the overthrow of the Avon County finally took place. The parish from this point on would be working with North Somerset, and become a 'Unitary Authority' (County Council and District Council combined) which means that, at the time of writing, we are outside the boundary of the (current) County of Somerset. This causes all sorts of problems, mainly for the councillors, but at last we were allowed to use our old address once more, 'Winscombe, North Somerset'.

Although it was anticipated that the new Council structure would result in less paperwork, this turned out to be far from true. The Council now has so many reports to read and act upon, so many forms to complete, and so many meetings to attend, that they have had to employ a full-time clerk. This is the first time that the role has been carried out by a woman, Mrs Xanne Blythe, who worked partly from home and for a couple of days a week from the Council Office at the Community Centre. Unfortunately for Winscombe, Mrs Blythe proved so good at the job that she was offered another post working for North Somerset Council. She was replaced by Mrs Lynne Rampton, so perhaps we have established a new village tradition of female clerks after a century.

When Television Came to Winscombe

Ever since Winscombe was able to tune in to radio programmes, complaints about the quality and variety of programmes have arisen. There follow extracts from letters of complaint and comments from notes in the parish records. Several protests were sent to the television company, a typical example being at the time when a 're-run' of a rugby match on the Welsh Channel was shown on the West Channel at the very time when the Queen was visiting the area, thus preventing thousands of viewers from seeing her. Complaints suggested that consideration be given to airing a programme from the Wenvoe transmitter showing the visit of Her Majesty so that it could be seen locally. In the end, an equitable arrangement was reached. The BBC agreed to show the film 'Welcome to the Queen' at St James Church Hall on 31 October throughout the afternoon and evening until 9p.m., thus enabling those concerned to have an opportunity of seeing this, even if they had to work during the day.

There was also a complaint about the lack of balance in the programmes transmitted from the Cardiff Broadcasting Station. Mr Tracy wrote:

My... complaint was that many people have wished for more London programmes, as they were lighter and more interesting. We had read in the 'Radio Times' that there was to be an evening given to an old-time musical hall show by many of the favourites in their original successes. We then find that this feature is for London only, not relayed to any other station, and even if you had a one hundred pound set, you could not get it here. My other complaint... was that it was a pity they did not include the news bulletin in the Sunday evening programme. I presume that it was left out because some of the Welsh religious cranks objected to news on the Sabbath. The funny part of it was that when the news did come, it was largely composed of the doings of the churches and chapels of all denominations. I am quite aware that the BBC cannot please everybody, but I often find myself getting on to Bournemouth...

One question that was still of considerable concern to the village was that of television reception. No matter in which direction we placed our aerials or how many of them there were, we could not get a decent programme in English on BBC One. At the Parish Annual Assembly of 1973 it was proposed that the Minister of Posts and Telecommunication should be asked to ban all Welsh programmes from the Wenvoe transmitter, or allow a reduction in the licence fee until a service could be provided for this area. The arrangement in place at that time meant that many villagers were deprived of ten hours' viewing time per week. During the coming years this pressure was continued and in the chairman's report in 1977 it was noted:

... the number of viewers in this area was about 20,000 and they were still having to tune to Wenvoe in order to see BBC One. This was, of course, predominantly for the Welsh and consequently much of it, at peak viewing times, was in the Welsh language... we have to endure this agony just to satisfy a small minority of Welsh speaking people... as less than 5 per cent speak the language and less than 20 per cent understand it... we are told it will be several more years before the necessary frequencies become available... (apparently) the Home Office are reserving the spare channel at Wenvoe exclusively for a Welsh-speaking programme.

Above: *Stile into Kings Wood on Railway Walk, 2002.*

Left: *The Strawberry Line brochure, 2000.*

Below: *A place to relax on the Millennium Green, 2002.*

It was not until 1978 that the Parish Council were informed that a new relay station at Hutton would be in place by the end of the year.

Cheddar Valley Railway Walk

At an inaugural meeting on 20 February 1978, the Cheddar Valley Railway Walk Society was formally constituted. The hon. secretary, Mrs Lois Brenchley, has provided most of the information regarding this walk. The initial aims and objectives were to provide a public route on the former Cheddar Valley Railway for leisure and recreation, and to conserve the land as a nature reserve. With the backing of the Parish Councils, together with many members and supporters, the society persuaded the District Council to purchase the seven linear miles within Woodspring, before going on to finance and set up this first phase of the scheme from Yatton to the A38 at Shute Shelve between 1983 and '85.

Phase two, the Axbridge to Cheddar Cycleway, followed in 1990 and was established by the Axbridge/Cheddar branch of the society in collaboration with Sedgemoor District Council. This provided a much-needed safe route to school for Axbridge children, avoiding the busy A38.

The 'Strawberry Line' remains a fitting title for today's popular ten-mile Yatton to Cheddar route. It is widely recommended as a major artery through the countryside of North Somerset and Somerset for leisure and recreation. The area is a mass of wild flowers and ideal for bird-watchers. The wide variety of linear landscapes of cuttings, embankments, moor and rhynes, woodland, hills and even a tunnel, all contribute to make this, at 74 acres, the largest Local Nature Reserve formally designated by English Nature in North Somerset.

The society and its branches continue to manage the land in partnership with local authorities. Conservation is important and recordings of plants, birds, butterflies and mammals are kept. New members and volunteers are always welcome.

Although our forefathers trembled at the thought of the railway line stretching through the countryside, perhaps they would be pleased to think that modern villagers are also concerned with conserving the natural beauty of the area. The remains of the station itself became the centre of attention for another group of people who eventually formed the Winscombe and Sandford Millennium Green Trust. Their aim was to bring the site into use as the 'Millennium Green'. Winscombe was fortunate for in 1998 the Green became one of the very few accepted in the national 'Millennium Green Scheme', and it acquired charitable status which was necessary for the group to retain the site as 'of County Importance for Conservation'.

After a great deal of work this area now provides a superb setting for many annual events – the May

Above and inset: *Railway Walk, 2002.*

Above: *Statue on the Millennium Green, 2000.*

Left: *Mrs S. Gunn cutting the first sod of the Millennium Green, 2000.*

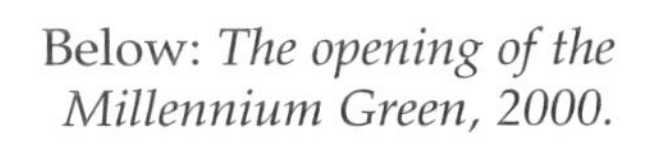

Below: *The opening of the Millennium Green, 2000.*

Left and below: *Inside the bus shelter at Sidcot, 2001.*

and Michaelmas Fairs among them. The plan of the old station has been laid out, using bricks from the original building, which provides an idea of the old structure for visitors. Brass plaques have been sponsored and these, showing dates relevant to the area, are placed around the edge. As well as giving historical information, the area also provides a place to sit and reflect.

As is the case with any such undertaking, without the constant attention of the members of the Trust, it would soon lapse into its former wild state, and everyone who enjoys the Green has a duty to ensure that it is not misused.

One event which proved to be a great benefit to the entire village took place in 1980. The school in Sandford Road, together with the attached cottage, was leased for 28 years to the Winscombe Community Centre Association. Together with the original school buildings, there was also a playing-field with one classroom. The lease was on an annual renewable licence of £20. It was later decided to hold fund-raising events to buy the property and the other buildings for £50,000 which, after many coffee mornings, jumble sales, other events and a great deal of hard work, was finally accomplished. The following year proved to be a great success story. After much hard work, largely engendered by Mrs Rita Hinton, the building has been transformed. It started with just a few chairs and tables, and small meetings for coffee or card games were arranged.

Gradually, more and more bookings were received and there was the beginning of an income from these 'lettings' and annual subscriptions. By 1981 the Centre had raised £2,500 and soon hoped to be self-supporting. In 1983 the Centre was awarded a cup for the most improved village hall in Avon. The WI scrapbook includes the comment: 'The Annual Michaelmas Fair (held in the Centre) successfully unites the entire village with competitions and entertainment.' This is possible due to the fact that, together with the actual school buildings, the Community Centre also has the large grassy area with some large timber buildings, which had been used as classrooms but which are are now used by many societies who may only require a smaller amount of space. One of the buildings is used by the Day Nursery and another by the Youth Club.

Every Thursday the market provides a venue for the sale of a variety of articles, from eggs and bread to flowers and plants. Stalls vary weekly as people bring whatever they have to sell, and, of course, it is always possible to have a cup of tea and a biscuit.

The villagers were pleased when they heard that the Countryside Commission proposed to extend the Mendip Hills AONB (Area of Outstanding Natural Beauty) right up to Winscombe village fence, as it was felt that this would preserve the character of the village by preventing further expansion. (In the preceding 20 years the population had risen from 2,530 to 4,041.)

Left: *Eric and Peggy who brought their van from Weare to the Community Centre, 1980.*

Right: *John and his wife selling repaired old tools at the centre, 1980.*

Left: *Doris selling unwanted clothing, 1980.*

Right: *Morris dancing on the Millennium Green, 2002.*

Below: *Maypole dancing on the Green, 2002.*

Below: *Poster for the May Fair in celebration of the golden jubilee, 2002.*

There were once three necessary but rather drab bus shelters in Winscombe that had been built in the parish following the silver jubilee, and these were to undergo a complete transformation from 'scruffy', graffiti-tempting areas, into places where waiting for a bus could be quite an interesting and pleasant experience. This happened when three local girls, Samantha Matthews, Laura Miles and Susanna Shouls, decided that they would like to decorate the bus shelter at Sidcot. The cost of the paint and varnish was rather more than was expected – £80 or £90 – but, as they were doing such spectacular work, the Council agreed to put no limit on the cost. When the work was finished, it was decided to give the girls a gift token of £10 each in view of the 'marvellous' job which they had done.

In November, the girls gave two other shelters the same 'treatment', depicting fish, flowers and butterflies. The fact that these shelters remained in their original condition from 1978 until they were replaced in 2002 demonstrates the fact that these topics must have appealed to all and sundry, and that sometimes an area that is of such interest is not destroyed 'just for something to do'.

Winscombe Primary School

The growth in population put great strain on the education authorities, and it was inevitable that changes would have to be made. An excellent site on the edge of the Moorham Road estate was reserved for a new junior school, and infants were to remain in the old primary school in Sandford Road. The new school was opened in 1971 with one head teacher in charge of both juniors and infants. The split caused difficulties so temporary caravan classrooms were brought to the site to accommodate the infants, and facilitate the closure of the old school.

From 1971, the gradual deterioration of the temporary buildings – which were far from new when they first arrived on site – caused increasing problems, so it was a great relief when the school was refurbished and extended in 2000.

At the time of writing the school has seven classrooms, and large kitchens which also supply meals to other schools in the district. The grounds are well laid out with two separate playgrounds for the 220 scholars. Any child who was in the group that moved from the old school to the new must have thought it was a different world!

The headmistress, Mrs Linda Grogan, has eight teaching staff and a part-time bursar and secretary, and the school also has some part-time 'learning support assistants' who work with the teachers in various classes. Most classes will have an assistant once a week. Many local people are involved with the school, mainly through the St James Helpers – a group which began in the late 1990s. The members all have varied experiences and interests, and they discuss these with the children. Parents also provide help with fund-raising activities.

Winscombe is proud of its educational results. In 2003, all Year 6 children achieved Level 4 in Science, and 62 per cent reached Level 5 – the highest achievable at this stage. Similar results were achieved in English with 97 per cent achieving Level 4 and 59 per cent Level 5. Winscombe is above the national average, as well as the average for North Somerset. This means that the children embarking on their secondary education each September should have a grounding that will serve them well in the future.

At the time of writing, the local authority is considering insisting that no class will have more than 30 pupils. The benefits of this are clear, but the move may cause a problem for future residents, and for those who already have young children who may want to join their brother or sister in the school.

When the old school building became the property of the Community Association new opportunities were opened up. Mrs Lilian Crook, headmistress of Winscombe Nursery School, explains:

The school started as a small enterprise in a private house in Hillyfields Way. In 1980 the Nursery School was over-subscribed, and the opportunity of moving to a double classroom in the annexe building on to what was the old school site in Sandford Road, and is now the Community Centre, became available. The building is ideally suited to the purpose and became a focus for children's activities.

The Nursery claims to provide a caring, stimulating environment where pre-school children can develop social, emotional and intellectual skills in preparation for starting school. Parents are always welcome and help with the daily sessions and fund raising.

Above and right: *Winscombe Primary School class, 2003.*

Top picture: *Winscombe Primary School playground, 2003.*

Left: *Winscombe Nursery School, November 2003.* Children enjoying storytime include: *Piers, Abigail, Fay and Luke.*

Below: *Winscombe Nursery School, November 2003.* Amongst those playing are: *Zack, Piers, Toby, Abigail and William.*

Left: *Circle time, November 2003.* Left to right, back row: *Fay, Annie, William, Abigail, Zack, Piers;* front: *Emma, William, Luke, Piers, Reece, Toby.*

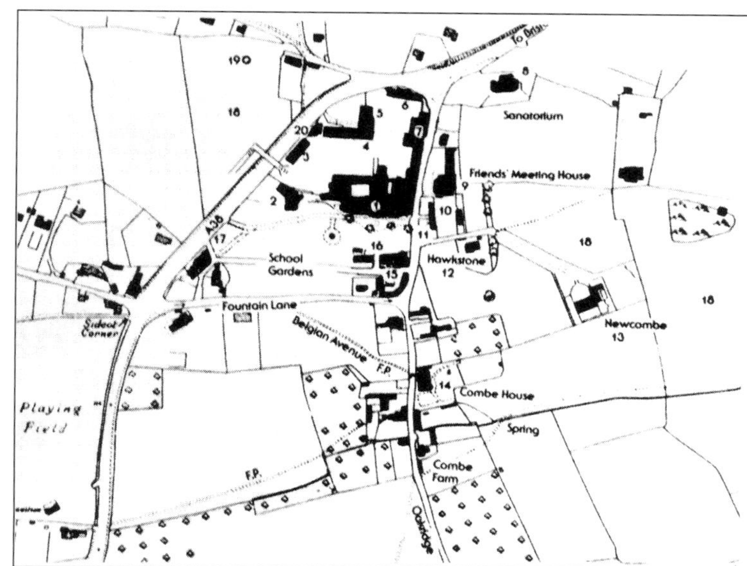

The School Site, 1983

1. Main entrance to central block.
2. The Wing (Boys' House).
3. Music School.
4. Classroom Block.
5. Arts and Crafts Block and Laundry.
6. Swimming Bath.
7. Science Block and Gymnasium.
8. Sanatorium.
9. Quaker Meeting House and School Hall.
10. Biology Laboratory.
11. Headmaster's House.
12. Newcombe (Girls' House).
13. Combe House (Mixed Junior House).
14. Yard and Maintenance Workshops.
15. Squash Court.
16. 'The Cottage' (Senior Girls' House).
17. Land let for grazing.
18. Observatory.
19. Drama Studio.

Nursery funding from central government was introduced for four-year-olds in 1996 to provide free nursery education. This has since been extended to three-year-olds. OFSTED has taken over nursery inspection from Social Services and Winscombe Nursery School is proud of its excellent inspection result in the year 2000.

The school has been well-supported over the years both by local families and others living a little further away. It has been interesting lately to have some of the earlier children return as students to carry out their work experience at the school.

Sidcot School & The Chestnuts in the Twenty-First Century

Sidcot School has always encouraged its pupils to participate in activities in their spare time. In the nineteenth and early-twentieth centuries, walks in the hills were popular and the children collected flowers, insects and birds' eggs and wrote beautifully illustrated diaries of their expeditions.

Nowadays, activities include sports, drama and music. Pupils are especially interested in charitable concerns and hundreds of pounds are raised each year for a variety of causes; most popular is the Wessex Walk for Save the Children. The computer age has placed more emphasis on technology-based activities, but there are still those who enjoy the outdoors – family rambles, abseiling and expeditions for Duke of Edinburgh awards.

Links between school and village are encouraged. Posters advertise concerts and plays, and there are courses and lessons to which local people are invited – learning Chinese for example! Pupils participate in such activities as debates, and ecumenical services are an opportunity to meet local people. Musical groups have performed at St James Church and the Community Centre, and the Quaker sale in November is a popular event. Although Sidcot is a small school, the pupils enjoy a wide range of activities.

The students also worked with the Millennium Green Committee to produce a piece of sculpture for the area. This is supposed to represent two railway lines bending away into the distance. The original thought was that it stood for 'SS' – 'The Strawberry Special' as the line used to be called in the past – but then, as happens with many sculptures, they are interpreted by the eye of the beholder.

Unfortunately, The Chestnuts School closed in 1980. In its place are some new houses built during the time of the general 'building boom'. The name is retained, however, as the road is called Chestnuts Close.

Above: *Sidcot School choir, 1983.*

Below: *Sidcot School's theatre, 1983.*

Top picture: *The first cricket clubhouse, which was opened by 'Digger' Weeks in 1961, with the First XI team.* Team members are: *Arthur Burton, Terry Fountain, Bill Varnham, Ken Body, John Cockerill, Doug Atwell, Adrian Miller, John Wilson, Ray Salter, Richard Humphries and Archie Wilson.* COURTESY OF *CHEDDAR VALLEY GAZETTE*

Above: *Opening of the clubhouse extension, 1972.* Left to right: *Chairman Colin Atkinson, Doug Atwell, Barry Palmer, Ken Perry, Brian Hancock, Chris Stephens, Mike Lilley.* COURTESY OF *CHEDDAR VALLEY GAZETTE*

Right: *Revd Tarr, who was vicar from 1946–60 and a supporter of Winscombe's cricket club.*

Sixteen

Outdoor Pursuits

Most of the village outdoor sports take place in the war memorial recreation-ground. This large and pleasant area was given over to the parish for a 'peppercorn' rent by Sidcot School after the First World War in memory of those who had served their country. The clubs lease the ground from the Council but the deeds are retained, in trust, by them. The memorial ground is now used by several different clubs; cricket, football, rugby and tennis. Each has played a part in fulfilling the purpose of this ground since its inception, and they each have a different tale to tell.

Cricket

The ground was first used by the cricket club as early as 1885. Little is known of the sport at that time, but it was certainly not used during the First World War. An account of the first meeting of this club includes the note:

> *In 1885 a meeting was held in the Woodborough Hall for the purpose of starting a Cricket Club in the neighbourhood, when about thirty were enrolled as members, out of whom the Committee Members were chosen.*

The first match was played on 13 June against Hutton. Unfortunately Winscombe lost, but this did not stop them continuing, and on 29 September the minutes read as follows:

> *The members of the club brought the season to a close on Tuesday with a match between married and single, and a dinner supplied by Mr W. Bird in his new dining room, the Rev R.F. Follett presiding. The 'married' team, winning the toss, went in, but the bowling of Rowntree and Guntripp quickly brought their innings to a close for 19. The 'singles' were more successful in putting together 38 in very short time. The second innings proved better for the 'married' team... scoring – 34. In the evening about 40 sat down to a good spread... The good things being disposed of, the Rev R.F. Follett proposed the health of the 'Queen and the Royal Family', the company responding in a hearty manner.*

After the meal, the evening concluded with music including some 'capital songs' and the president gave some encouraging and amusing remarks. The National Anthem brought the evening to a close.

The matches which had been postponed during the war were once again restarted on the cricket ground, often helped by the staff at Sidcot School in the early days, as members of staff taught local residents how to play the game. Play was suspended from 1913–20 but was restarted in 1922. Mickie Weeks has a special memory of those early occasions which is so representative of village life. The following appears in *100 Not Out* (edited by E. Averis):

> *My first memory of cricket teas in Winscombe was when, before I was married, I was invited to help with the refreshments. We sat on the ground in front of an old wooden shed, until about 4p.m. when Norman Bird drove up, opened up a 'flap arrangement' in the shed and produced boxes of food and urns of tea for us from a van.*
>
> *When matches re-started the tea-ladies were promoted to an archaic wooden structure, laughingly called 'the pavilion'. This consisted of two small changing rooms, divided by a reception area where tea was provided on an old trestle table. As rations increased, so teas improved and we made egg and salad sandwiches; scones and jam; fruit cake and sponges...*
>
> *The water for the teas and washing-up was supplied by Ernie Winslade – through a hole in the hedge from his cottage, and we were grateful for his help with a horror called a 'Primus stove', as it was often thrown through the open door in flames. I sometimes wondered why we didn't burn down the entire building.*
>
> *Our teas were very popular, and visiting teams were heard to say they were Winscombe's secret weapon – after eating them they felt too soporific to bat or field! We charged visitors 6d. for a cup of tea and one shilling for tea and cake. During the school holidays, we were allowed to use Sidcot's pitch. Again, we fetched water through a hole in the hedge from Jean Salisbury's house.*

I have many happy memories of the golden days spent on what must surely be one of the loveliest cricket fields in Somerset.

During the 1920s the Parish Council provided the club with a small hut which could be used as a changing room as Mickie Weeks mentions in her memories of some of the early matches. The club also received support from Sidcot School and the Revd Walter Tarr who was vicar from 1946–60 and often enjoyed a game himself.

There was no clubhouse on the ground and in 1960 Nigel Warren, who was manager of the Tiarks estate, donated a hut and also offered the club financial help with its removal. However, John Saxby and a team of 43 cricket club members helped to move the hut in sections to the new ground, and, several months later, a 36ft by 18ft clubhouse had been erected alongside the changing rooms, and a bar licence was obtained in the winter of 1961/2 when it was decided that the bar should open every evening. A television set was also hired at a cost of £2.3s.4d. per month.

The new clubhouse was opened by the then club president, 'Digger' Weeks, on 20 May 1961. Mr Weeks offered a bottle of champagne to the first player to break a window in his nearby house whilst batting, an offer which was never claimed!

Although the building officially belongs to the cricket club, other sporting organisations using the memorial ground used its facilities, paying a £4 membership fee to do so. By 1964 the clubhouse had become too small to accommodate those who wished to use it – particularly with respect to the skittle alley. There were teams who wanted to play every evening, and it became obvious that the building would have to be extended. Planning permission was given for another floor to be added and a second skittle alley was built.

As the changing rooms were available for any who used the sports ground, in 1964 they were improved and were opened by Mr 'Ernie' Winslade. Since then, they have been brought up to date with modern showering and changing facilities.

In 2000, a meeting was held to commemorate the centenary of the club, when it was shown that the alterations and improvements to the clubhouse through the years had meant that it could be used by many different sporting organisations. In the past, there were about 1,000 members and there are still 500 people who use these facilities at the time of writing. The only paid employee is the steward; everyone else is a volunteer.

Rugby Football

This club began in 1962 when a number of local men got together on 27 September to discuss the possibility of forming a Winscombe and District Football Club. At that time there were already sufficient supporters ready to join the club and to form at least one XV with ample reserves. The first chairman was Mr A.H.M. Stewart and the secretary Mr D. Davies.

The first ground that was used was at Home Field at the Woodborough Hotel, and the problem of the changing room was solved by an offer from the landlord, Mr Sidney Goss. At the rear of the hotel stood the old Drill Hall which had been used by the Army during the war, and this proved suitable for the purpose. The club's colours were to be a black jersey and black socks with white tops. The first order was for two dozen shirts. At this time, the club's income was £38.15s.0d.

After trial games in October and November, the first match took place on 10 November against a XV from Clifton RFC. Happily, Winscombe won by 26 points to 12. The refreshments were pasties, bread, butter, cheese, pickles and tea. The report of this match includes the note 'It was a night of undiluted euphoria.'

By June 1964 the club had a full playing list for both the 1st and 2nd XV, and by March 1965 there were sufficient members to consider running a 3rd XV. This situation led to the possibility of a further playing pitch. In May 1966 an agreement was

Mini rugby at the recreation-ground, 2003.

Left: *Winscombe Association Football Club, 1935–6, winners of the charity and knock-out competitions.* The team consisted of: *W. Weeks, M. Sims, F. Miller, D. Yeomans, T. Pratten, P. Glover, G. Westlake, H. Stephens, A. Westlake, R. Tripp and M. Weeks.*

Below: *Ready for football.* Left to right, back row: *Nicholas, Ashley, Ryan, Luke, William;* front row: *Luke, Joseph and Jamie.*
R & P PHOTOGRAPHIC SERVICE

reached with Reginald Pearce of Winterhead Farm, Sidcot, for using part of 'Longfield' from August until 30 April each year. In 1967, a stone-picking party was needed and more topsoil required for the pitch. Six loads were bought to finish the new ground, and the cricket club agreed to the use of their clubhouse after matches.

At their silver jubilee celebrations in 1987 the club held a birthday party on 5 September at the Weston-super-Mare Winter Gardens, and Kenny Ball and his band were hired for the night. Appreciation was expressed for the help of the ladies who worked so hard with their after-match entertainment, running jumble sales and other functions such as fancy-dress balls. Thanks were also given to the cricket club for their 'consideration, tolerance and help shown when we have approached them with problems at short notice.'

In 1992 the club decided that in order to secure their future, they should have their own ground. At the time of writing they play on pitches belonging to Sidcot School on a weekly rental basis, and are worried that it may not always be able to use them. They have been trying to find a permanent home for several years, and have inspected 12 possible fields in the parish and applied for planning approval three times. They have now found a site that would be suitable on ground near Yadley Way, adjacent to the recreation-ground.

Rugby is very popular with the young boys, and on a Sunday morning it is quite usual to see up to 150 youngsters playing 'mini' rugby. The local rugby club were the first to introduce this side of the game, and the idea was soon followed by others.

Association Football

Football in Winscombe began in the field adjoining the school in Sandford Road, but when the memorial ground became available this was the venue for the fast-growing sport. The president of the club is Mr Ray Tripp, who has been with the club since 1935 as the photograph *(above)* of the league shows. (He is the boy sitting on the floor on the right.) The other names and faces will be well known to many village people. The picture also illustrates the skill of the club at that time when they won the Valley League, Charity and Knock-out Cups.

At this time, most of the matches were played against local villages – Winscombe v Shipham; Winscombe v Banwell, etc. The sides all enjoyed strong support. Mickie Weeks remembers her husband, 'Digger', telling her about a match between Winscombe and Shipham several years ago. There was considerable rivalry at the time, and not only among the men, as this story of a woman supporter shows:

They used to have a lot of women supporters – their mothers, wives and even sisters – and most of them carried umbrellas. One day one of our players was having a good game and stopping their man from taking a 'throw-in' when one of these ladies walked up to him, shaking her umbrella in his face and said 'Oooh! Oi do 'ate ee!' – and she meant it.

One change since the earlier days is that then the women would serve teas at half-time, but this is no longer the case. However, since then the club has grown beyond all recognition and, at the time of writing, has 11 teams: the under-7 and under-10 boys and girls play 'mini' football, seven-a-side; the over-10 and under-14 boys play in the Woodspring League on Saturday mornings; the under-18s play mid-week under lights; and the 1st and 2nd Colts play on Saturdays. These teams all play on Sundays. On Saturday morning there are: the 1st team who play in Division I of the Somerset Senior League; the 2nd XI who play in the Weston and District; and the Colts who play in Division 4 under-18s.

A committee consisting of representatives from all the clubs undertake the organisation of the various sections of the game, and they also form part of the fund-raising committee. Once a year they hold a 'Fun Day', usually on August Bank Holiday Monday. Events, games and stalls are erected in the memorial ground, and the profits are divided among the teams who use the facility. In 2003, however, they decided to hold an 'It's a Knock-out' competition and 11 teams entered.

Another tradition which is rather unusual is the annual visit to 'Wolkersdorf' in Germany. This has taken place for over 20 years on an exchange basis, and in 2003 some 50–60 people took part.

During the year 2000 the three clubs combined with the Parish Council and obtained a major loan to enable the changing rooms, which had been in use for many years, to be refurbished. In addition to the original pavilion a new block of eight team changing rooms were added. There were also several referee rooms and a shower area – what a difference from the original clubhouse.

Bowls

On 27 May 1922 the *Weston Gazette* printed this report on the opening of the club:

WINSCOMBE BOWLING CLUB

SUCCESSFUL OPENING OF NEW VILLAGE GREEN

Under the most propitious circumstances Winscombe's bowling green was opened on Wednesday afternoon, and the Bowling Club received an enthusiastic send-off from a large company of villagers and visitors from Weston and elsewhere. 'Winsome Winscombe', as this charmingly located village has so appositely been termed, now possesses another up-to-date attraction by providing, paradoxically enough, an ancient game for the delectation of residents and visitors. The green is centrally situated on the Sandford road, and is a credit to all concerned with its construction. With due care and attention the club should next year possess a green that

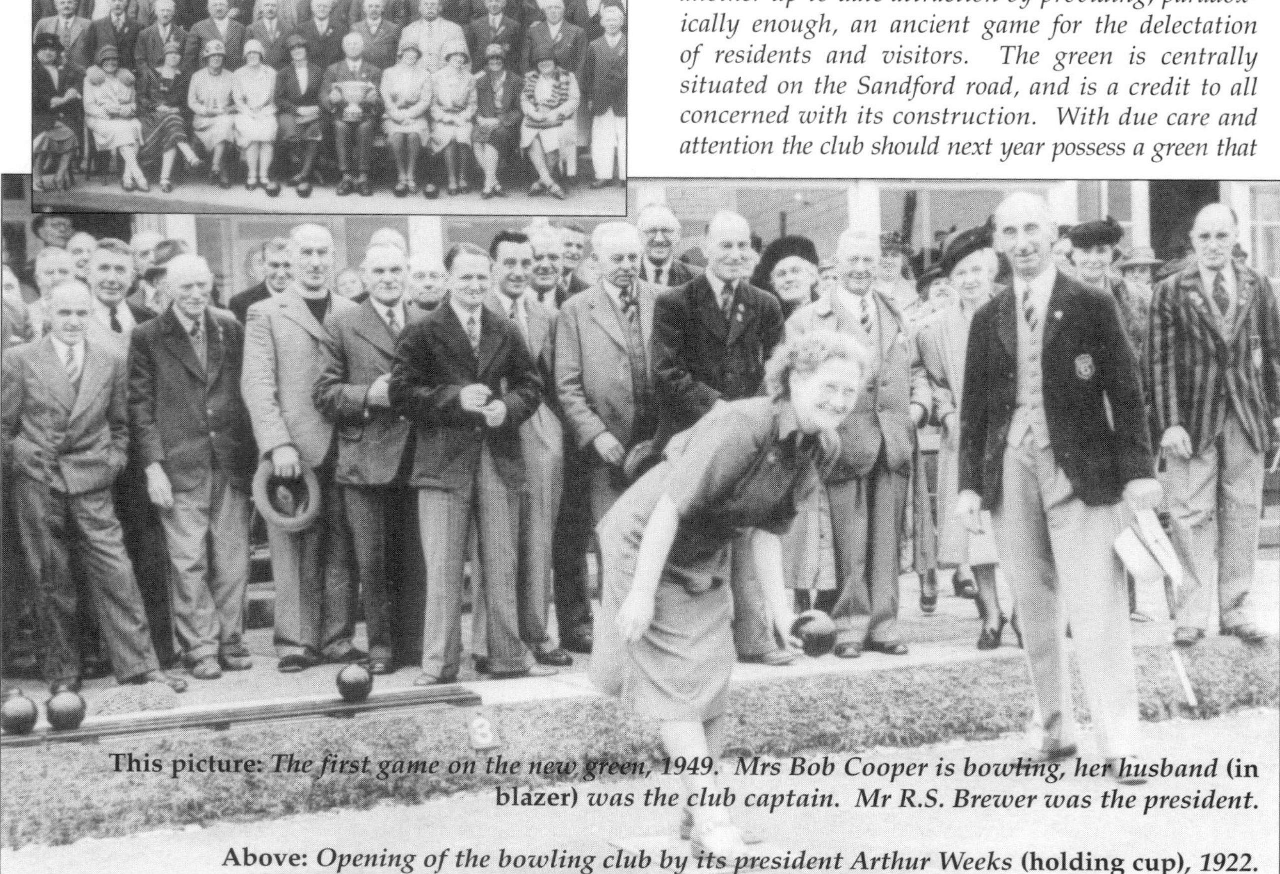

This picture: *The first game on the new green, 1949. Mrs Bob Cooper is bowling, her husband* **(in blazer)** *was the club captain. Mr R.S. Brewer was the president.*

Above: *Opening of the bowling club by its president Arthur Weeks* **(holding cup)***, 1922.*

Winning the Turnbull Cup, 1929. Left to right, back row: M. Atwell, E. Vowles, A.T. Tyler, J.T. Fowler, W. Pain, G. Hayes, J.R. Hird (?), J. Amesbury, A. Shopland, R.H. Kinsey, F.J. Mabbett; front row: T. Skitmore, C.R. House, H.R. House, K. Dunster, H. Moore, R. Weeks, W. Salisbury.

will be the envy of many older established clubs. At each end space is left for the provision of a terrace and club house.

The history of the movement to inaugurate the game of bowls at Winscombe was detailed in a speech at the opening ceremony, performed by Mr Walter N. Wake, the well-known Weston-super-Mare bowler. It might be mentioned that the green is full-sized (40ft square) and has been laid down by Mr Fisher the green keeper of the Victoria B.C. Weston-s-Mare. Local turf has been utilised. The club officials are as follows: President, Mr Richard Calvert; Captain, Mr J.K. Dunster; vice-captain, Mr A.G. Weeks. Committee; Messrs. H. Moore. F.M. Driver, R.H. Kinsey, J. Amesbury, W.H. Wake, C.H. Glanville, W.D. Compton, W. Todd and W. Organ. The hon. secretary and treasurer, Mr F. Anthony, with Mr H. Wilkins as Groundsman.

Mrs Kinsey the wife of a committee-man, threw the first jack – greeted with cries of 'Well bowled!' and Mr Wake trundled the first wood. His second bowl was the first 'ditcher'. He then expressed his pleasure at declaring the green open for future generations.

Play in a match – somewhat facetiously described as 'Mayor of Weston's team versus the Mayor of Winscombe's team' – was then proceeded with. Result: Weston 93 – Winscombe 126.

During an interval a sumptuous tea was provided by the Directors' wives.

In 1929 Winscombe recorded their first county honour by winning the Turnbull Cup, defeating Bristol in the final by four shots. One member of the club, M. Ronald Weeks, had the honour of not only playing for England, but was also captain of England in the Empire Games in Sydney, Australia, in 1918.

Although during the Second World War there is no 'official' account of matches being played on the green, it is thought that in all probability the local bowlers would have taken the opportunity of arranging 'friendly' games between the 'locals' and the visiting soldiers who are known to have used the clubhouse on occasions.

Throughout the coming decade the club gained more honours when Neil Westlake was selected for the English Junior International team. He also won the National Under-25s Singles Competition. Another important date in the club's calendar was 1949 when, after being ruined by 'leather-jackets', the turf was replaced.

Since this time, five members of Winscombe have held the office of president of the Somerset County Bowling Association: G.E. Attwood (1965), C.S. Westlake (1994), R.F.J. Tripp (1985), J.C. Bearman (1996) and J.A. Lukins (2003). Considering their size, the club is very proud of the fact that a small village such as Winscombe has seen so many members holding such high office. At the time of writing the club has 60 male players, 24 lady associates, and 14 non-playing members. They have two teams playing in the Somerset League and one team in the Weston-super-Mare Over Sixties Triples League. They also play about 50 friendly games each season. The club is also renowned for its hospitality – thanks to the assistance of the lady members.

Tennis

This game has been popular in the village since the early 1900s. Many of the large houses had their own courts and arranged matches with their friends; for instance, there was a court at Winscombe Hall and another at Kildare. By the 1930s there were two tennis clubs in the village – one was The Racketeers and the other the Winscombe Tennis Club which was formed in 1939.

The subscription was 12s.6d. and 7s.6d. for those aged 16–18. A court was hired from the War Memorial Committee at a cost of £2 per night per season. The club continued through the early days of the war, and in 1940 they made a contribution to the War Comforts Fund. There is no record of the game being played during the war, but in 1948 the two clubs combined to form 'The Winscombe Tennis Club'.

After the war the club wanted to find land in the centre of the village, where they could build an all-weather court which would be suitable for any who wished to join. Eventually, in November 1954, land at the rear of the Woodborough Hotel was chosen. This undertaking was not approved lightly, for it was

Left: *Spectators at the first hard tennis-courts. Just visible on the left is the corner of the Drill Hall, c.1950.*

Right: *Winners of the club competition, c.1970.* Left to right: *Ian Tanrett, John Kirk, Helen Beaulieu, ?, Peter Griffin, Margaret Hobbs.*

Below: *Mrs Lovell* (front row, centre) *presenting cups, c.1962.* Left to right, standing: *J. Gerrett, R. Smith, Joan Searle, D. Davis, I. Ross, 'Traffy' Wathen, Joan Langford, J. Stower, J. Thomas, B. Patterson, ?, Barney Lovell, I. Tabrett, Jean Patterson, J. Swain;* seated: *Margaret Hobbs, Lesley Swain, Hazel Church, Mrs Lovell, Penny Johnson, Sue Langford.*

Below: *'Last of the Summer Wine'*, 2002. Left to right: *Ray Sumpter, Ean Tucker, Maurice Morgan, John Kirk, Desmond Phippen, Orlando Giacich.*

Above: *'Salute' to John Kirk on his 90th birthday, 2003.*

estimated that the total bill would be £889.4s.0d. with annual running costs likely to be £172 including rates, rent, purchase of balls, interest and repayment of loans from well-wishers and the Lawn Tennis Association. The annual membership fee was set at £3, but for the first year, due to various delays, it was reduced to just £1.

Much delay was caused by the unexpected discovery of rock covering a large area of the site, the clearance of which could have increased costs by well over 50 per cent. Help was provided, however, by Mr C.F. Payne, a builder from Blagdon, who sent a man down with a portable drill, free of charge, except for the man's time. After several hours' trial, it was found that the rock responded to the drill. A compressor and two drills were hired from the local authority, and tools and machinery borrowed from various sources. Male members of the club volunteered for manual labour and eventually the greater part of the rock was disposed of. When sufficient clearance had been made, Mr Devensen of Priddy brought a bulldozer on to the site to clear the majority of the rock and level the ground as far as possible. At this point, the venue became 'The Woodborough Tennis Club'.

Finally, two courts were completed, as also was a reservoir, made necessary by the fact that the mains pressure was inadequate to power sprinklers to keep the surface watered. For several seasons, members had to change in an open-fronted garden shed, until a full pavilion could be constructed. They also had to cope with the limitations and problems caused by regular droughts and frosts. Fortunately, the conditions cannot have been too unbearable because the very first captain, Barney Lovell, remains a trustee, while several members who were in at the beginning as juniors are still active players today.

By the 1980s the club had to decide whether to completely refurbish their present club, or sell the land to a developer and rebuild in another area. Eventually the latter decision was made, and the club leased some land from Sidcot School abutting the present cricket ground. Work started before Christmas 1988, but due to heavy rain the project was delayed. (Drainage was to become a constant headache at the site and arrangements had to be made to ensure that the land did not flood.) During this period plans were made for matches to be played at Churchill Sports Centre and on some of the courts belonging to Sidcot School which are close to the ground.

The new positioning of the club seemed an apt time to change the name, and it became formally known as 'Winscombe Lawn Tennis Club'.

In 1987 the club moved to its present position in an attractive and well-sheltered site with four courts, two of which are floodlit – and with a clubhouse set in a landscaped area adjacent to the war memorial recreation-ground which is used by the other sporting associations. The club is used by people of all ages, from children of nine to adults of ninety. Despite its earlier struggles, the future of the club appears settled, and it is hoped that this will continue to be the case.

Other Activities

A major project for the future is the provision of a skate park. The idea was put forward by the youngsters themselves as being a high priority, and it is hoped that the cost will be covered by grants. The area is to be in the recreation-ground at the rear of the present children's play area (one reason for this being that the two areas can share administrative and organisational costs when it comes to insurance, etc.). Although some concern was expressed initially, it is now thought that, with the formation of a management committee who will be responsible for the park, there should be no problems. At the time of writing the Council are awaiting planning permission and, if this is granted, there is every hope that the building work will commence soon. An architect who specialises in this design was consulted, as the park is to be used for rollerblades and skateboards as well as skates. The area was chosen after considerable discussion, and it was largely due to the wishes of the youngsters that the Council agreed.

Hunting

In *Heart of Mendip* Knight mentioned that there was no fox-hunting in the district due to the fact that there were no foxes! However, many of the older residents believe that foxes were bred in the local woods for release for the hunt. In 1965 the local Women's Institute mentioned 'a popular annual event that attracted a large number of people to the village square... the Boxing Day Meet of the local Hunt.'

The increase in property development led to a diminishing amount of land being available for hunting. Additionally, several farmers had introduced 'game reserves' on which they reared large numbers of pheasants in order to let the shooting rights at high prices. These country activities had somewhat contradictory aims: the farmers employed gamekeepers who were responsible for keeping down vermin, which included foxes, but they objected to the hunt disturbing their birds, particularly on Saturdays during the shooting season!

The real story of the local hunt has been told by Dorothy and John Kirk in two booklets entitled 'Across Country with the Weston & Banwell Harriers' and 'Down Kennel Lane' (1973). Apparently there has been hunting in the area since the early 1900s:

> [It began in] *an old country lane in Somerset which takes its winding course below Crook's Peak to where*

Left: *Boxing Day Meet outside Woodborough Hotel, c.1950.*

Right: *John Kirk (Master) and Len Morse (Groom), from the Weston and Banwell Harriers, c.1980. The Master's horse is called 'Biddy'.*

a lively pack of hounds are quartered. Tucked away in a picturesque little world of their own, and sheltered from the cold north-east winds by the lofty Mendip Hills, they hunt far from the hurly-burly of fashionable Packs, where 'the field' may be counted in hundreds.

It is in the pretty hamlet of Webbington that the present Weston Harriers were formed way back in 1907. Of all the Masters and Huntsmen who have served the Weston Harriers since then, none have excited more popular interest than the founding Masters, Mr Frank Tiarks and his brother, Mr Herman Tiarks, who had built these kennels regardless of cost – an expenditure which our parents shuddered to contemplate.

There were originally two hunts in the area: the Mendip Farmers Hunt and the Weston and Banwell Harriers. They had various hounds – the Harriers hunted hares, and there were also foxhounds, deerhounds and beagles – the latter came from Portishead and hunted on foot.

The building of the M5 motorway divided the area of the hunt from end to end. The etiquette of hunting is extremely strict; it would be unthinkable to go over another hunt's territory without their full agreement but at the same time, from the hunt's point of view, it is equally unthinkable that this attractive hunt should end.

After considerable discussion a decision was taken:

Our sub-committee decided to approach the Masters of adjacent Hunts, with an appeal for permission to extend our boundaries; and our first approach was made to the Mendip Farmers. At their invitation, a sub-committee of four... called upon them one evening, and were most hospitably received. Indeed, hospitality was so good and the atmosphere so cordial that our hosts were genuinely concerned that they could help us so little. In common with other hunts, their own territory was being greatly diminished by ever-sprawling urban development, and the introduction of game preserves on many of the big farms on Mendip.

Hunting may be a controversial subject; and it is not the author's intention to enter into the debate on these pages, but what is undeniable is the fact that the 'hunting fraternity' is witness to a special comradeship that binds country people together.

Dorothy, the wife of a retired master, tells many tales which reveal a very different side to the whole sport. A popular occasion is the 'Gymkhana' which has grown out of the old village agricultural shows. In 1880 the Banwell Village Horse Show included many competitions for riding, driving and shoeing contests between blacksmiths, and marquees for the display of local crafts and dairy products. In 1914 the shire-horses won a silver entrée dish which is still used today. In the past there were also midnight steeplechases including one called 'The Webbington Bed Warmer Chase'. On one occasion this event was 'greatly enlivened' by the sudden appearance of a 'streaker' (although it was cold and rainy at the time). He came galloping out of the dark to join the race half way round, and then he vanished into the gloom again, hotly and hopelessly pursued by the local constabulary.

Another form of 'partnership' between the hunt and the farmers concerns the feeding of the dogs. Dorothy explains:

For the most part our hounds are fed on raw meat... Fetching 'flesh' from distant farms is an expensive and time-consuming operation. Collection must be prompt and unfortunately the animals give no prior notice of their intention to die... Very often (after collecting an animal from one farm) there has been a casualty on another farm in the same neighbourhood, and the journey has to be made all over again.

The kennel staff then have to skin the carcasses and carefully pack the skins as they represent a valuable part of a hunt servant's income. This relationship between the farmer and the hunt works well for both parties. The dogs are fed good fresh meat, and the farmer does not have to pay for his animals to be taken to the abattoir.

This aspect of hunting has suddenly risen to the forefront of discussion, due to the Government's new proposal that all animals which die on a farm should be taken away to the local abattoir. This could prove to be quite an additional expense, both for the farmer and the hunt.

Every November the Harriers hold their Annual Hunt Supper in Banwell Village Hall. The main purpose of the party is to show gratitude to the sporting farmers who allow the hunt to ride over their land. Such farmers are thus given priority in the allocation of tickets. Approximately 200 sit down to the meal which is prepared and cooked by a ladies' committee. Dorothy notes:

Some idea of the size of appetites can be judged by the fact that when ordering meat for this function, one pound per head is the requirement. Enormous joints of beef are roasted, boiled and pickled by the ladies, and delicious hams are cooked by the butcher. Thirty sherry trifles, thick with clotted cream, and gallons of fruit salad are followed by unlimited chunks of gorgeous cheese cut straight from a 56lb. truckle.

The hunt supper is a real country occasion. It is chiefly a meeting of old friends and neighbours, but it also represents a chance for both old and new subscribers to recognise and repay some of the kindness and generosity of the farmers. At the time of writing the hunt is alive and well and still going strong.

Left: *Paper collection, 2003.*

Right: *Bottle collection, 2003.*

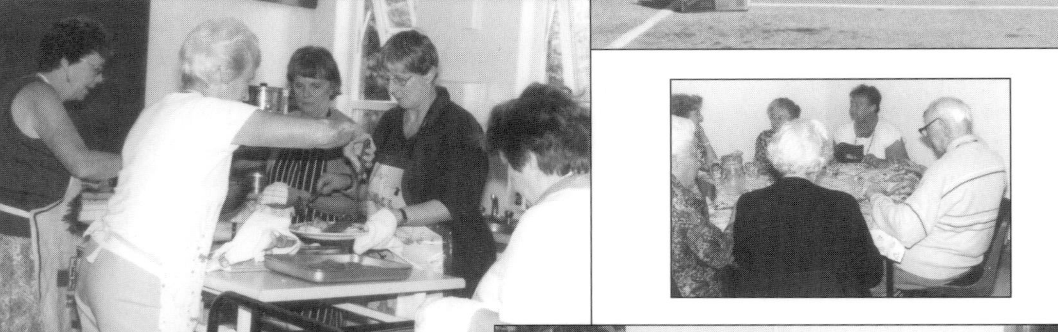

Above: *Serving meals at the Community Centre, Winscombe, 2003.*

Right and above right: *Luncheon Club at the Community Centre, Winscombe, 2003.*

Seventeen

Down to Business

After all the upset caused by the changes in local authority, the increase in the number of properties in the village, and the final acquisition of the Community Centre and the Church Hall behind them, the villagers settled down to do what they do best – finding ways of helping other people, whilst at the same time enjoying themselves. However, during recent years their thoughts have turned to more far-reaching issues such as recycling, salvage and other major concerns like global warming.

Once a month the local Scouts collect waste paper left by each householder outside their house. The Scouts have managed to get several fathers to use their cars to drive them round the village, and it is a common sight to see a car parked, with its boot open, waiting for the bundles to be collected. The loads are then taken to the recreation-ground car park, where they are put into the waiting container to be taken to Glastonbury.

Bottle Collection

The sound of crashing glass in the Sandford Road car park on a Saturday morning is a regular fixture in Winscombe. One may think that quarterly glass collections are a common feature in other communities around the country, but we know of no other!

It was in 1979 that the local Christian Aid group, in trying to relate to Third World poverty, came up with this original idea. It was to be a 'one-off' event to promote awareness of growing concerns regarding wastefulness of the earth's resources.

The response was so successful that it has continued ever since, albeit under a different organisation. Early collections were huge – probably twice the size of those at the time of writing, which average about six to seven tons. This initiative was ahead of its time in addressing what are world targets of Agenda 21. Local authorities are now accountable for reducing waste and the group receives financial credits from the District Council in acknowledgement of its contributions. Thanks to that early seed sown, many thousands of pounds have been raised for the local community groups which organise and man the collections. Small organisations have been helped through difficult times. Collections are held in January, April, July and October. Dates are posted locally. On the day, work continues cheerfully, come rain or shine, as boxes and bags arrive and are lifted into the lorry freely provided for us by a friendly haulier. As this account is written, the group is approaching its 25th birthday. Despite conveniently sited bottle banks, the independent collection is holding up well, thanks to undiminished support from local residents who realise that, by recycling this way, their community stands to gain financially whilst also benefiting the environment.

Winscombe Luncheon Club & More

The Luncheon Club was started by Mrs Eileen Blasdale and a group of friends in 1981, as it was felt there was a need for people who lived on their own to be able meet and chat together over lunch. There are now 36 people who come to lunch each week, and groups of four take it in turns to cook. There are groups of four teams and this arrangement means that the ladies take on the task once a month.

Two weeks before Christmas they have their Christmas lunch, with turkey and all the trimmings and home-made Christmas puddings. Entertainment is provided by some of the children from Winscombe School who sing carols and play their instruments. This is much appreciated by all the members. The less able are collected by volunteer drivers each week.

The cost is £2.50 and the food is freshly cooked at the Community Centre kitchen each week. The lunches are so popular that there is always a waiting-list of people wishing to join.

This was also the period when another task was set by the then 'Food and Figure Group'. In 1983 a talk was given by Tony Ferraro on the 'dustbin babies' of Calcutta. Apparently, when these babies were found they were put in a cardboard box with a

Below: *FOCUS, 2003.* Left to right, standing: *Gwen Burman, Olive Sydney, Melba Boulter, Madge Williams, Pauline Keen, Doreen Treasure, Tricia Hobbs, Brenda Pye, Margaret Bignold, Janet Hetburn, Barbara Hemmens;* seated: *Alice Crook, Bunty Tracy, Joyce Lindley, Mickie Weeks, Moira Cooper, Connie Burroughs, Barbara Roberts. Ellie Hingott is not in the photograph.*

Above: *Mother Teresa Group, with jumpers for India, 2002.*

40-watt bulb inside for warmth. If the baby survived for 24 hours, it then went into care. The first need was obviously for warmth, so the group set themselves the target of knitting 50 vests. To their astonishment, the final total was nearly 500, plus many sacks and boxes of baby clothes. The story of the babies spread throughout the district and help came in from many other sources.

The group decided that this experience gave them an opportunity of helping others in a very different way. They formed The Co-Workers of Mother Teresa and knitting began in earnest.

The leader of this group was Miss Gwen Burman and she kept in contact with the regional links. By now the items included many knitted or crocheted knee-blankets, and hundreds of cotton dresses (with matching knickers) which were made for the little girls, and trousers for the boys. Various items poured in: assorted woollen cardigans, gloves and bundles of bandages.

The preparation of these garments for shipping to India was a task in itself. The goods had first to be packed in plastic bags and then in hessian sacks. Each sack (known as a liner) could only contain items of the same kind. The sacks then had to be stitched in strong thread and the contents noted on the outside. Eventually, the sacks were sent to a central address in London prior to being loaded onto a ship.

For over ten years the group continued knitting and sewing items of clothing for those in need. One of the major problems was the storing of finished items, prior to despatch. Miss Burman's house became a temporary warehouse, not only for clothing, but also for the supplies of unused wool that were collected ready to be handed on to another 'knitter', or clothing that could be used by another person, and she became used to finding large packages being left on her doorstep. The one area that caused the greatest concern was the packing of goods. This meant dealing with up to 100 knitted blankets, innumerable dresses and bandages. It was heavy work and the sacks were difficult to sew.

It became obvious that this was a job for the young and, as the members of the Mother Teresa's Group inevitably found, it eventually became too much for them. With a sad heart it was decided that the group would no longer be able to carry on with this side of their charitable work. All was not lost, however, and in 1994 a group made up mostly of founder members sought a new beginning, and, after considerable discussion, a name was suggested by one of the members, Pauline Keen: FOCUS (Friends who are Optimistic, Curious, Understanding and Stimulating).

Although it has acquired several new members, it is essentially a 'social group' in which slightly offbeat members enjoy each other's company and look out for one another. Now well established, the group has continued to flourish, having changed its image and diversified using the considerable expertise existing within the group. Their programme is widespread and has covered such things as Chinese paintings, calligraphy and crocheting, or Somerset patchwork. They have also organised theatre visits and day-trips out. A wide-based magazine-type programme merges visiting speakers and in-house expertise and provides a stimulating, fun programme.

Save the Children

From the above accounts of the various activities organised in the village, Winscombe is, and always has been, a supporter of those less well off than themselves. Many 'good causes' are helped throughout the year, and several have already been discussed, but one in particular benefits from the efforts of 'Mo' Matthews. Below is an account of her yearly activities:

> *We are pleased to say that our Branch in Winscombe managed to send over £7,000 to headquarters each year through the various fund-raising events for which we have become famous.*
>
> *Kicking off in January with our famous 'sell-out' Burns Night, thoroughly enjoyed by those who manage to obtain tickets. March hails the Jumble sale. In June we have a new venture – an open-air play in the Community Centre grounds, preceded by a bring-your-own picnic. In September we have our second Jumble Sale, and a 'Travel Talk' and slides with supper in October. We have visited Russia and Cuba so far, with excellent slides and our suppers are in keeping with the countries.*
>
> *October heralds our Christmas Goods selling in various venues about the village. An Auction in the Community Centre comes in December and is well attended by local people. We then have a well-earned rest until next year.*

There is one event not mentioned in Mo's list and this takes place at her home in Belmont Road, when she opens her house and garden to the villagers. As the notice in the *Parish Magazine* states 'Come for coffee and stay all day.' Coffee, lunch and tea are available throughout the day, and the society she supports must be very grateful for her consistent help.

These are only some examples of the type of projects being undertaken in Winscombe. Some are far more complicated than others and, although intending to be long-lasting, require a large amount of money.

The Restoration of St James Church

In 1983, when the Revd Salmon was the vicar, a restoration appeal was launched in aid of the church. There were two specific items which required urgent attention, the first being the re-tuning of the bells.

The form of ringing practised today has been established for at least 350 years, and has now spread to much of the English-speaking world. The tower captain, John Matthews, is proud of the fact that there are still more towers with ringing bells in the Axbridge Branch of the Bath and Wells Diocesan Association of Change Ringers, than in the whole of North America!

In December 1983 the bells had been removed from the tower and taken to Loughborough to be re-tuned. This was the first time any work had been done on them for over 80 years, and about £7,000 had been raised to cover the cost of the work. A 'Watchnight Service' heralded in the New Year, preceded by a service that was broadcast on the BBC entitled 'With Iron Tongue'. The bells had previously been re-dedicated by the Bishop of Bath and Wells. After the service the bells rang out and mead and mince pies were served to the congregation which filled the church to capacity.

As the total cost of this restoration and the repair of some of the medieval glass in the windows was to run to around £10,000, many events had to be organised. One of the earliest was a church pageant held in 1996 when medieval clothes and skills were displayed, among the weaving, spinning and stonemasonry. Another, now lost skill, was that of story-telling and there is also a picture of a 'jester'. The local Brownies dressed up and sold posies of sweet-smelling herbs: lavender, thyme and rosemary. At a similar event in 2001 the Winscombe Orchestra provided musical accompaniment during the afternoon. Many other events have been held since then.

Another task, undertaken largely by the women in the congregation, but not exclusively so, was the replacing of the somewhat worn kneelers in the church. The project was instigated by Mrs Margaret Lister. The kneelers were to be of a similar size and worked with a cross-stitch pattern.

Removing the church bells, 1983. COURTESY OF BOB BOWEN

St James Church, 2002.

Above: *Taking the bells away, 1983. Note the reporters at the bottom right of the picture.*
COURTESY OF BOB BOWEN

Below: *Spinning in 2002.*

Below: *St James Church fête with Peter Whicher on the left, 2002.*

It was decided that it would be a good idea if everyone designed a kneeler that in some way reflected their own lives. There are many examples – some copied a badge which represented their personal concerns, and others used animals or fruit to express their particular interests.

Mothers' Union

The Mothers' Union in Winscombe has had a somewhat disturbed history. Although it had been closed in 1969 it was reopened again in 1996 with the encouragement of the vicar, Revd John Hubbard, and a membership of 15. By 1998 it had risen to 27. At the time of writing (2003) the membership is 24.

In Winscombe in 2001, 125 years of the life and work of the MU was celebrated in the church. Depicted in flowers and memorabilia, they remembered the inspiration and vision of Mary Sumner, a young wife and mother of three, who felt a need to share with others her faith and the great responsibility of bringing up her young family. If only she could have visualised how it would grow. Now, there are over one million members in 65 countries, continuing the work towards improving family life through practical action and prayer.

In the Winscombe branch, the members are strong in their commitment, but as they grow older it is not always easy to fill places of leadership. Now most mothers work, and there are many more organisations to join. Their children are involved with so many more events outside their school life, that parents seem to be busy ferrying their offspring to and fro in cars. Although the main aim of the MU is prayer, at meetings they have had speakers who have told them just how valuable their help has been, and what help is needed in the future. Over tea and biscuits they can chat amongst themselves and discuss the ways in which they can offer help. They feel sure, if it is God's will, that people will come forward to help them through the coming years.

The Women's Institute

One group of women who have only been mentioned indirectly so far is the Women's Institute. These women have had meetings in the village since the early 1920s and, at one time, there were two groups – an afternoon and an evening one. This catered for women with children and others who worked during the day, but in 2004 there is only one.

The WI is sometimes written off as a group of women interested only in cooking and knitting and with very little real grasp of the world at large. Although Winscombe WI may be a relatively small group, they have completed a great deal of hard work through the years. The work of the Institute is implied many times, and, if not mentioned specifically, their presence is conveyed time and time again through these pages.

Above right: *The Mothers' Union celebrated 125 years in 2001. The figure represents Mary Sumner.*

Right: *Example of a church 'kneeler', c.2000.*

Top left: *Mr and Mrs Hares on her 80th birthday.*

Above: *Alfred and Harriet Tripp, c.1970.*

Left: *Somerset Cottage, home of Mr and Mrs Tripp, c.1980.*

Eighteen

Country Tales

Ted's Tale

As previously mentioned the majority of the local children who did not go into further education started work as soon as they left school. One such village lad, whose school days are told in another chapter, explains how in his youth he helped his father in the garden, but at the age of 14 found his life being changed completely.

Ted Hares started work for Mr Fry of Sidcot Lane, who had a carter's business, but when Mr Fry was called up Ted took over his job to help his wife until the war was over. One of the jobs he had to do regularly was to collect a teacher in the horse and trap from Churchill at 7a.m. and return again at 5p.m. As he remarked:

> *In the winter it was too dark in the mornings to see which horse I had to collect from Hillyfields, so, if I wanted a special one, I would take a bit of cow cake and call. When the horses came I had to wait until it was light enough to choose the one I wanted.*
>
> *I did any of the jobs that the work called for – taking people from one destination to another, collecting parcels or delivering them. I also used to take people to weddings and funerals or baptisms in one or other of the traps belonging to Mrs Fry. Besides looking after the horses, I also used to make all the funeral arrangements. However, there were some advantages to the job. For instance, one gentleman who used to employ coachmen in Weston would sometimes let me have a warm coat for say, ten shillings. One thing I remember was that I never had any time to myself. I suppose you could say I had to learn to grow up fast.*
>
> *One job I had was to take the hearse to the Axbridge Workhouse and collect the bodies of the paupers and carry them to Weston for burial. It wasn't too bad in winter, but in summer (there being no refrigeration at the time) it could be very unpleasant.**

After the war, Ted took a job as a gardener at Webbington House and he used to cycle there and back daily. He later thought of becoming a special constable, but decided that it was not a good life.

After leaving his gardening job, Ted worked at the station where he earned about 30 shillings a week, and later, when the railways were remodelled, there was one stationmaster for two or three stations and he was given responsibility for Winscombe.

The station was opened up every day at 6.30a.m. to ensure that everything was ready for the goods train. Then the goods were taken from the van – say half or one ton – and moved to dry storage. Later they were collected by lorry for delivery in the village. Ted had a four-wheeled truck that would take half a ton, but he could save his energy by free-wheeling back to the station. He worked an eight-hour shift, but before he could lock up, all the tickets sold had to be listed, with the destination shown, and they had to be totalled and balanced with the ticket boxes. Thousands of pounds worth of tickets had to be checked every month and, if they did not balance, they had to be re-checked until the error was found.

Ted had a big piece of ground near the station, and both he and his wife worked on it. Not only did he grow his vegetables, he also showed them and once took all 16 prizes at Priddy. He had his first class certificates nailed on the walls of his garden shed.

His wife had left school at 14 and gone into service, although she had always wanted to be a nurse. Unfortunately, she was unable to do this due to varicose veins, and eventually she looked after her elderly parents at Priddy.

* *According to an item in the* Weston Mercury *of 19 September 1913, the price for the conveyance of the dead was nine pence per mile, and the allowance for bearers was four shillings, but Ted was not included in these wages. The price of coffins varied according to district.*

Alfred Tripp

What is life if full of care,
We have no time to stand and stare?
No time to stand beneath the boughs
And stare as long as sheep or cows.
William Henry Davies, b.1871.

This verse could be said to reflect the thoughts of several of our older villagers, but perhaps one in particular who is no longer with us. Alfred Tripp was born at Shipham in 1887 but moved to Somerset Cottage, Sidcot, at a young age and spent the rest of his life there. He attended the local school and his first job was as a baker's boy at Shipham. His great love in life, however, was gardening, and later he had the opportunity to take up this work, although his baking skills were to come in very useful later on. He and his wife, Harriet, lived at the cottage behind the Friends Meeting House. Alf was a keen sportsman and was a founder member of the Shipham Adult School Football Club.

The family was well known in the village, and is remembered by many today. Harriet loved singing and particularly enjoyed taking part in the local Christmas pantomimes. She was also a member of many of the other organisations in the village, particularly the Women's British Legion. Apparently, one of Alf's favourite sayings was 'So help me bob!' and he used to say that when, in the early part of the century, he came down to the village, although there may not have been many people about, he knew all their names. Latterly, there were a lot of people, but he didn't know many of them!

Early in his life, Alf drove garden produce to Bristol market by horse and trap. This entailed a very early start – around midnight – and then he usually stopped at The Darlington on the A38 at five o'clock for a drop of rum! Eventually, he became head gardener at Coombe House for Mrs Tregelles and then, for many years, he held the same post at Sidcot School. He is still remembered today by way of some trees that he planted in Newcombe Drive, and he also assisted the Belgian refugees who planted The Avenue during the First World War.

When he joined up he enlisted in the Royal Artillery, being a great lover of horses, but this was not the only part of his life that was to prove useful during his service. Apparently, on the Western Front one day, the unit had flour but no one to bake the bread. So Alf, recalling his days at the bakery, constructed a field oven, and although it could not be said to have been the best bread that he had ever tasted, at least no one starved.

The trenches profoundly affected Alf, as they did so many others. He did not like to speak of his time under fire during the Battle of the Somme, but he would talk about the time when his unit was moved to Italy and he got separated from the rest of the men. He spent some time wandering in that country until he was reunited. He also very much enjoyed his 'R & R' in Venice. It was always a mystery to him that, considering the carnage on the Somme where so many of his friends died, he had somehow been saved.

When he went home he was able to return to his work as a gardener. Whilst at Sidcot School, he produced fruit and vegetables for over 300 pupils and a variety of flowers for the house. His son Raymond remembers vividly his father's extensive knowledge of gardening (as well as his excellent bread). People would come to seek Alf's help for a variety of concerns, not only from the village, but also from further away. Had he lived in today's modern world, he could well have been our local 'Alan Titchmarsh', but he would probably have much preferred his own quiet life.

Alfred and Harriet lived a happy life together for many years, and his son says his father was the most contented man he had ever known. He could never really understand today's desire for money and the bustle of life. He lived a quiet and happy life, until he died at the good age of 93 in December 1980.

A Country Family

This is the story of a Winscombe family who have always been associated with the land, and three of whose members have worked as gardeners at Sidcot School. Edward James (Ted) Hembery was born in 1872 and lived at 'Gasworks Cottage' (now called 'Garden Cottage'), Sidcot, with his wife Florence and their son, Cyril, who was born in 1907.

In 1939 Cyril married Sara Margretta ('Gretta') and they lived at 'Brookside Cottage', Sidcot, with their four children: Robert John, Janet Florence, Stephen and David Raymond, who was born in 1947, and he has recalled many memories of his early life with his family.

The lives of Ted and his son, Cyril, are remarkably intertwined. Both were skilled countrymen and earned their living through gardening, thatching, laying hedges, and using their knowledge of animal welfare. The 'Hembery' skills were well known, and Ted worked for many years at Sidcot School. At this time, the school was completely self-sufficient – they grew all their own vegetables at the main school garden and also at Coombe House. Fresh flowers were always required for the headmaster's house and the Friends Meeting House, so the hedging and ditching had to be done at weekends.

Another responsibility during Ted's earlier years at the school was to keep the school gasworks

Edward 'Ted' Hembery with horse and cart at Sidcot School, c.1930.

Cyril Hembery and Gretta when they got married, 1939.

functioning – in those days, they made their own coal-gas, and if things were not working efficiently, there would have been no lighting or heating. In her book *Reflections of the Island* Christine Gladwin writes:

> *Ted Hembery looked after the gas works for over thirty years. Before that he was a Carter at Cheddar, carting stone from the quarries to Blagdon for the building of the reservoir dam. He only became a Carter again when the school changed from gas to electricity. The old man with his white, curly locks and his big black horse is now an institution, a part of our childhood.*

At the beginning or end of a school term there were numerous journeys to be made to the station, and Ted would carry the scholars' trunks and bicycles as well as anything else that had to be moved. Initially, this work was done with a horse and cart, but later mechanical transport was used.

During the early 1930s the gasworks closed and, as in the village, savings had to be made, and Ted was asked to take on the work on the games field instead. This saved the school £30 a year in wages. Apparently, Ted had been due to retire on 1938, but, because of the coming war, and the fact that some of the younger men looked likely to be called up, the school decided to keep him on. He worked for another 17 years, finally retiring in 1955 at the age of 83.

Cyril Hembery in his garden, c.1960.

Ted died in 1963 and his son Cyril carried on life as he had always known it. He worked as a gardener, initially for Alan Emery, a farmer, and then for many of the large properties in the area including Capt. Wills at Oakridge House, and Dr Boobyer at Hillyfields. Following this he worked for a Mr Walter Little, and of the several letters David has which refer to his father's ability, this is one example:

> *Cyril Hembery has worked for me for the past 5 years and I have much pleasure in testifying to his general all round skill and capabilities in Horticulture, Farming and Livestock keeping. While he has been working for me he has been responsible for maintaining the lawns and extensive flower beds in very good order and condition, with a succession of many kinds of flowers for cutting and bedding etc.*
>
> *His life-time experience in things connected with the soil makes him an asset to any farmer or grower and I would be pleased to recommend him for any job for which his exceptional ability makes him a suitable applicant.*
>
> *Walter Little*
> *'Uplands', Winscombe, 14 December 1949*

Cyril also worked as a gardener at Sidcot School until he retired, and his son Stephen also worked there. David remembers that during the school holidays the children of the families who had worked there were allowed to use the school premises, and this is where he learnt to swim. They were also allowed to use the gym and the workshop where the school's own furniture was repaired and other types of joinery work were carried out. In those days, nothing was locked up.

During the war, Cyril was in the Home Guard, and used to go to the Observatory in the evening to watch for planes. At that time, there were fewer trees, and from this site you could see down the valley to the coast. The family always suspected that this was rather a convenient excuse for a 'chat and a drink' with his friends – probably a little unfairly!

David has many memories of his life as a boy when his father showed him some of his skills. 'He was an outdoor man – always working in the garden and the orchards. He kept goats, sheep, ducks, ferrets – everything. He was also skilled at making rabbit nets.' Apparently, there are two kinds of net; one is a long net, which is used when the rabbits are in the pasture, eating. This is fixed across the end of the field with sharpened stakes, and then the rabbits are pushed towards it. The other way, using the short net, was to cover the entrance to the burrows and then send in the ferrets! Another use for his skills was the making of pigeon 'decoys'. He formed the shape on a mould, and then, using paper, fish glue and leather, he formed the shape of a bird's body. He then added a painted wooden 'head'. These apparently roughly made bodies, with their pigeon-like heads, were placed on wires among the long grass, and as they swayed in the wind, they looked incredibly like birds feeding, and so attracted other pigeons. David says he often remembers his father coming in with two or three brace of pigeons, which, if too much for the family, were taken to the pub and 'swapped' for some cider – naturally!

On one occasion when Cyril was working at the school hedging, he cut out a goldfinch's nest by mistake. Of course, the nest was ruined, but there were about 12 nestlings in it. Cyril brought them home and hand-reared them. He fed them on mashed boiled eggs and introduced the food to them by means of a sharpened goose quill – possibly the nearest thing to an original 'bill' that could be used. Unfortunately, most of the birds died, but two of them lived for five or six years in a cage, and they sang beautifully.

Another lasting pleasant memory David has is of the evenings when he and his mother would walk up to Callow, where his father was either hedging or ditching, and they would take food and a kettle with them. Then they would cut a few twigs, boil the kettle and brew up a cup of tea together.

A home-made mould for a pigeon decoy, c.1930.

Pigeon lures in the grass, 2003.

George Whicher

George Whicher, who was born in 1908, has left some very vivid memories of his first glimpse of the house that was to be his home in the village for 70 years. The property – The Brook in Church Road – was bought by his aunt, Gertrude Cookson (referred to as 'Aunt Gar' or 'the aunt'), and George first saw it just before the outbreak of the war in 1914. He writes:

The long room sticks in my memory as there was a wooden mantelpiece, which was rather ornate, and there was a crack in the wood that my father pointed out to the aunt. The other part of the house, which I remember particularly, were the two little rooms beyond the spare room. There was no staircase then but a ladder through the passage floor into the scullery. I was only six and these rooms leading one out of the other seemed endless.

It was not until 1917 that the family moved into The Brook, when the long room was extended and French windows to match the morning-room (which is now the dining-room) were put in and the garage was made into a bathroom. George's uncle had unfortunately been invalided out of the Army where he had been serving in India. He lived with them in the house, with the assistance of two nurses and other domestic help, until he died in 1922.

Although George went to school at Clifton College, he spent many happy times at Winscombe and tells of his adventures with a horse called 'Moti', which is Hindustani for 'little fatty', that his aunt had bought from Col Yatman at The Hall. The end of the tale is rather tragic, for he writes:

The gardener was an elderly man called Tucker who lived in The Square and his wife, who we called Tuckie, was a dear! I was very fond of her. She did the family washing and looked after me from time to time. Tucker looked after the pony and one hot summer's day he tied him to a stake in the field. The field was up for hay, otherwise he would have been free. Sadly he was stung by a horsefly and bolted down the drive and his head hit the large double gates at the bottom and killed him.

This picture: *The Brook, Winscombe, 2003.*

Inset: *An egg box and advert for Whicher & Searle.*

It was a Sunday morning and I remember walking to church with Aunt Gar who blamed me for the tragedy. Old Tucker I suppose had tried to 'pass the buck'. I remember walking close to the hedge towards the top of the field at the time so was nowhere near the pony when the horsefly had stung him.

George also comments on countryside sights which would have been common in those days. As he says, a hay field before being cut was a mass of wild flowers and butterflies, a very different sight from that which greets the walker today when modern farming methods have had a devastating effect on such plants as cowslips and even the bluebells which have largely disappeared from the hedgerows.

'Moti' was succeeded by a New Forest pony, a grey, called 'Swallow' (after Hereward the Wake's mare Swallow, in spite of his being a gelding). He was collected and ridden down from somewhere near Bristol:

When the pony reached the country roads by Ashton Court he did a dance for joy at leaving the city. Swallow and the pony carriage provided us all with much fun, both because of the drives we had in the carriage and also, when we were younger and not too heavy, riding him. He used to try and rid himself of his rider by ostensibly walking into a pond for a drink, his intentions becoming clear when his legs began to buckle under him and one was left in the pond.

Aunt Gar did all her shopping in Winscombe and Weston by pony carriage. The two spaniels, Bounce and Scinna, always sat in the front seat, and the shopping had to go elsewhere. One day, passing a charabanc in the Barton Road, the pony carriage went too near the ditch and tipped both the aunt and the two indignant spaniels into the hedge. No one was hurt.

Swallow had his favourite lanes for trotting down when it was felt safe to go all out. Shipham Lane from the A38 to Sandford was one of them. Jim Thoms and I used to career down this narrow lane with the carriage swaying from side to side; luckily we never met anything.

In 1923 George was confirmed in the Clifton College Chapel and his aunt drove to Clifton with Swallow who was then put up for the night in the old stables at their house in Bristol. Aunt Gar was George's godmother and attended the service at the Chapel, before returning to The Brook the next day:

At this time, Salter, our gardener and my friend, planted the yew just outside the coach house. In the first few days after planting Swallow tweaked it out of the ground and started to munch it. The yew was rescued and for many years carefully tended by Salter. He cut it to look like a hen. The work involved in keeping its shape was too great, so it lapsed into being a round bush.

The big field behind the house was divided into two, the smaller piece near where the nut copse is now, was Swallow's piece. The rest of the field was usually kept for hay for the winter keep. Haymaking was great fun and Salter used to make a haystack at the top of the field. The other important event was getting bracken for Swallow's bedding in the stable. Salter and I used to take the pony cart to the Barton Drove, in those days a grassy lane with bracken on either side...

We cut the bracken at the sides of the lane and brought it home to keep for his winter bed. As a boy I used to go out and I remember nutting in Shipham Lane. In those days the hedges literally met overhead and except for the odd cart we never saw anybody.

Salter came to us as a young man in 1921. He was then living in Axbridge but unfortunately he was dogged by ill health. He became a family friend and in 1923 when he married Nora Hemmens... the aunt built a bungalow for them. (It cost £300 to build in 1923.) Salter died in 1954 but his wife continued to live there until 1956. When anything went wrong, any human or animal was sick, or pipes leaked, the cry from the aunt was: 'Send for Salter!'

Swallow died in 1932 and the carriage was broken up as there was no room to keep it, cars being the order of the day. George commented:

In retrospect, how short-sighted this was. The shafts alone remain and they are used as handrails on each side of the steps going down to the little gate at the bottom of the front lawn.

I used to bicycle a great deal in those days and certainly did many trips between 115 Queens Road (where the rest of the family lived) and The Brook... One evening I rescued a stray cat from the pavement outside the house in Queens Road. Within a few days of my kind deed she rewarded me with kittens. We kept two and one we called Simpkins; the other we subsequently gave to friends in Redland. The mother was a poor thing and did not live very long. Simpkins was a great joy to me and used to come with me on my bicycle rides to Winscombe. He had a basket on the carrier and seemed quite happy with the arrangement.

The doctor who tended the family then was a Dr Lêche who lived in Axbridge. He was a charming Jersey man and very French in looks and manner. He had a surgery at Browns Corner for his Winscombe patients and perhaps to pick something up, he would park his car in the middle of the road with a quick application of the brakes. In 1919 traffic was almost non-existent except for horses so nobody minded. One day, about this time, my grandmother was sitting in the garden when Dr Lêche arrived with his new young partner – Norman Cooper. (He was destined to play a large part in village life in the future.)

In 1927 when I started the poultry farm at The Brook, Simpkins moved in with me and used to come into the fields when my father and I were making the chicken houses. Sadly, he died in 1929.

George was to combine with his friend, another George, to become the firm of Whicher & Searle. The apple side of the businesses was worked from land at The Brook together with some land belonging to George Searle, whilst the poultry side was run from The Brook. This is described as follows.

The Apple Orchard

Two young men, both called George, met at Cannington Agricultural College, at Bridgwater. George Whicher trained in poultry farming, George Searle in horticulture, and they became great friends. In the early 1930s George Searle went to work for the Long Ashton Research Station and married Joan, whose family farmed around The Square in Winscombe. George Whicher started poultry farming on his land at The Brook. Also on this land there was a large orchard and the two men decided to join forces and the firm of Whicher & Searle was born. Apples were grown in an orchard Searle had in Parson's Way, as well as in the orchard belonging to Whicher.

Later, George Whicher decided that he had had enough of the 'fruit business' and turned to his other love, politics, becoming the Conservative agent for the area, whilst remaining a 'sleeping partner' in the firm. George Searle took over the administration of the business, and, although he was, in many ways, somewhat reserved, during the war he visited many places and gave talks and advice to people to encourage them to grow their own food, and in this capacity grew to be an excellent and persuasive speaker.

According to George's very high standards, any fruit that did not meet his exact requirements was discarded. Many villagers remember the orchard in Parson's Way very well, as, every autumn, they would go and pick up the 'fallers', paying a minimal sum for them. It was normal to see several cars parked and women and children peering under the trees to find the best ones. The official 'packing station' was a wooden shed containing a 'sizing' machine on the corner of Barton Road.

The orchard was not only used for growing apples. There were also a great many blackcurrant bushes. George was fortunate enough to have a contract with Ribena* so, of course, the fruit had to be picked at its best. Those were the days when strawberries and other fruit provided a means for many women to get some 'pin money'. It was not easy work, but it was a common sight in the area in the summer season.

In the 1960s Peter Duckett, who had recently opened a grocery and vegetable shop in the village, became very friendly with George Searle, and, on seeing him discard so many apples because they were just a little too small, Peter decided to make him an offer to sell them for him at the shop. This relationship lasted for many years, and the two became good friends. Latterly, George began to find the orchard too much to cope with, and it was sold to Peter in 1985. His wife, Joan, retained her vegetable garden on the site until her death in 2001.

Peter kept the shop until it was sold, but he still owns the orchard at the time of writing. He has one problem which he would love to be able to solve.

Peter Duckett.

Sorting apples in the original shed; note the boxes from Whicher & Searle.

When he was walking over the ground one day, he found a beautiful gold signet ring, and it would make him very happy if he could find out who owned it. Possibly, it has been in the ground for many years; on the other hand, it may have been dropped by anyone popping in fairly recently to gather some fruit.

* *This contract has passed to Thatchers at nearby Sandford – they have been previously mentioned in connection with cider. The juice from the blackcurrants is now extracted here, and the remains (presumably skin and pips) are sent to China for medicinal purposes.*

The White Family

This is the story of the well-known family of Daisy and Albert White. Their two children Christopher and Christine have told us their story.

Daisy was the daughter of Winifred and Albert White. Albert was born in Treorchy in Wales and moved here when the mines started closing. Winifred was born at Pattinham, near Sidcot, and when they married they lived at Sycamore Cottage, where Daisy was born. Albert worked for the local Council, and, among other things, was involved with the clearing away of the earth that was left after the caves at Cheddar had been blasted. There are rumours that some of the stalactites that may have been accidentally broken were 'stuck' together again with cement.

Winifred did domestic work mainly at Coombe House, Sidcot, but also at The Hall for Mrs Gunn, the granddaughter of Revd Yatman. In fact, 'Granny White', as she was known, went to The Hall every Christmas day, even after she had retired, and did all the washing up for a number of years and would not accept payment for this.

Daisy went to the school at Winscombe where she met her future husband – another Albert White! When she left school she worked for Mr and Mrs Rusten Harrison at Zenner on The Lynch for a number of years. Albert, who was born in 1909, worked for the firm of John Scourse, builders, joiners and makers of strawberry baskets at Cheddar. After the death of the founder, the business was left to his two sons, and Albert went with John Scourse junr, who took over the basket firm. According to Christopher:

This is where Dad learnt his trade as a Sawyer. In the early days the Black Poplar trees were bought locally, but later he had to travel down to Exeter and other areas to cut them down. From 1962 the wood was imported

Winifred and Alfred White, c.1920.

from the Baltic. The trunks of the trees selected had to be completely straight. They were then cut into four foot lengths. The bark was then removed and peeled – like a pencil sharpener, into strips about one-sixteenth of an inch thick. They were then cut into different size strips to be interwoven into various sizes of basket, which ranged from one quarter of a pound to twelve pounds. They were used for strawberries and also mushrooms. When the plastic punnets came in they were so much cheaper that the firm could not compete.

In 1939 Dad had passed A1 for the Army, but was told he was in a reserved occupation, so he joined the Home Guard for the duration. His main duty was to keep watch on the reservoir at Cheddar.

In 1941 when the banns for Daisy's wedding were read they caused considerable confusion, for the name of the bride's father and that of her husband-to-be were the same – Albert White. The old saying 'change the name but not the letter, change for worse and not for better' was certainly untrue in this case, for Daisy not only kept the same letter, she also kept the same name, and only changed from Miss to Mrs White. They remained together for over 60 years.

Immediately after their marriage, they went to Sycamore Cottage with her parents for a while, but later they moved to Stable Cottage at Winscombe Hall where, for 48 years, Daisy also worked for Mrs Gunn. Albert's chief love in life was his garden, and when they later moved to Stone Cottage near the National Trust car park, he began a love affair with his garden which lasted for 28 years.

Albert carried on his trade for 42 years, and when the firm folded in 1968 he worked for Axbridge RDC and then Sedgemoor Council as a maintenance man, until he retired.

Daisy, who had spent all her life on the hill, had two wishes – one to see the Dutch bulb fields, and the other to go to Chelsea Flower Show. Thankfully she was able to fulfil both of these.

According to Christopher:

Mum was fond of animals and always had a mini zoo. At its height, her pet collection consisted of a sheep dog called Sandy, a tortoise called Monday and another called Friday. She also had two budgerigars called 'Bluey' and 'Tibby' plus two rabbits – 'Mousie' and 'Blackie'. Over the years there were many others, but these are the ones I remember most. When she became

This picture: ***Stone Cottage, c.1980.***

Inset: ***Daisy and Alfred White at The Hall, c.2001.***

Above: ***Daisy and Alfred, c.1980.***

ill with Parkinson's disease, she still had 'Monday', the tortoise, a rabbit called 'Silver' and a cockatiel called 'Bobo'. Her garden was her hobby, as it was with Dad. It was the simple things in life that were important. Dad used to make ornaments out of wood and these used to be in the garden along with the flowers. The two complemented each other.

Due to Mum's bad health she moved to 'The Hall' – now a Retirement Home – to live in the same place she had been for so many years. When Dad retired, he remained fit and active, working with me for several years on a part-time basis. He did not give up driving until he was 89 years of age. His interests were simple, and he enjoyed life to the full – football, gardening, and car boot sales were always popular, as was going out in his car. He died in 2002, one year after the death of Mum.

Chris is a self-employed gardener, and has retained contact with Mrs Gunn. He remarks that all the time the family worked at The Hall they never felt like 'staff'. He says everyone there appeared to be part of one large family. Mrs Gunn agrees with this, and she is still in touch with some of the next generation of villagers who worked for the family many years ago, some of whom are now living abroad.

The Doctor's Tales

During the First World War, Dr Norman Cooper joined a Field Ambulance Unit in 1915 and then the RFC. In 1919 he returned to Winscombe and started his general practitioner career as a part-time partner to the then local doctor, Dr Lêche. Dr Cooper was also on the surgical staff of the Bristol General Hospital and later he joined the staff at Weston-super-Mare hospital as senior surgeon.

Dr Cooper had lived in the village from the age of 11, and was educated at The Chestnuts and Sidcot School. He was much loved locally, and even children liked him. He used to take a little piece of plasticine with him on visits, and would make lovely little animals for them. He recalls his early 'doctoring' days when for the first six months he had to do his rounds on a bicycle, but later he used a motorbike.

Aside from his medical duties, he was very interested in local history and archaeology. Sometimes, he would dress up in an old smock and entertain audiences with local tales spoken in the original dialect. He was very keen to point out that the common 'ARH!' and 'Zomerset' that are heard nowadays on radio and television as part of the local accent are a fiction. He also commented that, in the early days, even the local hamlets would have different accents and use individual words for the same item; someone from Oakhill, therefore, might be very difficult to understand for those who lived at Barton. In those days, the various hamlets were completely separate. In Shipham, for example, some of the old people believed in witches, and the old woman who lived at the 'turnpike' suffered 'from the growing of the moon!' Next door to another of the doctor's patients there was a woman who definitely was a witch – according to Shipham people. They used to watch her and would not have anything to do with her. If she came out on the doorstep, they vowed she had a toad out there, and was talking to it, etc. Of course, they would not speak to anyone else about it, but they believed it was quite true.

Dr Cooper described 'haymaking' in the very early days of the twentieth century. Many times, the grass would be cut using scythes, before being turned with 'hay picks' and gathered into 'swathes'. When it had dried it would be put into 'pooks' (mounds of hay) before finally being made into the 'mow' (haystack). 'Longfield' was a huge oat, wheat or barley field, depending on the rotation, and in the summer it was just a mass of red poppies – a really beautiful sight.

Whilst it would not be possible to write some of his 'tales' in the appropriate accent, there is one that it may be possible to explain: this is a yarn about a man who got into a car, and stopped a labourer to enquire the way:

'Can you tell me the way to Shipham my man?'
'O-aa,' sed the yokel. 'Thiz go down thik road there, take the virst to the right, past the next turning and the second to the left – no – be dang'd if th' do. Thik takes this road back there, second – no – not that there neither. Well, tiz like this ere, if I were goin to Shipham I shouldn't start from ere!'

His favourite old Somerset comment was: 'Well, there 'tiz – can't be no tizzer.'

Sometimes, illnesses and pains were described to him in veterinary terms or other unusual ways, such as the man 'who had a pain in his 'hockle' joint, like 10,000 pigs grunting and 10,000 rats gnawing.' A woman who was troubled with insomnia wanted something 'to make I sleep at night. I do turn ee over in me mind awl night, and ere old man says to me – that's over-intelligence. That's wat tiz!' Finally, there was the woman who thought her daughter was suffering with the 'tubular galoshes'!

Dr Norman Cooper, c.1960.

When he retired after 50 years of service, Dr Cooper was presented with a teak seat, suitably inscribed, and later a tree was planted beside it to give shade to those resting there. At the time of writing this is still doing good service outside Winscombe Surgery.

Above: *Observatory Field, c.1999.*

Right: *Observatory Field, 2003.*

Left: *Harvest lunch in St James Hall, 1992.*

Nineteen

Then and Now

The idea for this chapter came from a note written by a farmer, John Mabbett, who has lived in the village all his life:

My memory, which may be faulty, as we tend to remember the good times and forget the bad, is that we could wander where we pleased, whether it was on a bike or on foot. At times we would bike along the A38 from Sidcot Corner to Shute Shelve. There would be five or six of us with dogs. The traffic was few and far between (petrol rationing was in force then) and we would go right over the top of Wavering Down and Crook Peak. The only other things on the hill would be sheep, and people were rare.

Now, if you go there, you seldom see a sheep, but people are there at times 'en masse'. There are also horse riders by the dozen and, with those, the ground gets chewed up and it would be impossible to ride a bike, and, in places, hazardous to walk. Even there, the sound of any birdsong is drowned out by the noise of the traffic.

He then goes on to describe his work on the farm in the early twenty-first century compared with his younger days:

The main difference is that then it was mainly physical, and done with at least two others. I expect for every hour on a tractor we would spend at least three doing physical work, and we would go to the nature and whims of the cows – for example, we used to milk by machines, but they were not as efficient as today's. So two men would follow behind to strip them out, and, as I recall, there was one cow who would not stand for the machine and had to be milked all the way by hand. Today, that cow would not be kept, as the herd has to fit the machine.

As for field work such as hoeing, hedging, hay making and any other jobs, these were all done by hand. Now you have precision drills for mangolds and a spray to get rid of the weeds.

Time-keeping was by the church clock, or the trains which we all knew the times of, but now – no trains, and the sound of the church clock is drowned out by traffic.

Then, the farm supported four families who all lived in walking distance. Of course, there were no televisions, washing machines, or any other modern gadgets that we take for granted today.

In my grandfather's day, there was a boy who had weak bones, and the doctor said he had to have a pint of milk a day. His family were too poor to afford that, so grandfather gave him a pint a day for years. Can you imagine a situation like that today?

But now my son runs that farm, which is double the size, by himself and spends 90 per cent of his time on a tractor. If something has to be done by hand, it just isn't done. So, today, everything fits the machine and yesterday, the machine fitted the man.

Harvest Festivals

The following story is taken from an article by John Bailey written in 1988 for the *Weston Mercury*. In 1893, according to Mr Knight, a well-known local author, this annual gathering was a great event:

Little knots of villagers file into the church. The porch is hung with oat sheaves and red apples. Over the door are hung boughs of wild hedge-row plums – bullace – not sloes, so thickly clustered and with so rare a bloom that they might easily pass for grapes.

The windows are heaped with fruit and vegetables, with apples and 'taters' and huge marrows, the best of each man's field or garden. The pulpit is draped with heather and bryony, while the font is lost in a great pile of ferns and flowers. The Chancel is a bower of green. Lectern and reading desk are wreathed with creepers and corn sheaves and trophies of the harvest.

It is nearly time for the service to begin. Young 'village beauties' conscious of admiring glances, are scattered here and there, bright reliefs of light and colour among the darker costumes of the men. The choirboys, conscious too, but more sheepish as they run the gauntlet of less sympathetic eyes, muster under the tower, where presently the tall curate joins them.

When the service is over, the villagers join in a procession which passes under the flags and streamers hung at intervals across the green lanes. They arrive

Left: *The corner of Woodborough Road, 2003.*

The corner of Woodborough Road, c.1930.

at the spacious meadow where the people of the hamlet, of all sorts and conditions, are to meet on equal terms – vicar and 'Lady bountiful' and dames of high degree on the one side, and farmers and farm labourers on the other.

Tea in the tent is the first business: a tent brave with festoons and flags and decorations. There is a hint in one of the mottoes at the shortcomings of the season: 'May the year '93, Be the worst we shall see.'

Follows then a game of rounders, in which the vicar, after much persuasion agrees to play, if another somewhat elderly pillar of the church will take a hand too... and if the vicar plays no very conspicuous part in the game, his boys are the life of it... as is his daughter too, who, in a far corner of the field, leads a dance of village children to the old world ditty 'As we go gathering nuts in May'. Later there is a dance and a hundred pairs of dancers are footing it merrily on the short, dry turf.

It is an orderly company, quiet and well behaved to the very last, breaking off their revels on the stroke of mid-night, trooping out of the tent that, with its multitudinous lamps, is bright against the moonless sky, its festoons, flags and creepers showing clearly through the canvas walls. They go their several ways across the wide parish, along the dim, unlighted lanes, to meet no more, under such conditions at any rate, until next year brings round another harvest home.

Nowadays the local churches still hold a harvest festival service in the autumn, when flowers and fruit are brought to decorate the church, and after the service a harvest lunch may be held, sometimes on the same day but not necessarily so. (The famous harvest suppers, when the whole village would meet and vast quantities of cold joints would be consumed, have gradually faded out – perhaps due to the increased population in so many villages.) In 2003 St James Church held a harvest lunch on the Sunday following the service. This meal was prepared and provided by members of the congregation and no charge was made. Donations towards the cost were added to the 'Harvest Help' mentioned below.

A generation ago, the fruit and vegetables taken to the service were distributed among the poor of the parish, but now there is a more modern concept for this 'bounty'. Now, the gifts are distributed depending on the form in which they have been given. Fresh produce brought forward at the harvest festival service is distributed to our residential homes for the consumption of the residents. Tinned goods, breakfast cereals, etc. are placed in the bins at the back of the church, to be donated to the vicar's pantry at St Andrews Church, Bournville, and the Breakfast Club at Bournville School. These are given to families in need of emergency food supplies and for children who are sent to school without having been given any breakfast. Flowers that are donated to decorate the church are made up into small posies and delivered to people in the village who have lost loved ones recently and those who have received pastoral care. Lastly, the cash from the collections at the service are sent to the charity 'Harvest Help' for their work in 'providing seeds of hope' in southern Africa.

The tides of change could be seen on the cover of the *Parish Magazine* for September 2003 which showed a harvest festival spread, including jars of pickled eggs (or onions?), bottles of sauce and tinned food – items which, years ago, would not have been thought of.

Despite all the changes that took place in the twentieth century, there are still occasions when 'the past meets the present'. One event that happened in about 1915 is, as this is written, about to be brought back to life. As previously mentioned, during the First World War a number of Belgian refugees were living in the village and they planted an avenue of trees, known as 'Belgium Avenue'. Recently it was decided that, as many of the beech trees have died (possibly due to a drought in the 1970s), it would be a good project to replace them. With the agreement of Sidcot School and after discussion with several experts, it has been decided that this may be possible. A report of the original occasion has been sent to the Belgian Embassy and, hopefully, one of their representatives may attend the replanting; the money has been raised by public subscription.

In 1867 Mrs A.V.B. Yatman, from The Hall, was asked to dig the first sod for the new railway line, and she was given a spade with an engraved silver blade.

Mrs A.V.B. Yatman, c.1900.

When the Millennium Green was being planned, Mrs Sue Gunn, Mrs Yatman's great-grand-daughter, used the same spade for a similar purpose.

Another, somewhat strange, echo from the past can be found in Compton's *Mendip Sketches* in a discussion of boys at play:

> *... as soon as the muscles of the arm grow stronger, exercise is found with sticks, and in stone-throwing; the pleasure being heightened by achievement... Then there is the propensity to scribble, with chalk or pencil, on walls and doors – a sad nuisance, as the chief attraction is always to new paint and clean whitewash. But the propensity is inveterate. Perhaps the best remedy would be the erection of a public hoarding, with a light surface for pencils, and a black one for chalk. Native talent might thus be developed, and private walls and doors kept from superfluous decoration.*

This could well have been an early form of the 'native talent' so much in evidence today – in other words, what started out as graffiti has since developed into an art form of its own.

Left: *The silver spade used to lift the first sod of the Millennium Green, 1999. The engraving reads 'Presented by the Mayor and Corporation of Axbridge In commemoration of the cutting of the first sod of the Yatton and Cheddar Valley Railway. 20th Feb. 1867.'*

Below: *Mendip Lodge behind the car park where the Drill Hall used to be, 2002.*

Left: *Cups and rosettes at the Michaelmas Fair, 2003.*

Right: *Vegetables at the Michaelmas Fair, 2003.*

Left: *Exhibition of mini rugby at the Michaelmas Fair, 2003.*

Left: *The modern fire station, 2003.*

Right: *Winscombe firemen, 1998.* Left to right, back row: *Kevin Rigley, Steven Hartshorne, Noam Perretz, Mark Pennington, Ian Hine, Brian Pearce;* front row: *Paul Newton, Peter Ballard, Norman Ebson, David Hares, Robert Bale, Phillip Birchell.*

Twenty

Winscombe Today

For a visitor approaching from the top of Banwell Hill, the village looks very similar to that of many years ago. The houses can be seen surrounded by the Mendip Hills, and the church still stands proudly on the hill. Despite the desire of many to keep the village unspoilt, the demands of employment and housing have inevitably led to many changes. For some of the older people whose stories are mentioned in this book, much of Winscombe today would be unrecognisable. Many of the green fields have gone and in their place houses and shops have appeared.

Often it is almost impossible to keep up to date with all of these changes. Many elderly residents might find it hard to imagine some properties changing hands ten or more times within a short space of time. The sawmill in Woodborough Road, which was once owned by the Eade family, is a case in point. When the business closed, two large semi-detached houses were built on the site. For many years they were private properties, but later they were used for a number of purposes. One of these was as a workshop for 'The House of Nesbet' who made expensive dolls. Following this there was an office on the site for several years for the local authority. When the building was eventually demolished, it became Dunster House. The name 'Dunster' probably refers to the gentleman who lived in one of the original properties and was a surveyor.

Browns, the grocery business, was taken over by Mason & Gillett for a while, but in 1985 the property was rented by 'Light Ideas'. However, this did not last long. In 1985 R.C. Adams, who had owned a shoe shop in Woodborough Road for a number of years, took over the front of the premises. The part fronting on to Sandford Road became a fish-and-chip shop and this adjoins an Indian take-away. Even though the structure has a long history, inside it is unrecognisable. It is a similar story when it comes to the Electricity Board showroom. Since those days it has been used as a clothes shop, a knitting-wool shop, a veterinary surgery and lately a charity shop for the local Cancer Hospice, to name but a few.

Photographic evidence helps to demonstrate change, but it also enables us to capture a history of Winscombe through the years. The needs of the inhabitants have changed. Whereas at the beginning of the period the housewife shopped locally, possibly daily, for her food, now it is more likely that a weekly trip to the supermarkets in Weston-super-Mare will suffice. This would help to explain the demise of so many of the old established grocery shops. Those shops that are open at the time of writing, apart from the Co-op and Roberts, tend to sell the occasional product that may have been largely forgotten, but they also provide a very real service to those who are unable to drive or get about easily. The latest change in this side of life is the growing interest in internet orders which can be delivered direct to the house. In a strange way, this reflects the past in modern guise; most purveyors of food would once have been willing to come around with their vans, baskets or trucks. Even as late as 1950 it was possible to have bread, meat, fish and vegetables delivered daily, and now, by the press of a key, the same service can be obtained.

We have, however, retained some of the traditional services: the milkman still delivers, although it is now three times a week instead of daily, the postman calls only once a day, and our refuse is collected weekly. So far, we have been able to retain our local Post Office (despite the fact that the 'stamp machine' has been sealed up), but the two banks that remain are only supplying a 'part-service' and many people are considering changing to 'on-line' banking.

Our library, which at one time contained only about 100 books, now boasts a large supply and also two computers for the free use of members. Despite this, the past is not forgotten – there is still an area with table and chairs where people may read the daily paper, and the mobile library service has been extended.

The whole point is that, although some things have changed, the structure and way of life has remained constant. The villagers have continued to get together and organise a lifestyle that takes into account the wishes of the majority. In the *Parish Guide* of 2000, some 80 organisations and activities are listed, and a selection of these are described below.

The Winscombe Club

Downstairs in this modern club, there is a lounge with a bar which incidentally serves a large selection of drinks of all descriptions, including some excellent draught guest Real Ales. The club was awarded CAMRA Club of the South West in 2002. Also in the downstairs lounge, should they be required, are various games such as pool, darts, table skittles, dominoes and, in the club's own alley, skittles (they have some very successful teams). There is also a large television set.

Upstairs there is a stage, a dance floor and, of course, a bar. There is also a kitchen with limited facilities. Should a member wish to hire the upstairs for a party or wedding, there is no charge to the member hiring the room. Drinks, however, are a little dearer in order to cover the wages of the bar staff. On Tuesday and Sunday evenings bingo is played in this upper room.

The club is run by a management committee that is elected annually and is always open to suggestions from fellow members. Live music is provided on the first and third Saturdays of each month. A raffle is held on Sunday lunchtimes consisting of all one needs to make an excellent dinner or big breakfast. On music nights another raffle is run by Keith Brooks with some great prizes to be won. All this and probably the cheapest drinks for miles around! Membership in 2004 is only £3 per annum and only £1 for pensioners, plus the price of your entry key.

The Winscombe Bell-Ringers

The group ring primarily for Sunday services, but also ring weddings, special occasions and celebrations. Because it is also a pastime requiring both mental and physical discipline, it presents a challenge and entertainment to all who participate from the youngest ringer to the oldest. Age is no barrier, the oldest ringer was aged 90 and our youngest learnt while in primary school. Contrary to popular belief, no great strength or stamina is required, only the ability to climb the tower stairs! The ringers are a band and fortunate in having long-standing members who are experienced ringing teachers.

There is also a social side to ringing. The Axbridge Branch of the association organises training days and outings provide a variety of social events. At Winscombe there is an annual outing and the club joins with other towers for practices and events. Supper and skittles always follow the Annual General Meeting. It is possible for a ringer to go elsewhere in the county to another tower and be made to feel at home. There can be few other pastimes that are so inexpensive yet can provide so much.

Visitors are always welcome, and anyone is invited to come and watch the group ring, and they encourage anyone who may be interested in learning to come and meet the band on the practice night, which is Thursday.

Winscombe Orchestra

The orchestra was formed in 1974 when 11 players were brought together through the efforts of its first conductor, the late Ronald Clarke. From this modest beginning, the playing strength has risen to some 55 musicians, which still includes three of the founder members. The leader at the time of writing is Christine Gladwin (who is a teacher at Sidcot School). Members come from as far afield as Bristol, Blackwell, Clevedon, Burnham and Wells, as well as from Winscombe itself.

Winscombe Orchestra, 2003. Left to right: Christine Gladwin (leader), Brian Morris (oboe), Elvina Trinder (violin), the late Rupert Bottomley (conductor), Diane Keast (clarinet). All except the conductor are founder members.

The orchestra performs six concerts a year, three of which are given in aid of charity at the Friends Meeting House, Sidcot. A different charity is chosen each time (this is often a local one). In the early-twenty-first century the proceeds of the summer concert were donated to the Winscombe Community Association in recognition of the loyal support the orchestra receives from the local community. Each concert is repeated at All Saints Church, Weston, in the winter and spring, and at Mark Church in the summer.

The aim of the orchestra is to explore a wide range of music and to perform it to the highest standard possible. Members believe that the making of music should be a pleasurable experience for players and listeners alike and, as the Winscombe Orchestra approaches its 13th birthday, it is their hope that their audience will continue to share in their enthusiasm and enjoyment.

Sadly, in 2003, the conductor, Rupert Bottomley died whilst on holiday at the age of 52. He will be greatly missed as he gave so much to the orchestra for several years. However, members plan to continue, using temporary conductors until a replacement can be found, and hope that the future will be as rewarding as the past.

Winscombe Probus Club

Retirement can be a very busy time and especially so for Winscombe men and women. There are so many thriving clubs and societies that evenings at home, should they be needed, can be few and far between. However, there are times when the men of the village, in particular, would like to get together and discuss issues specific to themselves. The Probus Club offers them an opportunity to do this. Such groups are organisations for people who have retired or semi-retired from their profession or business, and wish to maintain a social network with others in the locality who have similar interests. There is no central governing body and operating costs are met by members' contributions.

Winscombe Probus Club was founded in 1976 with Mr Frank Adams as the very first chairman. Like all other Probus Clubs it is quite independent, non-sectarian and non-political... whatever do they all talk about?! At the age of 80 members become 'honorary' and, while still able to take an active part in all proceedings, relinquish full membership and so allow 'younger' men to join and make up the numbers to a maximum of 45.

In this way, the organisation of the Winscombe group is completed mainly by these 'younger' folk with the 'elders' sitting back, advising where necessary, and knowing that they have made their contribution in previous years. This type of organisation has much to recommend it as all members' fees go towards running the club and a source of younger 'officers' to do the running is guaranteed.

The Probus Club usually meets twice a month. Each meeting includes coffee, conversation (usually informational, brisk and entertaining) and a talk given by either members or non-members on a variety of subjects. For members and their partners there are several optional trips, lunches, dinners and a short annual holiday. For the holiday a single hotel is used as a base where in the evening all meet to dine and socialise. On one day of the holiday all visit some local place of interest together, but otherwise members spend the days doing whatever they wish.

While the purpose of the group is not charitable, it has, over the past few years, included in its activities an annual fund-raising event in support of 'Sight Savers'. A considerable amount of money has been donated to this charity.

Winscombe Youth Club

The club was set up seven years ago to provide a safe environment for young people aged 11–17 from Winscombe and Sandford to 'hang out'. It is a 'drop-in' centre providing snooker, table tennis, computer games, PlayStation 2, air hockey and other games, as well as opportunities to try different arts and crafts. Music and 'tuck' are also popular features. Since 1999, many of the youngsters have become adept at glass painting and the sale of their work has provided cash for a music system and up-to-date CDs. They also help at the Michaelmas Fair and have a stall at the Scouts' Christmas bazaar.

Winscombe and Sandford Parish Council have paid for a youth worker for the past three years, and will also offer training to anyone who would consider working as a volunteer for one session per month. At the time of writing they have over 60 members with about 25 attending each week, and are pursuing plans to build an extension to provide more space for arts and crafts and a lounging area. In 2003, the club is fortunate to have six young people working there as part of their training to be youth workers.

Another hut-type building in the Community Centre field is the Meeting Place – a place where the young can just gather and chat, rather than hang around in the streets.

Left: *Meeting Place for youngsters to 'hang out' near the Youth Club, 2002.*

Winscombe Youth Club, glass and china painting, 2002.
Left to right: *James, Tamara, Roxanne and Thomas.*
COURTESY OF DAVID WYATT

Winscombe Youth Club, 'PlayStation', 2002.
Left to right: *Garry, Daniel and Nathan.*
COURTESY OF DAVID WYATT

Top left: *Setting for 'The Promise Ceremony', 2002.*

Above: *Christmas cakes for Sewell House, 1997.*

Left: *Winscombe Brownies toasting marshmallows around the campfire, 1995.*

Winscombe Brownies

In 2003 Gillian Smith, the 'Brown Owl', related the story of the present pack. She has been with them since 1978, during which time things have changed hugely, a fact which can be seen from a photograph of the pack when she first joined them. The most obvious change came when Jeff Banks designed the uniform that has been used since 1990. The khaki culottes, yellow sweatshirts, badge sashes and baseball caps soon became the norm. The 'Promise Badge' changed as well, from a silver trefoil to a round yellow badge depicting a trefoil; and a new 'Promise' accompanied these changes to reflect a multi-cultural Britain. The name of the association also changed to become the Girl Guide Association, and now 'Girl Guiding UK'.

Brownies always celebrate 22 February – 'Thinking Day' (joint birthdays of Lord and Lady Baden-Powell). This takes the form of an 'International Evening' with crafts, games and food from around the world. Lighted candles are placed on a map and members 'think' of Brownies and members of the movement in those countries.

The Brownie Pack is an active, energetic and happy group. They enter into many of the village events – the fund-raising for the Millennium Green fête with cake stalls, sideshows and a lucky dip. They rehearse a Nativity play and perform for the residents of Sewell House. Usually, a small gift is given to each resident. They also make table decorations or calendars and even a Christmas cake for everyone. The photograph *(opposite)* shows the girls with their 'Christingle' gifts, having previously taken part in the service at St James Church by forming a Nativity tableau, doing the readings and prayers and taking the collection.

When Baden-Powell founded the movement in 1909, he may have doubted that it would still be thriving almost 100 years later, but it seems as popular as ever, with waiting-lists for all sections. One problem which has remained constant over the years is the difficulty in finding willing volunteers to run units.

Right: *Brownies dressed as Flower Girls at a church fête, 1996.*

Above: *Winscombe Brownies, c.1980.*
COURTESY OF BOB BOWEN

Left: *Winscombe Brownies at the Millennium Green, during the Jubilee Fête, May 2002.*

Christingle

A very special gathering is the annual Christingle service in the church, a candlelit family celebration in which the Christingle itself symbolises the light of Christ's love and it being turned into practical action for vulnerable children. St James Church was one of the first in the country to hold such a service and has made it an annual part of their preparations for Christmas. Traditionally, an orange represents the world but, since we don't grow oranges in Winscombe, we have always used an apple which is supplied every year by Winscombe Orchards next to the church.

The Christingle consists of an apple, to represent the world; the four cocktail sticks portray the four seasons; the fruit and sweets attached illustrate God's love in providing 'the fruits of the earth'; the red ribbon depicts the blood of Christ; and the candle, the Light of the World.

The Children's Society

The Church of England's outreach to underprivileged children and young people in the country is the Children's Society, and St James Parish Church has given its full support since the early 1950s.

Scouting in Winscombe

The first record of Scouts in the village dates from 1913, with Cubs following on shortly after that when the Wolf Cub movement was formed in 1916. The first 'official' record of Scouting was in 1924 when the Seven Wolf Cubs and Seven Scouts were registered with a group headquarters address c/o Mr Haynes, Sandford Road, and run by George Hutchings (Scoutmaster) and Miss Hilda Clothier (club mistress). In 1931 the 2nd Winscombe Scout Group was formed, meeting at Sidcot School, and this continued until 1970.

In 2003 the group still flourishes and comprises three sections which were joined by a Beaver Colony in 2001 (which runs for boys between six and eight) and, along with the Cubs (for boys aged between eight and ten-and-a-half) and Scout sections (for boys and girls aged between ten-and-a-half and fourteen), number over 70 young members along with six 'warranted' leaders. There was, at one stage during the late 1980s and early '90s, a Venture Scout Unit which met in Winscombe under the name of Anglo Saxon VSU. The 1st Winscombe also had, at this time, two separate Scout groups – one meeting on a Tuesday, and one on a Friday.

The Beavers, who are easily recognisable by their distinctive turquoise sweatshirts, meet on a Wednesday and have evenings of games and crafts, as well as outings, stories and camp fires. They put on a show for parents involving circus skills which they had learnt. They have also joined in with other Beavers in the district to have a 'sleep over', staying overnight in a hut together.

On Monday Cub evenings, the boys learn new skills, including lighting fires and cooking on the fire, navigation, using compasses and maps, first aid and weather. This is all mixed in with fun, games and many other activities.

In Scouts, the young adults start taking on new and exciting challenges that are held either during their Tuesday-evenings meeting or at weekends. This gives them opportunities to put into practice some of the skills they have learnt – for example, building rafts, climbing and abseiling, and orienteering day and night hikes.

The group is supported by an executive, whose main preoccupation is fund-raising – the majority of which comes from the village paper collection and the annual 'Christmas Fayre'. The boys working on the monthly paper round have, over the years, collected in excess of 1,000 tons of paper, which has involved a lot of shifting and helping. This has raised thousands of pounds for the group, enabling them to buy equipment and subsidise outings and camps.

As with the Brownies, although many things have changed since the early-twentieth century, particularly since the new uniform, logos, programmes and age groups were brought in, the ideas of Baden-Powell still hold true, and it is great to see so many children and young adults getting so much out of the movement. Sadly, as with their sister organisation, the number of leaders that are available to help is always a problem and any adults that could come forward to help would be very welcome.

The Winscombe and Sandford Local History and Archaeology Society (LHS)

The LHS was formed in 1990 to promote the study of the history of Winscombe and Sandford, both by co-ordinating the work already being carried out by individuals, and by initiating new studies on various aspects of the past. These projects have included oral history – in which people's memories of Winscombe over the years have been recorded, the history of the shops, a graveyard survey and the collection and study of tobacco clay pipes from the villages. Various members have collected archaeological material from fieldwork, and members have slowly built up a collection of archaeological artefacts and historical material including documents, maps and old postcards.

Anyone with an interest in any aspect of the history of Winscombe and Sandford is very welcome to join the society which has about 100 members in 2003 and publishes at least five newsletters each year. The group also holds lectures and meetings, organises trips and puts on displays. (Please contact John Gower on 01934 842945.)

Above: *Temple Meads; waiting for a train to the Lake District, 2003.*

Left: *Brownsea Island, 2001.*

Below: *Scouts testing a raft at Ferny Croft, New Forest, 2001.*

Left: *Eade's Sawmill, c.1910.*

Below: *Demolition of local authority buildings, c.1988.*

Below: *Dunster Court – in 2003 this now replaces the buildings shown in the two pictures above and right.*

Right: *Rebuilding shops in Woodborough Road, 1950.*

Below: *Shops in Woodborough Road, c.1950.*

Above: *Shops in Woodborough Road, 2002.*

Twenty-One

A New Millennium

Over a century ago, Winscombe was largely a place of two worlds – one where the so-called gentry lived, and the other mainly occupied by farmers or shopkeepers. This book has traced the gradual growth of the influence of both the old and new families in the area, and the introduction of other businesses. Everyday life in the village then, when even one hamlet's dialect might have been completely different from that of a mile or so away, did not lend itself to a cohesive society. The area was largely united through the Church. The coming of the railway opened up village life to a considerable extent – initially by the introduction of new labour for the actual building of this massive operation, and then the gradual acceptance of this form of transport as a way of life, which brought travel to so many people.

Much of the physical change that has taken place during this period can be demonstrated with photographs; but the question for the future generations is how they will go about coping with the increasing load of economic and other problems that are bound to come. The first challenge concerns the growth in new buildings, with the inevitable increase in population and traffic which this brings, together with the loss of farm land. There are also many other, less obvious, changes that are already impinging on our quiet lives and the ways in which these affect us, and our children, is one of the most important questions for the future.

One major change is the character of everyday life for the women of Winscombe. Early in the twentieth century, it was generally assumed that the role of the wife was looking after the home and children. It was at this time that women such as Hannah Moore, Mary Sumner, Mary Watt, and many others, took it upon themselves to create groups for women with common interests, and so give them an opportunity to meet and discuss items of mutual concern away from the closed life of the home.

There are many examples of this: the Mothers' Union, the Red Cross, and, perhaps the best known, the Women's Institute. For well over 70 years these varied groups of women had an enormous effect, not only locally but also on a national front, the best known being the 'Women's Suffrage' movement. As has been shown in earlier chapters, many of the events that take place outside the home have been organised for, and by, women, although they have also gradually brought a larger population under their umbrella.

Whereas in the past any 'little jobs' that women did were thought of in terms of the 'pin money' they generated, these days it is usually the case that the wife's wage forms an integral part of the family

Above: *Rebuilding the garage at the bottom of Woodborough Road, c.1910.*

Right: *Passey & Porter Garage, c.1945.*

economy. So, apart from housework and children, the women are often engaged in part-time or full-time employment. This, of course, prevents them from having much spare time and the organisation of some of the groups in the village has suffered.

However, it is not only for women that life has changed. In earlier days men usually lived near their place of work, or at least within a few miles. Now, with the arrival of the motorway, it is not unusual for men to live 30 or 50 miles away from their place of business and some of the hours that may have been spent in other ways have to be used for travel.

Although the parish has tried hard to find ways of uniting the community, and there are many such organisations, some of them are finding it difficult to keep going, not because they are not popular, but due to a lack of organisers.

This leaves the future generations with a great problem that will have to be overcome if the life of the village is to continue as it did throughout the twentieth century. The challenge to be faced is that, although there are many choices to make, and many people who would like to take part in village life, the organisers of these associations are not getting any younger. There is a limit to the amount that a person of 70 or 80 can do, no matter how much they may wish to contribute. Unless some of the newer, younger villagers 'take up the batton', we stand a very real chance of losing the things that have made Winscombe such a wonderful and friendly place in which to live. Unless we care for these things that we all enjoy, and are prepared to give a small amount of time occasionally, it makes one wonder what a future historian will find to pass comment upon when writing this type of book.

Browns Corner, 2003.

Birds Assembly Rooms, 2003.

View of Winscombe from Wavering Down, 2003.

Left: *Farmec Central Garage and Woodborough Hotel, c.1950.*

Below: *Modern garage, c.1990.*

Left: *The house in Woodborough Road which was demolished to make way for the Midland Bank, c.1960. It is now HSBC.*

Below: *Woodborough Hotel, c.2003.*

Subscribers

Adrian Adams, Winscombe
Peter and Janet Alletson, Winscombe, Somerset
Mrs Maura Aston, Winscombe
Professor Mick Aston, Sandford, Winscombe, Somerset
Brenda Austin, Grimsby, N.E. Lincolnshire
Mr Anthony Avery, Winscombe
Philip and Alsana Baird, Sandford, Somerset
Brian Bancroft, Winscombe, North Somerset
Ellen (Nell) and Fred Bancroft
Anne and Richard Banks, Winscombe, Somerset
Colin J. Banks, Winscombe, Somerset
Dave R. Banks, Winscombe, Somerset
Heather and John Bearman, Winscombe
Alice Bignell (Nurse), Winscombe, Somerset
Cyril A. Binning, Winscombe, North Somerset
Graham Body, Nut Tree Farm, Barton
Trevor and Melba Boulter, The Lynch, Winscombe
Mrs Denise Bowler, Worle, Somerset
Mandy Brading, Winscombe
Mike and Jacquie Bravery, Winscombe
Mike and Dianne Bridges, Sidcot Gate, Winscombe, Somerset
Eliot Buckland
Gwen D. Burman, Winscombe, North Somerset
Dr Peter S. Burr, Munich
Dr and Mrs W.G. Burrows, Winscombe, Somerset
Mary Butlin, Cardiff
Penny Callow, Winscombe, Somerset
Martin and Belinda Carwardine, Winscombe
Dr Andrew J. Chandler, Winscombe, Somerset
Nigel, Sue, Elena and Jessica Chapman, The Square
Enid E. Clark (née Ellis), Sidcot, Winscombe, Somerset
Dorothy F. Cooper, Winscombe
Phyllis Cram, Parish Councillor, Winscombe
Mrs Joan Crook, Winscombe
Margaret Crystal (née Nipper), Rainham, Kent
Alan and Mary Cuthbert, Winscombe
Steven Robert Davies, Banwell, Somerset
Jack Denning, Winscombe, Somerset
Richard and Iris Dew, Winscombe
Julie Edmondson (Woodhead), Bristol
Julian and Grace Evans, Winscombe, Somerset
Emma Fanthom, Knapps Close, Winscombe
Jon Feltham
Mr Owen John Foord, Yatton, North Somerset
Grace Freem, Winscombe
Nancy and George Friday
Linda Gardiner, Winscombe, Somerset
Samantha Gardiner, Winscombe, Somerset
Victoria Gardiner, Winscombe, Somerset
S. Glanfield, Winscombe 1948–1978
John and Marian Gower, Winscombe
Capt. J.H.G. Grant, Co-Founder of Winscombe British Legion, Inglewood, Winscombe
Susanna Gunn
Clive Hannam, Winscombe
Christopher Harris, Mooseheart Gardener
Miss E. June Harris
K.E.C. Headford, Winscombe, Somerset
Frank and Belinda Hellard and Family
D.R. Hembery, Sandford, Winscombe, Somerset
Ian A. Hine, Winscombe, Somerset
Phyllis Hopkins, Winscombe
John Horne, Somerset
Jim and Joyce House, Winscombe, Somerset

Geoff and Anne Hutchings, Sandford
Andrea G. James, Winscombe, Somerset
Sally James, Winscombe, Somerset
J. and W. Jenkins, Winscombe, Somerset
Graham D. Jones, Ilford, Essex
Kevin and Tina Joyce, Longfield House, Winscombe
The Key Family, Winscombe, Somerset
Joan and Arthur Langford, Winscombe, Somerset
George C. Leigh, Winscombe, Somerset
Tom Lewis, Winscombe
Jane Lloyd (née Mabbett) and Gerald Lloyd, Winscombe
Mr and Mrs D. Love, Winscombe, Somerset
Jim Lyon, Winscombe, North Somerset
James and Sandra Macqueen, Winscombe
Michael Martin, Winscombe
Roseanne and Ronnie Morgan, Winscombe, Somerset
Mary Naylor, Winscombe
John D. Neesham, Winscombe
The Neill Family, Winscombe
Sylvia Mary Newton (née Nipper), Kingsley, Western Australia
Alan and Barbara Nipper, Llandrillo-Yn-Rhos
Dennis G. Nipper, Smethwick, West Midlands
Betty M. Pain, Winscombe
Mr Maurice E. Phillips
Stanley Pickett, Weymouth, Dorset
John Popham, Nr Winscombe, Somerset
Mrs B. Pring, Bridgwater, Somerset
Mr and Mrs Rawlings and Family, Woodborough Crescent, Winscombe
Alice L. Reed, Lynch Crescent, Winscombe
Mrs M. Richards, Almondsbury, Near Bristol
Miss Rita Richards, Winscombe, Somerset
Jean Laura Richardson, Winscombe
The Rudge Family, Winscombe, Somerset
Robert Sadler, Winscombe, Somerset
John and Marjorie Salter, Winscombe
Mrs Christine Salvage, Winscombe, Somerset
Mr and Mrs R.C. Salvage, Winscombe
Bert and Eunice Sandford, Winscombe, Somerset
Lorna Scherer, Winscombe
Wendy, Charlie, Ebba and Freya Scherer, Church Road, Winscombe
Effie Shopland, The Lynch, Winscombe, Somerset
Sidcot School, Winscombe, Somerset
Ronald and Mary Sinnett, Winscombe, Somerset
Jenny Sisman, Winscombe, Somerset
Revd Mike Slade, Vicar of Winscombe from 1999
Mrs Gillian Smith, Winscombe, Somerset
June D. Smith (née Nipper), Stroud, Gloucestershire
Sue Spencer (née Hill), Dover, Kent
Julian Stephens, Winscombe, Somerset
Michael Stephens, East Riding, York
Ian Studley, Shipham
Tim and Jenny Sykes, Winscombe, Somerset
Joyce May Syms, Southleaze Cottages, Winscombe
Judith Taylor, Brooklands, Hillyfields Way, Winscombe
May Taylor, Winscombe, Somerset
Stewart R. Tennent, Winscombe, Somerset
The Thomas Family, Ashford, Kent
Mrs Grace Gwendolyn Thornton, Winscombe, Somerset
Win Threasher, Winscombe, Somerset
Brian Tilly, Winscombe, Somerset
Carol Ann Tucker
Catherine E. Tucker, Winscombe Hill, North Somerset
Betty J. Turbitt, Winscombe
R. Uffindell (née Hancock), Winscombe, Somerset
K.M. and P.Y. Vigus
Gladys E. Vowles, Winscombe, Somerset
Mr John Vowles, Broadleaze Farm, Winscombe, North Somerset
John F.W. Walling, Newton Abbot, Devon
Mickie Weeks, Winscombe
John Westlake, Masida, Winscombe
Peter G. Whicher, The Brook, Winscombe
Janet E. White, Winscombe, Somerset
F.J. Wilkinson, Winscombe, Somerset
Winscombe & Sandford Local History & Archaeology Society,
Martin Woodhead, Exeter
Molly Young, Winscombe
Wendy Young, Winscombe

Community Histories

The Book of Addiscombe • Canning and Clyde Road Residents Association and Friends
The Book of Addiscombe, Vol. II • Canning and Clyde Road Residents Association and Friends
The Book of Ashburton • Stuart Hands and Pete Webb
The Book of Axminster with Kilmington • Les Berry and Gerald Gosling
The Book of Bampton • Caroline Seward
The Book of Barnstaple • Avril Stone
The Book of Barnstaple, Vol. II • Avril Stone
The Book of The Bedwyns • Bedwyn History Society
The Book of Bickington • Stuart Hands
Blandford Forum: A Millennium Portrait • Blandford Forum Town Council
The Book of Boscastle • Rod and Anne Knight
The Book of Bramford • Bramford Local History Group
The Book of Breage & Germoe • Stephen Polglase
The Book of Bridestowe • D. Richard Cann
The Book of Bridport • Rodney Legg
The Book of Brixham • Frank Pearce
The Book of Buckfastleigh • Sandra Coleman
The Book of Buckland Monachorum & Yelverton • Pauline Hamilton-Leggett
The Book of Carharrack • Carharrack Old Cornwall Society
The Book of Carshalton • Stella Wilks and Gordon Rookledge
The Parish Book of Cerne Abbas • Vivian and Patricia Vale
The Book of Chagford • Iain Rice
The Book of Chapel-en-le-Frith • Mike Smith
The Book of Chittlehamholt with Warkleigh & Satterleigh • Richard Lethbridge
The Book of Chittlehampton • Various
The Book of Colney Heath • Bryan Lilley
The Book of Constantine • Moore and Trethowan
The Book of Cornwood and Lutton • Compiled by the People of the Parish
The Book of Crediton • John Heal
The Book of Creech St Michael • June Small
The Book of Cullompton • Compiled by the People of the Parish
The Book of Dawlish • Frank Pearce
The Book of Dulverton, Brushford, Bury & Exebridge • Dulverton and District Civic Society
The Book of Dunster • Hilary Binding
The Book of Easton • Easton Village History Project
The Book of Edale • Gordon Miller
The Ellacombe Book • Sydney R. Langmead
The Book of Exmouth • W.H. Pascoe
The Book of Grampound with Creed • Bane and Oliver
The Book of Gosport • Lesley Burton and Brian Musselwhite
The Book of Hayling Island & Langstone • Peter Rogers
The Book of Helston • Jenkin with Carter
The Book of Hemyock • Clist and Dracott
The Book of Herne Hill • Patricia Jenkyns
The Book of Hethersett • Hethersett Society Research Group
The Book of High Bickington • Avril Stone
The Book of Ilsington • Dick Wills
The Book of Kingskerswell • Carsewella Local History Group
The Book of Lamerton • Ann Cole and Friends
Lanner, A Cornish Mining Parish • Sharron Schwartz and Roger Parker
The Book of Leigh & Bransford • Malcolm Scott
The Book of Litcham with Lexham & Mileham • Litcham Historical and Amenity Society
The Book of Loddiswell • Loddiswell Parish History Group
The New Book of Lostwithiel • Barbara Fraser
The Book of Lulworth • Rodney Legg
The Book of Lustleigh • Joe Crowdy
The Book of Lydford • Compiled by Barbara Weeks
The Book of Lyme Regis • Rodney Legg
The Book of Manaton • Compiled by the People of the Parish
The Book of Markyate • Markyate Local History Society
The Book of Mawnan • Mawnan Local History Group
The Book of Meavy • Pauline Hemery
The Book of Mere • Dr David Longbourne
The Book of Minehead with Alcombe • Hilary Binding and Douglas Stevens
The Book of Monks Orchard and Eden Park • Ian Muir and Pat Manning
The Book of Morchard Bishop • Jeff Kingaby
The Book of Mylor • Mylor Local History Group
The Book of Narborough • Narborough Local History Society
The Book of Newdigate • John Callcut
The Book of Newtown • Keir Foss
The Book of Nidderdale • Nidderdale Museum Society
The Book of Northlew with Ashbury • Northlew History Group
The Book of North Newton • J.C. and K.C. Robins
The Book of North Tawton • Baker, Hoare and Shields
The Book of Nynehead • Nynehead & District History Society
The Book of Okehampton • Roy and Ursula Radford
The Book of Ottery St Mary • Gerald Gosling and Peter Harris
The Book of Paignton • Frank Pearce
The Book of Penge, Anerley & Crystal Palace • Peter Abbott
The Book of Peter Tavy with Cudlipptown • Peter Tavy Heritage Group
The Book of Pimperne • Jean Coull
The Book of Plymtree • Tony Eames
The Book of Porlock • Dennis Corner
Postbridge – The Heart of Dartmoor • Reg Bellamy
The Book of Priddy • Albert Thompson
The Book of Princetown • Dr Gardner-Thorpe
The Book of Probus • Alan Kent and Danny Merrifield
The Book of Rattery • By the People of the Parish
The Book of Roadwater, Leighland and Treborough • Clare and Glyn Court
The Book of St Day • Joseph Mills and Paul Annear
The Book of St Dennis and Goss Moor • Kenneth Rickard
The Book of St Levan and Porthcurno • St Levan Local History Group
The Book of Sampford Courtenay with Honeychurch • Stephanie Pouya
The Book of Sculthorpe • Gary Windeler
The Book of Seaton • Ted Gosling
The Book of Sherborne • Rodney Legg
The Book of Sidmouth • Ted Gosling and Sheila Luxton
The Book of Silverton • Silverton Local History Society
The Book of South Molton • Jonathan Edmunds
The Book of South Stoke with Midford • Edited by Robert Parfitt
South Tawton & South Zeal with Sticklepath • Roy and Ursula Radford
The Book of Sparkwell with Hemerdon & Lee Mill • Pam James
The Book of Staverton • Pete Lavis
The Book of Stithians • Stithians Parish History Group
The Book of Stogumber, Monksilver, Nettlecombe & Elworthy • Maurice and Joyce Chidgey
The Book of Studland • Rodney Legg
The Book of Swanage • Rodney Legg
The Book of Tavistock • Gerry Woodcock
The Book of Thorley • Sylvia McDonald and Bill Hardy
The Book of Torbay • Frank Pearce
The Book of Truro • Christine Parnell
The Book of Uplyme • Gerald Gosling and Jack Thomas
The Book of Watchet • Compiled by David Banks
The Book of West Huntspill • By the People of the Parish
The Book of Weston-super-Mare • Sharon Poole
The Book of Whitchurch • Gerry Woodcock
Widecombe-in-the-Moor • Stephen Woods
Widecombe – Uncle Tom Cobley & All • Stephen Woods
The Book of Williton • Michael Williams
The Book of Witheridge • Peter and Freda Tout and John Usmar
The Book of Withycombe • Chris Boyles
Woodbury: The Twentieth Century Revisited • Roger Stokes
The Book of Woolmer Green • Compiled by the People of the Parish

For details of any of the above titles or if you are interested in writing your own history, please contact: Commissioning Editor, Community Histories, Halsgrove House, Lower Moor Way, Tiverton, Devon EX16 6SS, England; email: katyc@halsgrove.com